Adolescent Substance Abuse
Assessment, Prevention, and Treatment

Oscar Gary Bukstein
Western Psychiatric Institute and Clinic

A WILEY-INTERSCIENCE PUBLICATION

JOHN WILEY & SONS, INC.

New York • Chichester • Brisbane • Toronto • Singapore

To my wonderful wife, Yvonne and
my children, Rachel and Eric

Library of Congress Cataloging-in-Publication Data:

Bukstein, Oscar Gary, 1955–
    Adolescent substance abuse : assessment, prevention, and treatment
/ Oscar Gary Bukstein.
        p.   cm. — (Wiley series on personality processes)
    Includes bibliographical references and index.
    ISBN 0-471-55080-9 (acid-free paper)
    1. Teenagers—Substance use.   2. Substance abuse.   I. Title.
II. Series.
RJ506.D78B85   1995
616.86´00835—dc20   94-40264

Printed in the United States of America

10 9 8 7 6 5 4 3 2 1

Series Preface

This series of books is addressed to behavioral scientists interested in the nature of human personality. Its scope should prove pertinent to personality theorists and researchers as well as to clinicians concerned with applying an understanding of personality processes to the amelioration of emotional difficulties in living. To this end, the series provides a scholarly integration of theoretical formulations, empirical data, and practical recommendations.

Six major aspects of studying and learning about human personality can be designated: personality theory, personality structure and dynamics, personality development, personality assessment, personality change, and personality adjustment. In exploring these aspects of personality, the books in the series discuss a number of distinct but related subject areas: the nature and implications of various theories of personality; personality characteristics that account for consistencies and variations in human behavior; the emergence of personality processes in children and adolescents; the use of interviewing and testing procedures to evaluate individual differences in personality; efforts to modify personality styles through psychotherapy, counseling, behavior therapy, and other methods of influence; and patterns of abnormal personality functioning that impair individual competence.

IRVING B. WEINER

University of South Florida
Tampa, Florida

Preface

The purpose of this book is to provide a comprehensive review of what we know about substance abuse in adolescents and to provide a guide to the assessment, treatment, and prevention. While there is a consensus as to the severity of adolescent substance abuse in our society, there have been surprisingly few books that cover this topic in a scholarly, yet practical and accessible manner.

While adolescent substance use and abuse is often described in simplistic terms, it remains a complex problem created and often maintained by a host of factors. To truly understand adolescent substance use and abuse, the reader needs to appreciate the historical and cultural context of adolescent behavior. A discussion of normal adolescent development and the developmental context of substance use and abuse is also necessary for understanding the risk and resilience to substance abuse. Based on this background, I will present the various theoretical underpinnings on the etiology, prevention, and treatment of adolescent substance abuse. Due to the importance of psychiatric or mental health problems in the etiology, assessment, and treatment of substance abuse, a detailed discussion of comorbid or coexisting psychiatric problems is provided.

There are several special features of this book. The first is the discussion of the research support for the material presented. If we are to approach and ultimately succeed in dealing with the problem of adolescent substance abuse, we must make certain that our assumptions about etiology, prevention, and treatment are supported by research utilizing sound methodology. The second feature is the discussion of a number of theory-based approaches and their practical application. These approaches range from traditional approaches grounded in Alcoholics Anonymous and 12-step philosophy to the aggressive use of biological treatments, such as medications.

Returning to my initial proposition that adolescent substance abuse is a complex phenomenon, this book attempts to synthesize theory and research to provide a useful guide to a clinical approach to assessment, treatment, and prevention. A number of various modalities are discussed and suggested.

The first chapter, an historical and theoretical overview, provides the reader with the historical-cultural context for understanding the nature of adolescence substance use and abuse. Chapter 2 presents the issues of diagnosis and the theoretical and practical problems encountered by using different types of diagnostic criteria. Chapter 3 discusses trends and the current prevalence of substance use and abuse in adolescents in the United States. In an attempt to review risk factors for adolescent substance use and abuse within a developmental framework, Chapter 4 describes types of risk factors, consequences, and the natural history of substance use by adolescents.

Chapters 5 through 9 are more clinically oriented. Many clinicians working with adolescents recognize the importance of behavioral and emotional problems coexisting with substance use and abuse. Chapter 5 reviews what we know about "dual disorders" or the comorbidity of substance abuse and other psychiatric disorders in adolescents. Chapters 6, 7, 8, and 9 discuss assessment and treatment issues, respectively. Finally, we end at the beginning; that is, how can we prevent substance abuse in adolescents before it starts? Chapter 10 outlines the current status in the prevention of substance abuse.

Our knowledge of substance use and use disorders is changing rapidly. I have attempted to be as current as possible in my review of the literature as well as to anticipate coming changes and issues.

OSCAR G. BUKSTEIN

February 1995

Acknowledgments

I have many people to thank for their time and effort to this volume. First, I thank Herb Reich, my editor at John Wiley & Sons, and his staff for their effort, understanding, support, and assistance. I thank my colleagues in the field of addiction and psychiatry for their stimulation and contribution to my career and to my understanding of adolescent substance abuse. These colleagues include: Vince Van Hasselt, Ph.D.; Ralph Tarter, Ph.D.; John Donovan, Ph.D.; Nancy Day, Ph.D.; Ada Mezzich, Ph.D.; Shirley Hill, Ph.D.; Jan Pringle, Ph.D.; Yifrah Kaminer, M.D. and David Brent, M.D. I also thank the staff at the Pittsburgh Adolescent Alcohol Research Center (PAARC) for their help and support.

I am enormously grateful to a series of secretaries who made my writing comprehensible: Tracey Eck, Mary Dulgeroff, Shelly Parker, and Tammy McLaughlin. Finally, eternal thanks and devotion by my most critical editor and faithful supporter, my wife Yvonne.

O.G.B.

Contents

CHAPTER 1

Historical and Theoretical Perspectives

AN HISTORICAL OVERVIEW OF ADOLESCENT SUBSTANCE USE

No medical, social, or any other kind of problem exists or develops in a vacuum. Substance use and abuse by adolescents is no exception.[1] Throughout the history of humankind and certainly throughout the history of the United States, youth have used alcohol and other psychoactive substances and have sometimes developed problems resulting from this use. Like almost every other behavior, people have sought to explain the behavior of substance use and abuse by adolescents and adults. The social and political history of our country has influenced and shaped not only the use of alcohol and other drugs by young people, but also society's explanation of and response to this behavior. This opening chapter will review the history of substance use and abuse by adolescents in the United States and the development of theories to explain such behavior among youth.

An Emerging Concept of Adolescence

The concept of adolescence as a distinct developmental period of life has come into focus only recently. Since antiquity, poets, philosophers, and historians have referred to adolescence, or vaguely to a period of "youth" succeeding childhood and preceding full adulthood. What we now call adolescence was an early part of adulthood when an individual learned the role of an adult while assuming most, if not all, of the responsibilities and privileges of adulthood. For the greater part of history, people could only appreciate the gross physical changes occurring during puberty in determining the responsibilities and

---

[1]For the purpose of simplifying the discussion, I have chosen the term "substance abuse" as a generic term indicating pathologic use of drugs and/or alcohol (includes both DSM-IV substance abuse and dependence) unless other terms such as psychoactive substance dependence are specifically mentioned as part of a specific, formal classification system or the abuse or dependence of a specific substance, for example, alcohol abuse or cocaine dependence.

1

privileges in a particular society or culture. While little was expected of children prior to six or seven years of age, the period between seven and puberty was marked by increasing expectations in terms of work and assistance in the household. Finally, after puberty and attainment of adult physical size, the adolescent obtained both the privileges and responsibilities of adulthood.

Alcohol and other substance use, whether illicit or as part of sanctioned social or religious purpose, is rare for prepubertal children of any culture or historical period. At puberty, many cultures included alcohol or specific ceremonial substance use as part of puberty rites (Lourie, 1943). Following these rites or the passage of puberty, youth were considered a part of adult society with rights, including the right to use alcohol or other substances if such use was an accepted part of that society.

Adolescent Roles in Early American History

After puberty, the individual youth could expect incorporation into society as he or she could now handle adult work and be productive. In colonial America, the census of the population would often include those 16 years or older (Kett, 1977). After puberty, which occurred over a longer period of time and later than it does presently, a youth would be expected either to remain with the household and provide an adult's provision of labor or to depart and sustain him- or herself as an apprentice to a trade, a servant or, in rare cases, as a student in higher education. Youth was a transition period at best, with usually some level of "semi-dependence" to a family, a master, or a school. By his twenties, a young adult male could be expected to have set up an independent household and a vocation as a farmer, tradesman, professional, or servant. By this age, almost all females would be married.

Similarly, the period following puberty marked the development of adult-like social relationships with young men entering into courtship with young women, both sexes with the intention to meet and marry as opposed to dating for amusement and socialization. Upon marrying and obtaining a more independent vocational status, the young person was rapidly exposed to and incorporated into the existing political, civic, and religious institutions of the day. The age of consent for marriage—12 years for girls and 14 years for boys—is a prime example of early entry into adult responsibilities for youth (Kett, 1977).

During the colonization of America, alcohol was incorporated into the daily lives of almost all settlers as a normal part of community and personal habits (Lender & Martin, 1987). Colonists drank alcohol at meals and even while working. By today's standards, most colonists could be considered moderate to heavy drinkers with adults over 15 years of age drinking an average of just under six gallons of absolute alcohol per year (Lender & Martin, 1987).

Although the drinking habits of youth are rarely mentioned in written histories of colonial and post-revolutionary America, it is logical to assume that youth who were treated as adults also drank with similar quantity and frequency as their elders. Drinking itself did not appear to be an important concern for colonial America, although overt drunkenness was condemned and punished. The law included acceptable patterns of consumption and limits on taverns' provision of alcoholic beverages. The American Revolution brought a breakdown of past allegiances and respect for authority, as well as the availability of large amounts of cheap domestic whiskey. As a result, alcohol use increased dramatically into the early nineteenth century. Accompanying this increase was an increase in the negative effects of alcohol consumption, including widespread drunkenness and its consequences.

Toward the middle of the nineteenth century, a number of historical developments, including the Industrial Revolution and increasing urbanization, served to change society's expectations of youth. The Industrial Revolution greatly expanded the range of potential vocational paths. Many of these paths would require a higher level of preparation, training, and/or education. As public education became more established, youth were remaining at home for longer periods during which their contribution to the economic well-being of the household often decreased. This was a sacrifice by the household in terms of not only the real cost of education and training, but also the cost of lost work and the need to sustain a less than fully productive household member. In order to repay these costs, parents demanded obedience to the rigors of education and put more emphasis on achievement.

By the mid-nineteenth century, American society began to view youth or adolescence as a time of character-building. Moral and education advocates of the day saw protection from the overindulgent vices of adulthood and the perceived increasing pressures of modern life during the nineteenth century as part of this character-building process. The environment of youth was increasingly regulated; society now denied youth the experience of past social outlets, such as alcohol use.

Although colleges attempted to prohibit drinking and activities, such as gambling, which were thought to promote drinking, the authority of colleges was limited. Into the nineteenth century, advantaged youth attended colleges mostly as boarders. Gambling, fighting, riots, and especially drinking were common activities. Later in the century, the increasing demands for achievement and moral rectitude in the guise of character-building led to increasing college authority and a more restricted, insular student life.

The legal responsibilities of youth had a similar transition. At the beginning of the nineteenth century, youth over 14 years had full responsibility under the law. However, by the middle of the century, separate detention facilities for youth were opened; by the beginning of the twentieth century, a series of court decisions in several states established the special status of children, including most adolescents, in terms of legal rights and responsibilities.

The Rise of Victorian Values and Prohibition:
Alcohol Use by Youth

During the last half of the nineteenth century, the increased concern about the developing moral character of children turned to an examination of parental management and supervision of youth. The Society for the Protection of Cruelty to Children, a forerunner of subsequent child protection agencies, was founded to address the needs of neglected urban children—especially those with drunken parents. Parents commonly modeled drinking behavior for their children and regularly sent them to the corner saloon to fill a pitcher with beer. Although laws forbid the serving of patrons under 16, there was usually nothing said about drinking off the premises as the "parent's beer" was returned.

In response to the problems generated by alcohol, the temperance movement gained sizable support, in large part by pointing to the threat of alcohol to the nation's youth. Temperance supporters described a vicious cycle in which drinking made parents irresponsible and neglectful. Their children would then grow up without discipline and would inherit or learn both a craving for alcohol and a tendency toward social deviance (Rothman, 1971). The Women's Christian Temperance Union (WCTU), founded in 1874, developed an elaborate curriculum of "scientific temperance" which often became mandatory teaching in the schools. This forerunner of modern prevention efforts described the medical and social consequences of alcohol consumption and replaced the strictly moralistic propaganda that was previously taught to students of the day.

Alcohol use by youth remained widespread through the end of the nineteenth century. The rise of Victorian values and mores, as well as the increasing influence of prohibitionists, led to a steady fall in overall alcohol use and alcohol problems in both adolescents and adults from the turn of the century until the 1940s and 1950s. After the onset of Prohibition and the Volstead Act in 1920, alcohol was much less available and its costs often beyond the means of most youth. Alcohol consumption and alcohol-related problems declined considerably for the entire U.S. population; adolescent use probably showed even greater decreases, as availability was sharply curtailed. Even after the repeal of Prohibition, the decline in alcohol use continued through the Depression and World War II. Many states or localities remained "dry" for all citizens; other states began to pass laws restricting the purchase and use of alcohol by minors, usually those under 21 years of age. Other than local crusades and occasional expressions of concern by parents and public officials, adolescent alcohol use took a back seat to a rising concern about the use of other substances by adolescents.

Narcotic and Other Drug Use by Youth in the Twentieth Century

Opiates

Before the turn of the century, proprietary medicinal products containing opiates were popular and commonly used by all segments of the population, including infants. Eventually the dangers and addictive nature of opiates became known and public opinion produced laws, such as the Pure Food and Drug Act of 1906, which forced manufacturers to state whether products contained opiates. As the actual or perceived addictive nature of specific substances became known, public acceptability changed. Cocaine or cannabis, as well as opiate use (usually in the form of morphine and later heroin) became deviant behaviors consigned to ghettos and lower socio-economic segments of the population.

Once the dangers of a substance—whether alcohol or other drugs—became known, large segments of society would censure the use and distribution of that substance. When opiates and cocaine lost their acceptance in the mainstream of society, the need to regulate their use became clear to reformers in the early part of the twentieth century. However, judicial interpretation of the Harrison Act of 1914 allowed physicians to prescribe narcotics. In fact, during the second decade of this century, numerous narcotic maintenance clinics were organized. Much like the methadone maintenance clinics of today, these clinics would provide addicts with narcotics. In New York City, the maintenance clinic operated by the Department of Health enrolled about 7,500 persons; 10 percent were under the age of 19 years (Hubbard, 1920). Later, the notorious Harry Anslinger, commissioner of the Federal Bureau of Narcotics from 1930 to 1962, would blame the maintenance clinics for the rise in teenage drug addiction and would insist upon interdiction and confinement as the best way to handle addicts (Courtwright, Joseph, & De Jarlais, 1989). Almost all of these early narcotic maintenance clinics would eventually close by the 1920s and 1930s. After coming into contact with addicted boys, Jane Addams and Hull House in Chicago struggled to help enact laws against the sale of cocaine and cocaine-containing products.

Following the first World War, there was an outbreak of drug addiction among juveniles. A substantial number of youth were among the estimated million addicts in the United States. In the early 1920s, youth, age 15 to 19, comprised 28 percent of patients treated in a New York City narcotic clinic. Although addiction rates appeared to decline for the entire population during the 1930s, there continued to be reports of youth in drug treatment facilities. In 1936–1937, 16.5 percent of the addicts admitted to the U.S. Hospital in Lexington were 19 years of age or under (U.S. Public Health Service, 1938).

Marijuana

In the late 1920s and 1930s, federal and local officials and organized moralist groups among the public focused attention on marijuana as the latest drug threat. Until the 1920s, marijuana use was confined to Mexican-American communities in the southwestern states. However, in about 1926, marijuana use among lower socioeconomic groups, both African-American and white, and its use by youth in New Orleans appeared to stimulate a sensationalistic response that would be characteristic of later public responses to each subsequent emerging drug trend (Bonnie & Whitebread, 1974). From 1915 to 1933, most states passed laws to prohibit the distribution of marijuana for nonmedical purposes. Many newspapers were active in focusing attention on the dangers of marijuana use and the need for additional anti-marijuana and anti-drug legislation. In 1929, the *Chicago Tribune* pointed out the ease with which marijuana could be obtained and stated, ". . . it has become widespread among American youths . . . even among school children" (*Chicago Tribune*, 1929).

Newspapers, magazines, and congressional testimony portrayed marijuana's threat to youth and its alleged role in precipitating violent crime. Anecdotes described widespread use by adolescents throwing marijuana parties and committing all sorts of heinous acts while under the influence of marijuana. The issue was popularized by Harry Anslinger and the Federal Bureau of Narcotics in speeches and magazine articles such as "Marijuana: Assassin of Youth" which appeared in the very popular *American Magazine* in 1937. Although there was little proof of widespread marijuana use among adolescents or scientific proof of its alleged dangers, the sensationalistic claims influenced the public and state legislatures, many of which included marijuana provisions in their adoption of the Uniform Narcotic Drug Act during the 1930s. Similarly, Anslinger's claims about the effects of marijuana on youth were more than a match for the minimal scientific evidence of the day, as Congress passed the Marijuana Tax Act in 1937.

Anslinger was hardly finished in protecting youth from the dangers of marijuana use. While many people thought that jazz musicians were among the more common marijuana users, Anslinger's attempt at cracking down on more prominent musicians was unsuccessful in the 1940s. Pointing to the following that jazz musicians had among youth, Anslinger attempted to publicly discredit this type of music. This effort represents the first of many efforts to tie the influence of a form of music and its musicians to drug abuse.

Into the Modern Era: Substance Abuse
after World War II

Alcohol use showed gradual but steady increases among adolescents after World War II. In a 1941 survey of high school students, nearly 80 percent of students reported never drinking (McCarthy & Douglass, 1949). This percentage of students abstaining decreased to 71 percent in 1945 and 66 percent in 1947. The percentage of students reporting occasional use increased from 16 percent in 1941 to 30 percent in 1947; students reporting frequent alcohol use increased from 0.9 percent to 3.5 percent. The authors of this study concluded that: Frequent drinking among students was negligible; occasional drinking usually meant only once or twice; and the period of most frequent initiation of drinking was immediately *after* high school. In the late 1940s, following the Second World War, addiction among youth appeared to increase. Substantial increases in narcotic arrests and hospitalizations among adolescents occurred between 1946 and 1952 (Prosser, 1954). Twenty-seven juveniles or 17 percent of the total number of youths admitted to the California Youth Authority had a history of use (consisting of mostly marijuana and lesser numbers of opiate users) or transportation of narcotics. The number of teenagers admitted to state institutions in New York State increased over 900 percent between 1947 and 1950 (Kreig, 1951). The increase in adolescent addiction rates, while substantial, was confined to large urban areas, particularly the ghettos of Chicago and New York. However, the idea of "child addicts" received the attention of the press and headlines proclaimed "dope epidemics." In this excitement, parents brought their children to family doctors to be checked for possible addiction. Children, also impressed, would prick their arms with pins and pretend to be "junkies" (Deutsch, 1952).

Much of the hysteria was unwarranted as only large metropolitan areas and severely deviant youth were affected by substance use. Although a popular press report estimated the number of teenage narcotic addicts at 15,000 and 25,000 in New York and Chicago, respectively (Whitman, 1951), investigations revealed a total of only 154 drug-using youth or about one out of every 200 students in New York schools. Most adolescent narcotic addicts were not in school.

Despite the episodic sensationalism of the popular press, scholarly reviews of the subject during the 1950s began to reveal a basic understanding of the risk factors for substance use and abuse in youth. Questions remained about the relationship between deviant behavior, that is, delinquency, and substance use. Some reports stated that drug use led youth to quit school and commit crimes to support their habit (Goldstein, 1952). The Federal Bureau of Narcotics presented the view that most of the drug-using youth were "hoodlums" or delinquents first and that drug use was part of a pattern of delinquency (Kogan, 1950).

In response to the rising level of drug use in adolescents, many schools began at least cursory instruction on narcotics. Prevention programs trained teachers and other school personnel in detecting drugs and addiction, and in appropriate methods of reporting these findings to the authorities. Community efforts included such campaigns as the "Dope Must Go" by the South Side Community Committee of Chicago (U.S. Senate Special Committee, 1951). Altogether, the educational, community, and public responses to the problem were sincere but superficial and did not address the underlying problems of poverty and neglect that help to produce delinquents.

As in the past, the popular press would occasionally sensationalize the threat of drug use by adolescents. Whether drug use was widespread among youth, drug use among the entire population was increasing during the early 1950s. Usually, the reaction was demands for more laws and stronger penalties for trafficking and use. In 1951, the U.S. Congress responded by passing the Boggs Act which increased penalties for all drug violations and put marijuana and narcotic drugs together in the same class for the first time in Federal legislation. The testimony leading to the Boggs Act's passage was filled with horror stories about the threat of marijuana and other drugs to youth (Bonnie & Whitebread, 1974). In 1956, Congress increased penalties further by passing the Narcotic Control Act. Following the federal lead, the states also increased penalties for the possession of substances.

A panel of physicians, lawyers, and judges questioned whether this emphasis on the threat of jail or prison was actually deterring addicts. This panel of the Joint Committee of the American Bar Association and the American Medical Association authored a report on Narcotic Drugs (1961) that recommended research and trial programs to emphasize treatment. Unfortunately, such informed efforts received little attention from lawmakers and the public at this time.

The Current "Epidemic"

After 1965, superimposed on existing patterns of inner-city narcotic use and addiction, there developed a pattern of mostly recreational and nonopiate drug use by middle class white youth. The social upheaval during the 1960s and 1970s affected almost all Americans. The Vietnam War, protests, the civil rights struggle, and riots in our inner cities exposed hypocrisy in the values of many of our leaders. Youth began to challenge traditional values, attitudes, and social norms. In this social and cultural rebellion, youth sought to develop their own values and lifestyle or to merely escape the perceived cultural chaos. The search for self-understanding, greater physical pleasure, or escape from boredom are only a few of the major reasons for the rise in widespread drug use among youth during the late 1960s and 1970s. In the United States, the number of 12- to 17-year-old adolescents who had tried marijuana increased from almost zero in 1960 to 3 out of every 10 students in 1979. In a study of substance use patterns in 10th grade boys in 1966, 23 percent of the boys reported alcohol use one to two times a month (Johnston, 1973). Approximately 20 percent reported having used marijuana, with 4.1 percent reporting use one to two times per month.

Drug use was now out of the ghetto. Increasing numbers of middle class and upper class citizens, especially middle class and suburban youth, became involved with drug use and abuse. After the publicity surrounding the jailing of the children of several prominent citizens for marijuana possession or use, the medical establishment and even law enforcement officials became increasingly uncomfortable and unwilling to continue to support the notion that marijuana users were criminals.

By the end of the 1960s, the need for a revision in the Federal drug laws appeared obvious. The country had to respond to changes in societal attitudes and behavior, including the increasing rate of drug use in the country. Congress passed the Comprehensive Drug Prevention and Control Act in October 1970. This act put all controlled substances within a uniform framework, eliminated mandatory sentencing, reduced simple possession of drugs to a misdemeanor offense, and appointed a commission to study marijuana and its effects. Subsequent state legislation reflected a more flexible approach to sentencing and proposed treatment as an alternative for those caught possessing illicit substances. State and local governments changed laws with felony convictions and long jail or prison sentences for marijuana possession to misdemeanors.

It is uncertain what difference these legislative changes made in the growing rate of substance use among adolescents and adults in the United States. The percentage of high school students trying various substances and using them regularly continued to grow through the early 1970s. However, as more scientific information about the potential dangers of these substances became known and as more adolescents experienced the negative social, physical, and psychological consequences of substance use and abuse, the perceived harmfulness of these substances increased and the use among high school students decreased, despite little change in the ready availability of these substances.

In the mid-1980s, cocaine became more available to youth, resulting in an increase in its use. As its adverse effects became known to adolescents, cocaine use has declined since the late 1980s. However, the increase in cocaine use among the entire population as well as the crack cocaine epidemic of the late 1980s and its accompanying increase in violent, urban crime prompted much public outrage and concern. The National Drug Control Strategy of 1989 was similar to past responses in that much more attention was paid to interdiction and enforcement and less to treatment. There is little evidence to support the effectiveness of these efforts. Recent declines in substance use patterns among youth can be attributed to education and public awareness of the danger of substance use rather than to the availability of substances which has shown little change.

From this brief history of adolescent substance use, several recurring trends have emerged. First, adolescent substance use mimics adult patterns. In times of early exposure to novel psychoactive substances of abuse, use among adolescents rises with that of the rest of the population. Second, in times of repression of behavior, such as Prohibition, adolescent use is probably more restricted and thus declines more than adult use patterns. Third, as with adult use in lower socioeconomic groups, a certain amount of regular adolescent substance use appears to be endemic. Finally, adolescents in upper socioeconomic groups, including middle class, appear to be responsive to the perceived harmfulness of substances as proven by scientific studies and conveyed by education and experience. Youth from lower socioeconomic classes may show less change in substance use, as they may have less knowledge about the harmfulness of psychoactive substances and be less concerned about the consequences of use.

THEORIES OF ADOLESCENT SUBSTANCE USE AND ABUSE

The view of the cause or causes of substance use and/or abuse in adolescence has undergone an evolution similar to the explanation of use and abuse in adults. Throughout American history, society has dealt with substance abuse alternatively as a moral failing or a disease. Colonial America condemned those drinkers at the extreme levels of abuse. Later, Benjamin Rush, the father of American psychiatry, described intemperance as a disease. For the next century or so, alcoholism, and later drug addiction, went back and forth from being considered a pathetic condition deserving of compassion to a deviant, stigmatized behavior deserving of censure. Prior to the last half of this century, most people considered abuse of substances to be deviant behavior that was usually the result of moral failings or the failure of proper moral development. If use or abuse by an adolescent was considered at all, the parents or adults in the adolescent's life were blamed for failing in their responsibility to teach the adolescent appropriate behavior. In the late nineteenth century, the blame for substance use and abuse was extended to include other environmental factors such as poverty, lack of education, or lack of parental guidance in the case of orphans or runaways. The usual manner in which society dealt with such problems was punishment; that is, deviant or substance-abusing youth were subject to criminal sanctions.

A significant change in societal attitudes did not take place until the last 20 to 30 years. Since the 1960s, research has identified some of the correlates and potential causes of substance use/abuse by adolescents. The search for effective treatment and prevention strategies would require such research to explain why adolescents use or abuse substances. As an appreciation of substance abuse as a disease or pathology took hold, schools of psychology began to incorporate substance abuse behavior within the broader theoretical schemes of their disciplines. Contemporary theories of adolescent substance use/abuse can be arbitrarily divided into one of four major groups: (1) the disease model, (2) psychological theories, (3) behavioral theories, and (4) biological theories.

The disease model and the psychodynamic and similar psychological theories competed as the most influential explanations for substance abuse from the period immediately preceding World War II until the past two decades. Since the 1970s, research establishing learned behaviors as critical to the onset and development of substance abuse has focused attention on behavioral theories. Finally, investigators have developed both biological and integrated theories to provide more comprehensive explanations for substance use behavior.

The Disease Model

It is difficult to classify the *disease model* of substance abuse or addiction either within psychological theories or within a behavioral/environmental framework. Despite its name, the disease model is not a medical or biological model either. Yet, in terms of its influence on the treatment of substance abuse or addiction during the past 50 to 60 years, the disease model remains the pre-eminent model of the substance abuse treatment community.

Unfortunately, no consensus or complete explanation of the disease model or specific explanation of the development of substance abuse according to the disease model exists. The essence of the disease model is that substance abuse or, more specifically addiction, is a disease. Addiction is a separate disease— not a symptom or part of another disease. Addiction as disease is not an explanation so much as a statement of fact about the maladaptive use patterns and the risk of repetition of these patterns throughout the life of the addict. Although many adherents to the disease model may disagree with many, if not all, of the tenets of other theoretical models, there does not appear to be a significant level of inconsistency between the disease model and other models of substance abuse etiology (Dodes, 1988).

Psychological Theories

Although psychological theories attempting to explain adolescent substance use and abuse could potentially cover a very wide range of theoretical perspectives, psychology will be defined here to mean the study of the internal mental processes of the individual adolescent. Included in psychological theories are psychodynamic perspectives, such as the self-medication hypothesis. Although environment, especially early experiences, may have significant influences on substance use behavior, psychological theories support the role of internal processes such as feeling, emotions, and personality as the primary causes of pathologic behavior, including substance abuse.

Psychodynamic Theory

Although psychodynamic perspectives on substance abuse have minimal influence among the substance abuse treatment community, psychodynamic theories have shaped attitudes and treatment approaches within the mental health treatment community until the past one to two decades. Similar to a number of other theories, psychodynamic approaches view substance abuse as a symptom rather than a cause of other behavior or emotional problems (Nystrom, Bal, & Labreque, 1979).

There are several major schools of thought within the psychodynamic literature that attempt to explain substance abuse. The role of "oral fixation" is proposed to explain the relationship of substances to impulse satisfaction, particularly in the case of alcohol abuse or dependence (Glover, 1956). The inability of the mother or family to meet the child's dependency needs at the earliest stage produces uncertainty in the child as to whether these needs will be met; therefore, the child does not develop the ability to delay gratification. Eventually, this low frustration tolerance manifests itself as impulsive behavior, such as anger or withdrawal, and through the abusive use of substances which is an immature way to achieve oral gratification (Blane, 1970).

Variants of the oral frustration perspective include Menninger's view (1938) that because the oral needs have not been met, the individual becomes angry with the parent(s). Being unable to express these hostile impulses toward the parent(s), the anger is turned inward and manifested in the self-destructive behavior of substance abuse. Latent homosexual feelings represent another psychodynamic view (Abraham, 1926). When the mother is unable to meet the child's needs, the child turns to the father for emotional attachment. Latent and unacceptable homosexual feelings are suppressed by alcohol or other drug use.

According to many psychodynamic theorists, substance abusers often share certain additional personality characteristics such as dependency, impulsivity, narcissism, emotional isolation, and feelings of inadequacy and depression. These characteristics or traits indicate ego deficits. Alcohol and other drugs are seen as a method of meeting dependency needs and alleviating the resulting psychological discomfort. Psychoactive substances act as "ego protheses" (Wieder & Kaplan, 1969).

Additional formulations of psychodynamic theory propose the substance as a psychological object and addiction as similar to dependencies on other people (Meeks, 1987). In addition to being a source of emotional gratification and a means of regulating adverse affective states, addiction is viewed as the avoidance of human relationships which are potentially conflictual and dangerous. Avoiding relationships only serves to retard the adolescent's development of interpersonal skills and further reinforces the avoidance of relationships. The interpersonal and dependency needs of substance abusers often manifest themselves in behavior which attempts to hide or mask dependency motives.

The *self-medication hypothesis* is another prominent psychological theory used to explain substance use. Both psychodynamic theorists and others, including some behavioral theorists, have described the use of alcohol and other drugs to control intolerable affective states. Khantzian (1985) proposed that certain substances are preferentially chosen on the basis of their specific ability to control certain affective states. Some individuals use stimulant drugs to manage depression, boredom, or emptiness while others use depressants for anger or rage. These affects usually result from ego deficits.

Behavioral, Learning, and Environmental Theories

Behavioral/learning theories are those theories or explanations which seek to justify behaviors, that is, the use or abuse of substances, on the basis of an individual's interactions with the environment and the effects of certain environmental variables on behavior. Important behavioral perspectives include social learning theory, interactional theories, and aspects of expectancy theory, tension reduction theory, and stress response dampening.

Social Learning Theory

Social learning perspectives assume that all substance use is governed by operant and learning principles, including cognitive factors (Abrams & Niaura, 1987; Bandura, 1969). As we shall explore further in Chapter 4, learning to drink alcohol or to experiment with certain psychoactive agents is an important part of psychosocial development within modern western culture. Adolescents are exposed to substance use attitudes, beliefs, and models of use; adolescents learn to use substances. Upon exposure to substances, direct experience allows use to be either positively or negatively reinforced by its effects which may include tension or stress reduction, management of negative affective states, and enhancement of social interactions. If substance use persists, increasing tolerance to the reinforced effects will require greater quantities to achieve the same effects. Obtaining greater quantities may produce preoccupation with obtaining the substance. Similarly, physical dependence may result and require further use to avoid withdrawal symptoms. Obtaining the short-term reinforcers may overwhelm the desire to avoid the negative reinforcement from the resulting negative consequences of substance use.

More recent modifications of social learning theory have given more importance to "distal" factors including personal characteristics, cognitive factors, and deficits in psychosocial coping skills (Abrams & Niaura, 1987).

Interactional Theories

Interactional theories propose that behavior, including substance use behavior, is the result of reciprocal effects among the individual person, and the person's environment, and individual behavioral repertoire. As contrasted with social learning theory, the individual is an active agent who is influenced by cognitive, affective, and motivational factors as well as by the environment. A continuous process of interaction and feedback between the environment and the individual will influence behavior (Savada, 1987). Much of modern interactional theory is based on multivariate statistical models, and is represented most prominently by the *problem behavior theory* of Jessor and Jessor (1977), the *domain model* of Huba and Bentler (1982), and the *developmental model* of Zucker (1979). Each is a model of adolescent development and deals with a broad range of adolescent behaviors rather than substance use or abuse, per se.

Briefly, for Jessor and the *problem behavior theory,* problem drinking is but one of many problem behaviors. These problem behaviors are the result of an interaction between three systems within the individual: personality, perceived environment, and behavior. Within each system, there are characteristics or variables which represent a "proneness" to deviance or problem behavior. Like other problem behaviors, drinking behavior, whether it be abstinence or problem drinking, is a continuous variable rather than a discrete state. Jessor says nothing about pharmacologic effects or biological vulnerability.

In Huba and Bentler's *domain model,* drinking is one of a larger set of behavioral tendencies or adolescent lifestyles. These tendencies are the result of interactions of several domains: biological, intrapersonal, interpersonal, and socio-cultural. Thus, the domain model appears to be more comprehensive than other interactional theories by including substance use in a broad framework of behavior and influences by both environmental and biological factors.

Expectancy Theory

Expectancies are cognitive processes which tie events, or more precisely, the anticipation of events, to certain outcomes. Through learning principles, the individual learns to anticipate relationships between events or objects in an upcoming situation. To expectancy theorists, what is learned is the relationship between substance use and certain outcomes that are desired because they are reinforcing. Substance abuse occurs when the adolescent has positive expectancies of use that are greater in number or value than negative expectancies. These expectancies may be reinforced in short-term experience. Due to their limited amount of experience and vulnerability to the influences of popular culture and its myths, adolescents may be more prone to develop expectancies which are not valid in the long term. The content of adolescent expectancies will be explored further in Chapter 4.

Tension Reduction Theory/Stress Response Dampening

Although the idea of alcoholics being tense due to frustrated oral and dependency conflicts originates in the psychoanalytic literature, *tension reduction theory* is largely based on learning principles in which the substance use behavior is rewarded (Conger, 1956). The main elements of the tension reduction theory state that alcohol reduces tension, which includes fear, anxiety, conflict, and frustration, and that alcohol is used for these tension reduction properties (Cappell & Herman, 1972). More recent research has shown that the tension reduction properties of alcohol are noted within only a circumscribed area of the alcohol dose response curve and that tension reduction is not a valid, single-factor explanation for use or abuse (Cappell & Greeley, 1987).

Stress response dampening is similar to tension reduction theory. The individual learns that substances can decrease the physical response to stress, thus prompting and reinforcing substance use in similar stressful situations (Sher, 1987). Cognitive processes, including expectancies, and individual characteristics such as response and sensitivity to stress may be important in determining susceptible individuals.

Self-Handicapping

Individuals who are unsure about their competence in certain situations may consume alcohol or other drugs in order to have their poor performance attributed to their intoxicated state rather than their actual competence (Jones & Berglas, 1978; Tucker, Vuchinich, & Sobell 1981).

Self-Awareness

Alcohol and other drugs affect cognitive processes, including the state of self-awareness (Hull, 1987). The individual becomes less able to evaluate his or her own negative experiences including failure and the negative consequences of continuous substance use or abuse; therefore, use and abuse can continue. For the adolescent, recognition of the negative consequences of substance use is essential in order to be able to either avoid use altogether or to avoid the progression from experimental to substance abuse.

Biological Theories

The disease concept of substance abuse is a prominent one in the substance abuse treatment community. Most of us feel that substance abusers, adolescent or adult, are sick and need treatment. However, a narrow but popular definition of disease implies an underlying physical abnormality—be it anatomical, biochemical, physiological, or infectious. Until recently, the inability to point to a specific, underlying physical abnormality has led some to question the notion of substance abuse or dependency or whatever one wishes to label it, as a disease.

In the past several decades, evidence increasingly points to biological traits or abnormalities as underlying a vulnerability to substance abuse (Tarter, 1992). Genetic studies, including adoption and twin studies, show a substantial genetic component independent of environmental influences. With evidence of genetic predisposition, investigators have searched for biological markers by comparing children of substance abusers (high risk) with children of nonsubstance abusers (low risk) (Schuckit, 1985b, 1987). Differences in event-related potentials, electroencephalography, certain neuropsychological tests, intensity of reaction to alcohol, and body sway between high- and low-risk groups point to a variety of biological factors which may be markers or may actively predispose the individual to the development of alcohol or other drug abuse.

Investigators have proposed several biogenetic theories including abnormalities in neurotransmitter function (e.g., serotonin or catecholamines) or differences in the metabolism of alcohol. The absence of overwhelming evidence for any of these biological markers makes a single-factor biological cause or theory unlikely.

Integration of Theories

The more research findings allow us to understand about the nature of substance abuse, the more complex the factors underlying its development and natural history appear to be. This complexity should hardly be surprising given the resistance of substance abuse problems to prevention and treatment efforts. Few theories appear to lack at least some merit. An integrated theory combining elements from a variety of psychological, behavioral, and biological theories is worth consideration. Based on existing evidence, substance abuse in adolescents is the result of a complex interplay of psychological, social, interpersonal, and other environmental influences and biological factors that create a level of probability for the initiation of substance use and progression to abuse. The relative contribution of factors varies between individual adolescents as do the outcomes. If the relative contributions from environment and biologic vulnerability are high, the probability of a substance abuse outcome is also high.

On the other hand, high biologic vulnerability may be counteracted by certain positive environmental factors, such as consistent discipline by parents or absence of exposure to substances.

None of the theoretical perspectives reviewed appear to be exclusive. Each explores a part of the vulnerability to attainment of and maintenance of substance use and abuse in adolescence. There appears to be some kind(s) of biological vulnerability to substance abuse. However, environment plays an important and necessary role. Although we cannot account for the internal or psychological motivation of the adolescent, what a child or adolescent learns from the environment influences both cognitive processes and overt behavior. Behavioral or learned factors may be more important at certain stages of the progression from initiation of use to dependence. For example, social learning may be most important in the initiation of use. Expectancies may be more important in maintaining regular use. Self-medication and other biological reinforcement mechanisms may be more important in maintaining substance abuse.

Interactional theories show the complex nature of individual-environment-behavioral interaction on substance use behaviors. In Chapter 4, we will discuss some of these theories in greater detail and how they might explain psychoactive substance use and abuse within the context of the developing adolescent.

Explanations of psychoactive substance use behavior among youth have evolved in response to an expanding scientific knowledge base about the nature of psychoactive substance use and addiction. This evolution has occurred within a social and legal context which greatly affects the manner in which society and individuals view psychoactive substance use and abuse.

THE TREATMENT OF ADOLESCENT SUBSTANCE ABUSERS

The treatment of adolescent substance abusers differs little from treatment for adults. Until the past two decades, youth were placed in adult treatment settings without significant modifications based on age or developmental level. As adults formed the overwhelming majority of these patient populations, treatment was usually directed to adult problems and concerns. Treatment programs considered adolescents as merely younger substance abusers. Adolescents were expected to attend the same treatment modalities, including self-support groups such as Alcoholics Anonymous (AA) or Narcotics Anonymous (NA). Given the self-help nature of the existing treatment process, it is not surprising that adolescents often had difficulty relating to their often much older substance abusing "peers."

The modern era of substance abuse treatment began in Minnesota with a self-help, 12-step model now known appropriately as the *Minnesota Model* (Cook, 1988a, 1988b). Substance abuse treatment directed specifically toward adolescent populations and based on the same self-help model also began in Minnesota with programs such as St. Mary's Hospital program. The 1970s brought increased attention to substance use problems in adolescents. This was soon translated into the development of more programs for adolescents. This trend exploded in the late 1970s and in the 1980s as hospitals, both nonprofit and proprietary, rushed to take advantage of the improved insurance and third-party payment for substance abuse treatment. The development of inpatient programs, usually 28 to 35 days in length, became somewhat of a cottage industry. By 1989, almost 70,000 youth under the age of 18 were clients in drug and/or alcohol treatment units during the preceding year (U.S. Department of Health and Human Services, 1991a).

The treatment philosophy of adolescent substance abuse treatment programs has largely followed the self-help, 12-step philosophy of adult programs. In addition to an ample number of Alcoholics Anonymous (AA) or Narcotic Anonymous (NA) meetings, youth are exposed to psychoeducation about the negative consequences of substances, work 12-step programs largely through work books, and attend confrontational-style groups.

By the early 1990s, an increased scrutiny of both substance abuse and mental health treatment programs and the arrival of managed care in controlling the access to these programs not only slowed the growth of adolescent programs, but has actually resulted in many programs closing, downsizing, or developing more outpatient or intensive outpatient alternatives to inpatient treatment. Given the usual absence of significant coexisting medical problems, justifying the inpatient treatment of adolescents is becoming increasingly difficult.

The need to develop additional modalities, particularly in the inpatient programs where the trend is toward much more severely affected youth, has resulted in more behavioral-focused treatment, an increased emphasis on family issues (including parent management training), and more attention to psychopathology and the specific treatment of coexisting psychiatric disorders when indicated.

The future of adolescent substance abuse treatment is uncertain. Severe restrictions in the type and length of treatment may significantly limit the efficacy of treatment. Ultimately, treatment planning will have to be backed up by research demonstrating the effectiveness of various types of treatment for various populations of adolescents who differ on a variety of demographic, social, behavioral, and psychological characteristics.

CHAPTER 2

Diagnosis

This book is about adolescent substance abuse, yet here at the beginning of this second chapter, the author still has to define what exactly is adolescent substance abuse. How do we define it? Do past or current definitions or descriptions of adolescent "substance abuse" make any practical sense? Do these definitions help in identifying and treating adolescents with substance use problems or guide us in making public policy decisions for prevention or interdiction? Despite prevailing views that we are experiencing an epidemic of drug and alcohol abuse in adolescents, little agreement is present about the definition of adolescent substance abuse disorders. This difficulty in finding a standard definition is hardly surprising given the diversity of opinion about the nature of substance abuse itself. Unfortunately, the absence of a valid, reliable and practical definition for adolescent substance use disorder(s) has likely slowed efforts aimed at studying the prevalence, natural history, genetics, and treatment outcome of adolescent substance abuse.

In this chapter, the author will discuss efforts to define adolescent substance abuse and the many problems inherent in attempting to devise a valid, meaningful diagnosis for substance use problems in adolescents. The basic criteria for the substance use disorders listed in the *Diagnostic and Statistical Manual of Mental Disorders,* fourth edition (DSM-IV) (American Psychiatric Association, 1994) will be reviewed.

LABELS AND DIAGNOSES FOR SUBSTANCE ABUSE

There are perhaps as many names or labels for adolescent substance abuse disorders as there are definitions. Despite efforts to achieve a consensus or convention(s) as to what one should call substance abuse disorders, a wide variety of labels exist to describe this problem. These labels include: problem use, substance abuse, substance dependence, chemical abuse, chemical dependency, alcoholism, and addiction.

The most official nomenclature and most widely used system of diagnosis that is accepted across clinical and research settings is the American Psychiatric

Association's *Diagnostic and Statistical Manual of Mental Disorders.* The most recent version is the fourth edition or DSM-IV (American Psychiatric Association, 1994). Despite its breath of use, DSM-IV and its substance-related disorders are not the only diagnoses or labels used to define substance use problems in adolescents. A variety of concepts and terms are in wide use by diverse groups of professional disciplines which are involved with research, treatment, and education about substance use disorders and related problems (Rinaldi, Steindler, Wilford, & Goodwin, 1988). While this book broadly deals with substance use by adolescents, the primary concern is with pathological use or disorder(s) of use by adolescents.

DSM-IV defines mental disorder as a clinically significant behavioral or psychological syndrome or pattern that occurs in an individual and is associated with present distress or disability or with a significantly increased risk of suffering death, pain, disability, or loss of freedom. Taking a broad view, adolescent substance abuse must meet these criteria involving distress or dysfunction to be considered a disorder.

As stated in the previous chapter, the author has chosen the term "substance abuse" as a generic term indicating pathologic use of drugs and/or alcohol unless other terms such as psychoactive substance dependence are specifically mentioned as part of a specific, formal classification system or note the abuse or dependence upon a specific substance, for example, alcohol abuse or cocaine dependence.

THE EVOLUTION OF DIAGNOSTIC CLASSIFICATIONS FOR ADOLESCENT SUBSTANCE ABUSE

The concept of substance abuse, particularly alcoholism, has evolved within both historical and social contexts such as Benjamin Rush's first description of alcoholism in terms of a medical disorder (Levine, 1978). Unfortunately, substance abuse diagnoses have been developed and described in terms of adult disorder. Very few studies have sought to describe a valid nosology for adolescents. There is little or no empirical evidence or conceptual justification to apply adult concepts of alcohol abuse, for example, to adolescents (Mayer & Filstead, 1979). The various substance abuse diagnostic systems proposed for adults suffer from their own problems. However, no historical attempt to describe a diagnostic system for substance abuse, including Jellinek's "species" of types of alcoholics (Jellinek, 1969), discusses the classification of alcoholism in adolescents.

The third edition of *Diagnostic and Statistical Manual of Mental Disorders* (DSM-III) of the American Psychiatric Association (1980) represented a synthesis of the Feighner and Research Diagnostic Criteria (RDC). DSM-III defined substance abuse in terms of pathological use and impairment in social or occupational functioning due to such use. Substance dependence is defined by the presence of tolerance or withdrawal and either pathological use or impairment in social or occupational functioning due to substance use. The DSM III diagnosis of substance dependence, and especially alcohol dependence, could rarely be applied to adolescents due to the rarity of significant specific withdrawal symptoms and the overemphasis of DSM-III on the physiologic symptoms or later stages of alcohol abuse/dependency (Filstead, 1982; Vingilis & Smart, 1981). The attribution of troubles, problems or consequences is particularly problematic with adolescents. With the DSM-III criteria possessing questionable specificity and construct validity in an adult population, one must further doubt its utility for adolescents.

The Alcohol Dependence Syndrome and DSM-III-R

The World Health Organization's ninth review of the International Classification of Disease (ICD-9) included the alcohol dependence syndrome as part of its criteria for substance abuse disorders (Edwards, Arif, & Hodgson, 1981; Edwards & Gross, 1976). This syndrome also forms the model for the revised third edition (1987) of the *Diagnostic and Statistical Manual* (DSM-III-R) of the American Psychiatric Association.

DSM-III-R criteria for psychoactive substance use disorders represented a substantial change from the DSM-III criteria (Rounsaville, Spitzer, & Williams, 1986). Among the changes were: (a) change of disorder class name from substance use to psychoactive substance use disorder; (b) broadening of the definition of dependence to include clinically significant behaviors, cognitions, and symptoms indicating a substantial degree of involvement with a psychoactive substance; (c) inclusion of criteria for severity of dependence; and (d) elimination of the reliance on physical parameters of possible abuse, that is, tolerance and/or withdrawal as necessary for the diagnosis of dependence. Thus, many adolescents formerly meeting DSM-III criteria for a diagnosis of substance abuse would likely meet DSM-III-R criteria for psychoactive substance dependence. By including behaviors and cognitions, the DSM-III-R diagnosis of psychoactive substance dependence probably includes increased numbers of adolescents as compared with DSM-III. With the exception of those criteria dealing with withdrawal and desire to quit use, adolescents with significant and problematic use could frequently meet the other dependence criteria relating to preoccupation with a substance, the acquisition and compulsive use of a substance and inability to fulfill role obligations due to use. DSM-III-R criteria can take into account adolescents' highly variable use patterns, while preserving the concept of a dependence syndrome across all age groups. However, implicit in the concept of dependence in both DSM-III-R and the *alcohol dependence syndrome* are impaired control over use and craving. Craving and impaired control over use have received little attention as phenomena in adolescents.

The abuse category in DSM-III-R was retained due to a perceived need for a diagnosis when substance use-related impairment was present without dependence criteria (Rounsaville, 1987). The implication is one of abuse as a mild prodromal condition to dependence. Such an abuse category would enable clinicians to give a diagnosis for adolescents referred to treatment due to episodic, excessive drinking without a pattern of dependence as well as provide a continuum of severity (Rounsaville, 1987; Rounsaville, Spitzer, & Williams, 1986). A diagnosis of abuse is not given if the adolescent meets criteria for dependence. The longitudinal study of male drinkers by Hasin and colleagues (Hasin, Grant, & Endicott, 1990) found that alcohol abuse often had a distinct course from alcohol dependence. This finding calls into question the notion of substance abuse as a prodrome or milder form of substance dependence.

DSM-IV

In the recently released DSM-IV, the category of substance-related disorders (American Psychiatric Association, 1994) shows a seemingly subtle but significant change in the criteria for dependence and more significant changes in the criteria for abuse. The authors considered several options for significant change in the diagnoses, including a return to a physiological basis for the diagnosis of dependence or adding criteria involving recurrent legal or interpersonal problems due to use. The eventual changes in dependence criteria for DSM-IV consist of: (a) elimination of the DSM-III-R criteria for frequent intoxication or withdrawal symptoms when expected to fulfill major role obligations, (b) addition of subtyping according to the presence or absence of physiological signs of dependence (tolerance or withdrawal), and (c) elimination of duration criteria. It is difficult to predict the effect of the revised dependence criteria on the diagnosis of adolescents. While the preservation of behavioral and cognitive criteria in a diagnosis of dependence in a subtype without physiological dependence allows for substantial numbers of youth to meet dependence criteria, the elimination of the criteria for inability to fulfill role obligations due to substance use may reduce the number of adolescents meeting DSM-IV substance dependence criteria.

The DSM-IV criteria for substance abuse represent a substantial change from DSM-III-R. DSM-IV expands the criteria of maladaptive pattern of substance use to require clinically significant impairment or distress, and provides two additional examples of a maladaptive pattern of use which include recurrent use resulting in a failure to fulfill major role obligations (omitted from DSM-IV dependence criteria) and recurrent substance-related legal problems. As with the diagnosis of substance dependence, DSM-IV no longer require duration criteria to establish a substance abuse diagnosis. Among adults, surveys using DSM-IV criteria have found a low prevalence of abuse diagnosis, especially alcohol abuse (Schuckit et al., 1991). This may be the result of the DSM-IV substance abuse diagnosis being possibly too restrictive and the substance dependence diagnosis not being restrictive enough. In both DSM-III-R and DSM-IV, the substance abuse diagnosis has more potential for disagreement between different evaluators (Rounsaville, 1987).

Perhaps the most significant change in DSM-IV is the addition of a requirement that the maladaptive pattern of substance use lead to clinically significant impairment or distress. In the past, the presence of a maladaptive pattern of substance use, by whatever subjective criteria, was sufficient to meet diagnostic criteria. The requirement of impairment or distress will likely present the difficult problem of whether to attribute the impairment or distress to substance use rather than to the variety of problem behaviors, psychopathology, or adverse environmental circumstances which are often observed in adolescents who use psychoactive substances. Failure to meet even a minimal level of impairment or distress despite a perceived maladaptive pattern of use may reduce the number of adolescents who meet criteria for a DSM-IV diagnosis of substance abuse.

For the DSM-IV diagnosis of substance dependence, elimination of the criteria for frequent intoxication or withdrawal symptoms when expected to fulfill major role obligations at work, home, or school may reduce the number of adolescents receiving a dependence diagnosis. Halikas (1990) noted that drinking at school and drinking or taking drugs while truant or missing school due to drinking are behaviors which are very commonly seen in adolescents with alcohol or other drug problems. In DSM-IV, this criteria of substance use interfering in role-fulfillment is transferred to the diagnosis of substance abuse where it serves as an example of a maladaptive pattern of substance use. However, the wording of the item is changed to require a failure to fulfill major role obligations due to use rather than recurrent use while expected to fulfill major role obligations as in DSM-III-R psychoactive substance dependence. The essential change in DSM-IV substance abuse and dependence criteria is away from the behavior(s) of substance use toward evidence of psychosocial dysfunction. This change may be more significant in the diagnosis of adolescents as substance use and related behaviors may be much more prevalent and obvious than dysfunction directly attributable to substance use.

In summary, there is absence of research establishing either the validity or reliability of past and current nosologic efforts towards adolescents. The assumption that DSM-III-R or the DSM-IV substance use disorders apply to adolescents requires further support by research data. While an emphasis on substance use causing or exacerbating psychosocial dysfunction is important, investigators have not established a basis for the current criteria differences between substance abuse and dependence in adolescents.

ADOLESCENT AND ADULT SUBSTANCE ABUSE: THE SAME DISORDER?

It is largely assumed that criteria for adult substance use disorders should apply to adolescents. The assumption is that the substance use disorders in both adolescents and adults represent the same disorder or pathological process. Do we truly know if this is the case: Are substance use disorders in adults *and* adolescents fundamentally the same disorder or do they represent different disorders with one or more phenomenologic similarities? One way of answering this question is to find chronological continuity in abuse from adolescence into adulthood. Some studies suggest that adolescent "problem drinkers" form the core of those who develop adult alcohol abuse (Donovan, Jessor, & Jessor, 1983). Other studies show evidence of discontinuity in drinker status between those labeled as problem drinkers in adolescence and problem drinkers in young adulthood (Jessor, 1984) and the lack of a predictive relationship between young adult drinking status and middle age problem drinking (Cahalan & Cisin, 1976; Filmore, 1974). Frequent heavy drinking in adolescents and the problems resulting from drinking appear to be self-limiting and are not highly predictive of alcoholism in adults (Blane, 1976). Similarly, patterns of involvement with marijuana and other illicit drugs peak in late adolescence (Kandel & Logan, 1984).

Many aspects of substance use, including patterns of consumption and consequences of use, vary between adults and adolescents. Blane (1976) observed that chronicity and pervasiveness of alcohol use distinguished frequently heavy drinkers in young adulthood from alcoholics in middle age, while similar patterns of drinking were not as frequent or prevalent among adolescents. Wechsler (1979) noted similar differences in use patterns between youth and adults. The chronicity of alcohol use disorders is not supported by the literature (Clark & Widanik, 1982) with many symptoms of abuse and dependence in adolescence and young adulthood spontaneously remitting later in life without the progressive course described in some definitions of alcoholism (American Society for Addiction Medicine, 1990). Numerous studies strongly suggest a maturational or developmental process as an essential element of a natural history which contrasts to course of substance abuse observed in later adulthood (Bukstein & Kaminer, 1993).

FORMULATION OF A DEFINITION OF SUBSTANCE ABUSE IN ADOLESCENCE

In attempting to develop a valid, reliable diagnostic classification for adolescent substance use disorders, one needs to consider the basic goals or purpose of diagnoses. Millon (1987) suggests four major goals of diagnoses: (1) reliable communication to allow the exchange of useful information about patients,

(2) providing prevalence and incidence data about the problem, (3) providing practical clinical utility by describing the natural history or typical course of the problem as a guide for treatment decisions, and (4) providing a framework for organizing and using research data. Unfortunately, the many diagnostic systems used for diagnosing substance abuse in adolescents are not empirically derived; nor has research established the utility of these diagnoses in describing outcome and separating those with from those without the described condition of adolescent substance abuse or whatever term is used.

Several variables offer a basis for operational definitions of adolescent substance abuse (Pandina, 1986): (a) extreme levels of drug or alcohol use in terms of quantity and/or frequency of use or frequency of intoxication, (b) criteria-based "symptomatic" use behaviors, and (c) negative consequences presumed to be due to substance use. The first potential basis for diagnosis, high levels of quantity and frequency, appears to be of limited usefulness when considered by itself. In view of survey data showing over 30 percent of high school seniors drinking heavily at least once during a two-week period (Donovan & Jessor, 1978) and epidemiological surveys indicating a high lifetime prevalence of substance abuse disorders during adolescence (see Chapter 3), assigning pathologic status to a behavior with such a large prevalence becomes dubious. In many of these cases, we are likely observing a range of normal adolescent behavior and development within the context of our modern society.

The second potential basis for adolescent diagnoses, criterion based on symptomatic behaviors, offers a way of eliminating a reliance on both quantity and frequency measures, or on more advanced complications of substance abuse such as withdrawal symptoms or medical consequences of use which are rare in adolescents. However, symptomatic behaviors of psychological dependence, such as impairment of control, craving and preoccupation with use, are not well-studied in adolescents.

The third option to consider as a basis for a definition of substance abuse is the presence of negative consequences of use. The DSM-III, DSM-III-R, and DSM-IV definitions of abuse, as applied to adolescents, are largely based on the presence of a pattern of negative consequences. Impairment in functioning forms the basis of our concept of disease and, indeed, most diagnostic systems use impairment as a basis for one or more of their criteria. However, basing a definition of adolescent substance abuse upon impairment or negative consequences in functioning is problematic. Inclusion of criteria for impairment in social functioning often assumes that negative social consequences are the result of substance abuse and not due to preexisting or concurrent factors such as another psychiatric disorder or family dysfunction.

Social consequences for adolescents differ from those experienced by adults. By virtue of their age and legal status, alcohol and drug use by adolescents is illicit; therefore, certain negative consequences follow from this legal proscription rather than from the properties of the substance being used. Often parents or other adults will attribute many or most of the problems of an adolescent to substance use which may appear to be the most overt problem behavior. Conflict due to limited familial tolerance, rigid family expectations, or intolerance of any adolescent substance use is influenced by such factors as the family's religious affiliation, prevailing cultural mores, and level of supervision of the adolescent, as well as a variety of other psychosocial and socioeconomic factors. Problems in the families of substance-abusing adolescents may be a function of these variables rather than of drinking or drug use, per se.

In attempting to explain the peak of alcohol or other drug-related problems in this age group, the adolescent developmental task of achieving autonomy and independence should be considered. Younger adolescents do not have the opportunity to drink with the frequency of young adults due to the younger group's greater level of supervision at home and at school, less available means to purchase alcohol, and the legal proscription against use and purchase. With increased independence and more opportunity, rates for heavy drinking increase and peak (Clark & Widanik, 1982) and, correspondingly, rates of problems peak also. Normal developmental maturation and increased social responsibility provide an explanation of the subsequent decrease in use and negative consequences after age 24 (Donovan, Jessor, & Jessor, 1983). Young adults have an improved ability to handle drinking and consequence in a socially acceptable manner (Kandel & Logan, 1984).

Despite the ascendance of a primary disease model of addiction, substance use or abuse may truly be a symptom of a more inclusive syndrome in many cases. For example, the research of Donovan and Jessor (1978) points to problem drinking as only a part of a larger syndrome of deviant behavior in adolescents. The same pattern of psychosocial variables which account for much of the variance in problem drinkers can also explain the use of marijuana and other deviant behaviors. Subgroups of substance-using adolescents may not have a "disease," but rather are best seen as violating established or prevailing societal norms or rules.

Adolescent Development and Diagnosis

This chapter has described several salient differences between substance use in adolescents and use in adults. These differences include: (a) discontinuity between adolescent problem use and adult abuse and dependency, (b) differences in patterns and consequences of use, and (c) differences in the social, peer, and developmental context of use. The latter distinction or the social and developmental context of substance use in adolescence is essential to understanding patterns of adolescent use abuse and dependence, and formulating a practical, valid nosology.

The need for developmentally specific criteria and substance use disorders is supported by the existing literature and by a societal view of a developmental progression of substance use. Criteria relying on quantitative criteria for frequency, amount, or duration should be adjusted according to age and/or developmental level. Similarly, a valid classification system for substance use problems should reflect salient developmental differences.

Diagnosis in Clinical Settings

Debate will continue about the appropriate definition(s) of adolescent substance abuse based on research. These efforts may be for naught if researchers do not consider the often minimal effect their efforts have had on most treatment providers. Many treatment programs are run by professionals who are guided by the framework provided by Alcoholics Anonymous (AA) and a unitary disease concept rather than the concept of addiction provided by the alcohol dependence syndrome or DSM-III-R and DSM-IV. In the popular professional literature, clear, concise operational definitions of adolescent substance abuse or dependence, or even specific diagnostic criteria, are rare. Generic labels such as "alcoholic" or "chemically dependent" abound and are based on vague definitions, if definitions exist at all. A distinction is rarely made between the diagnosis for substance abuse in adults and the one for adolescents.

It is possible that the treatment community sees little value in using more specific criteria or common diagnostic terms, if this does not provide any advantage in their perception of assessment or treatment outcome. If a uniform, standard diagnostic system for adolescent substance abuse is to be adopted by the substance abuse treatment community, the diagnoses must be practical in terms of the identification of affected adolescents, the selection of treatment modalities, and the prediction of treatment outcome.

Clinical Application of DSM-IV Criteria to Adolescents

Given our current level of knowledge about substance abuse in adolescents, the new and "improved" DSM-IV may represent a reasonable compromise for categorical diagnoses of substance abuse disorders on the way to a more valid and useful nosology for adolescents. *Psychoactive substance dependence* represents one level of substance "abuse," consisting of a core of negative consequences in addition to signs, symptoms, or behaviors indicating physical dependence preoccupation with psychoactive substances and/or compulsive use. *Psychoactive substance abuse* represents a lower level of abuse indicating the presence of direct negative consequences of use. Using these definitions as a departure point, we can explore the specific criteria of DSM-IV and focus on the relevance of each diagnostic criterion for adolescents.

Substance Dependence

Substance dependence is characterized by a maladaptive pattern of substance use, leading to clinically significant impairment or distress with three criteria occurring together at any time in the same 12-month period. Substance dependence is further specified by the presence or absence of tolerance or withdrawal, indicating with or without physiological dependence, respectively.

1. *Tolerance* is defined as the need for significantly increased amounts of a substance to achieve the desired psychoactive effects or the development of decreased effect with the same amount of the substance. Extreme levels of tolerance as manifested by use of large quantities of a particular substance is evidence of more advanced levels of use. Tolerance may also represent a compulsion to use to the point of achieving a given desired effect.

   Tolerance is very common for many substances and among any substance user who uses beyond very modest levels. While helpful at extreme levels of use (for example, the adolescent who needs a case of beer or a fifth of hard liquor to achieve intoxication), tolerance at low or modest levels of use may have limited utility as a diagnostic criteria to distinguish substance abuse or dependence from nonpathological levels of use.

2. *Withdrawal* indicates the presence of the characteristic or specific withdrawal syndrome for that particular substance, or taking the substance—or a similar substance—to relieve or avoid withdrawal symptoms.

   The presence of withdrawal symptoms and the continued use of a substance to avoid withdrawal are evidence of true physiological dependence. While significant withdrawal symptoms are rare in adolescents, even with other dependence criteria, the clinician should inquire about their presence.

3. *Substance often taken in larger amounts or over a longer period than the person intended.* This symptom or criteria suggests loss of control; that is, once a substance use episode has begun, it become difficult, if not impossible, for the adolescent to control use or stop despite any initial intention for control or abstinence.

4. *Persistent desire or unsuccessful efforts to cut down or control substance use.* Inability to control substance use through previous efforts to abstain, relapse, or previous treatment experiences, despite recognition of one's excessive or pathological use is another sign of loss of control. Unfortunately, recognition of a problem with substance use or previous efforts by adolescents to quit are infrequent. Many adolescent substance abusers may acknowledge attempts to cut down or even quit in response to pressure from family or peers, or negative consequences such as arrest for possession of substances or driving while under the influence of a substance.

5. *Much time spent in activities necessary to get the substance, using the substance, or recovering from its effects.* Preoccupation with substance use and related behaviors is evidence that substance use is beginning or has already taken over the adolescent's life. In severe cases, virtually all of a person's daily activities revolve around getting, using, or recovering from substance use.

6. *Important social, occupational, or recreational activities given up or decreased due to substance use.* The neglect or withdrawal from previously desired and important activities also illustrates the preoccupation with substance use.

7. *Continued substance use despite knowledge of having a continuing or recurrent social, psychological, or physical problem that is caused or worsened by the use of the substance.* The inability to abstain or cut down despite negative consequences in one or more areas of the adolescent's life supports the concept of loss of control. Meeting this criterion involves surveying a list of negative consequences of use and their repeated occurrence accompanying or following substance use. The adolescent may not specifically admit to experiencing these negative consequences or may not attribute these consequences to substance use.

Four remission course specifiers can be applied only after none of the criteria has been present for at least one month. *Early full remission* or *sustained full remission* can be given if none of the criteria are met during a period of remission, depending on the length of time elapsed since no criteria have been present. *Early partial remission* and *sustained partial remission* are given after a period of full remission (at least one month), if at least one criteria for dependence is met. *On agonist therapy* or *in a controlled environment* are additional specifiers. The latter is applicable to many adolescent substance abusers who are in residential placements. While abstinent and not meeting dependence criteria for some period of time, their intent to use substances is limited only by the limited accessibility due to placement.

Substance Abuse

Substance abuse is defined by DSM-IV as a maladaptive pattern of use leading to significant impairment and distress, as shown by at least one of four criteria during a one-year period.

1. *Recurrent use resulting in inability or failure to meet major role obligations at work, school, or home.* This criteria involves substance-use related social, occupational, and/or psychological impairment. The clinician should be careful to include only those behaviors or areas of dysfunction directly attributable to the adolescent's substance use. The replacement of major role obligations again suggests that substance use

has taken over as the focal point of the affected youth's life. This criteria item was previously contained within the DSM-II-R diagnostic category of psychoactive substance dependence.

2. *Recurrent use in physically hazardous situations.* Driving a motor vehicle or participating in a recreational activity such as swimming while under the influence of a substance are common examples of use in hazardous situations. Recurrent use in such situations is evidence of use despite the risk of harm.

3. *Recurrent substance use-related legal problems.* Underage drinking is a status offense where the adolescent is arrested by virtue of age and not necessarily due to immediate risk of danger to self or others. However, a pattern of substance-related offenses should be considered a maladaptive pattern of use.

4. *Continued use despite continuing or recurrent social or interpersonal problems caused or worsened by the effects of the substance.* This item continues the general focus of substance abuse, that is, the repeated use of a substance or substances despite negative consequences due to use. Common examples for adolescents are physical fights, conflict with family, peers, or others while under the influence, or conflicts about the adolescent's use.

Patterns of Symptoms in Adolescent Substance Abusers

How do the DSM-IV criteria usually fit together in adolescents receiving diagnoses for psychoactive substance abuse or dependence? Examining a sample of 181 adolescent drinkers, Martin and colleagues (submitted for publication) found that a substantial number of subjects with alcohol dependence met criteria for tolerance, drinking more than intended, much time spent drinking, alcohol-related loss of social activities, and repeated unsuccessful attempts to quit. Some level of alcohol withdrawal was present in only 23 percent of adolescents diagnosed with dependence, a relatively high percentage, but less than half of that noted in alcohol-dependent adult samples. Tolerance was less specific to the diagnosis of dependence than other dependence criteria. For adolescents diagnosed with alcohol abuse, problems or inability to fulfill role obligations were frequently observed in family contexts, followed by peer contexts, and school contexts. There was minimal endorsement of problems within work context. Reports of problems in school contexts may be decreased due to preexisting school problems or school dropout preceding a pattern of abuse. Patterns of alcohol abuse symptoms were heterogenous among adolescents diagnosed with alcohol abuse. Alcohol abuse symptoms tended to be only weakly associated with measures of alcohol consumption.

Although a significant number of alcohol-dependent adolescents endorsed craving (35.5 percent), it was uncertain whether this construct is useful in adolescents due to significant developmental variability to introspect.

SUMMARY

Regardless of what one chooses to call a pathological pattern of substance use by adolescents, such patterns of use by adolescents can produce serious dysfunction in one or more life areas, as well as a potential pattern of use-associated behavior demonstrating a preoccupation with use of one or more psychoactive substances. Before one assigns a diagnosis or label of substance use disorder, either substance abuse or dependence, one must consider the developmental role and context of substance use by the adolescent. The frequent coexistence of other problems such as deviant behavior, psychopathology, and environmental stressors may confuse one into believing the resulting dysfunction is due entirely or in part to substance use rather than to the coexisting problem.

Is there or isn't there a substance abuse problem? Ultimately, substance use must be related to impairment or dysfunction in one or more life domains secondary to a pattern of substance use. While a continuum of use patterns can be observed in adolescents, the necessity of some kind of cut-off and label to describe an unacceptable level of substance use is necessary for identification of adolescents in need of treatment or intervention. In order to use diagnostic labels in a practical, appropriate manner, clinicians and researchers should be aware of both the strengths and weaknesses of current diagnostic systems.

CHAPTER 3

Epidemiology

In the first chapter we followed the significant variations in substance use by adolescents during the early history of the United States. During the first half of the twentieth century, significant adolescent substance use and abuse could be found in only a very small portion of youth. Due to the social upheaval, the increased availability of many substances of abuse, and the increased questioning of authority, adolescents began to show dramatic increases in substance use in the 1960s. The perceived increases in substance use by adolescents beginning in the 1960s prompted the support of large-scale surveys of adolescents and their substance use behavior.

EARLY STUDIES: 1960s AND 1970s

Wechsler (1979) studied alcohol consumption among students, grades 7 through 12, in New England in 1965 and again in 1974. In 1965 and 1974, 41 percent of the 9th to 12th grade boys reported frequent use of beer; frequent was defined by use 12 or more times (11 or more times in 1974). Twenty-three percent and 26 percent of boys reported frequent use of wine and liquor, respectively, in 1965. Thirty-four percent of boys reported at least one episode of intoxication on any beverage during 1965. This rate of alcohol use increased to 70 percent in 1974. For 9th to 12th grade girls in 1965, 16 percent reported frequent use of beer, 15 percent for wine, and 13 percent for liquor. These rates increased to 36 percent for beer and 20 percent for liquor in 1974. Intoxication rates for girls rose from 14 percent in 1965 to 69 percent in 1974. For younger students in the 7th and 8th grades, intoxication rates from 1965 to 1974 increased for boys from 14 percent to 33 percent and for girls from 8 percent to 27 percent.

Rachel and associates (Rachel, Hubbard, William, & Tuchfield, 1976) conducted a national study of drinking behavior in 1974 under contract with the National Institute on Alcohol Abuse and Alcoholism (NIAAA). In their study, junior and senior high school students in grades 7 through 12 completed a self-administered questionnaire. Based on this survey, Rachel found that 18.6 percent of adolescents did not drink alcohol, 2.4 percent of students drank every day, 23.3 percent drank at least once a week, while another 31.5 percent of students drank at least once a month, but less than once a week. Main drinking level (MDL), consisting of quantity-frequency indices, described adolescent drinking levels. According to their MDL classification, 27.3 percent of adolescents are considered abstainers, 32.9 percent are infrequent or light drinkers, 15.5 percent are moderate drinkers, and 24.3 percent are moderate-heavy or heavy drinkers who drink at least 2 to 4 alcohol units at least once a week, or 5 or more units 3 to 4 times a month. The study also defined problem drinking as drunkenness four or more times in the past year, or two or more reported areas of negative consequences of drinking behavior. According to this definition, 27.8 percent of students were problem drinkers, 45 percent were non-problem drinkers, and 27.8 percent were minimal drinkers or abstainers. Seventy percent of problem drinkers were classified moderate-heavy or heavy drinkers and approximately 85 percent of these problem drinkers reported drinking about once a week or more frequently.

ADOLESCENT SUBSTANCE ABUSE AND DEPENDENCE

Estimates of the prevalence of substance use disorders in adolescents are limited by few epidemiologic or community studies measuring pathologic use. The few existing studies of general or community population samples of adolescents are based on arbitrary definitions of problem use or on one of the earlier versions of the *Diagnostic and Statistical Manual of Mental Disorders*—DSM-III or DSM-III-R which are based on adult criteria. The diagnosis of substance abuse in adolescents is discussed in more detail in Chapter 2.

Kashani and colleagues (Kashani et al., 1987a, 1987b; Kashani, Orvaschel, Rosenberg, & Reid, 1989) in a community study of 15-year-old adolescents found a prevalence rate of 5.3 percent for DSM-III alcohol abuse/dependence and 3.3 percent for drug abuse/dependence. In a community study of 386 older adolescents, ages 17 to 19 years, Reinherz and associates (Reinherz, Giaconia, Lefkowitz, Pakiz, & Frost, 1993) reported that alcohol/abuse and dependence had the highest lifetime prevalence rate (32.4 percent) among DSM-III-R diagnoses. Among this group, alcohol abuse/ dependence was significantly more prevalent for males than females (37.6 percent versus 26.8 percent), although equal numbers of each gender (over 90 percent) had tried alcohol. Almost three fourths of the adolescents were classified as either moderately or severely dependent while only 15 percent had mild dependence on alcohol. For drug abuse/dependence, 9.8 percent met diagnostic criteria. A majority of these youth (61 percent) met criteria for marijuana only. More than one third (34 percent) met drug abuse/dependence criteria for marijuana and at least one other drug, usually cocaine or hallucinogens. Five percent met criteria for cocaine abuse/dependence only. Most of these adolescents were classified as either severely (18 percent) or moderately (76 percent) dependent, while only 5 percent had mild dependence.

Results from another epidemiologic study of children from New York State show alcohol abuse rates of 4.1 percent for boys and 3.1 percent for girls in the 14- to 16-year-old age group (Cohen et al., 1993). In the 17- to 20-year-old age group, the rates increased to 20.3 percent and 8.9 percent for boys and girls, respectively. Rates for marijuana abuse were 4.1 percent for boys and 1.8 percent for girls in the 17- to 20-year-old age group. Abuse rates for other drugs were 1.4 percent for males and 0.9 percent for females. Cohen and associates also reported that substance abuse diagnoses made after 14 years of age were fairly persistent upon follow up two and one half years later.

The results from the community survey by Reinherz and associates (1993) show a very high prevalence of substance abuse/dependence in older adolescents. These rates are higher than those for similar diagnoses in the Epidemiological Catchment Area (ECA) study of adults (Helzer, Burnam, & McEvoy, 1991). While the high prevalence found in the Reinherz sample raises questions about the appropriateness of DSM-II-R psychoactive substance use disorder diagnostic criteria for adolescents, other surveys of problem drinking found that approximately 30 percent of adolescent males reported a pattern of problem drinking (Donovan & Jessor, 1978). Similarly, data from the "Monitoring the Future" annual survey of high school seniors shows that approximately one third of seniors report drinking at least five consecutive drinks in the previous two-week period (Johnston, Bachman, & O'Malley, 1992).

Surveys of substance abuse disorders among specific populations are more common. Consistent with the adult literature, adolescents with serious emotional problems have increased prevalence rates of problem substance use or substance abuse (DeMilio, 1989; Elliot, Huizinga, & Ageton, 1985; Greenbaum, Prange, Friedman, & Silver, 1991). Among juvenile offenders, the prevalence of substance abuse is very high, reaching over 80 percent in some studies (Milan, Halikas, Meller, & Morse, 1991). These studies involve nonrepresentative populations with significant risk factors, particularly deviance and psychopathology, for substance abuse. Both risk factors and comorbidity or coexisting psychiatric disorders are discussed in Chapters 4 and 5.

RECENT SURVEYS OF ADOLESCENT SUBSTANCE USE

Recognition of these significant trends in the use of alcohol and other drugs by adolescents prompted government support of several large-scale, ongoing surveys of adolescent substance use. As those surveys were planned and executed, researchers confronted several methodologic problems. Measurement of substance use is complicated by the fact of adolescent substance use being illicit. The deviant nature of substance use and feared consequences of affirmative reporting may influence survey results. Some youth may exaggerate their substance use. However, the available data suggest that adolescent self-reports are reliable and valid (Oetting & Beauvais, 1990). Among the factors possibly affecting accurate survey self-reports are problems with definitions of drugs and quantities for use (Johnston & O'Malley, 1986). As many studies are based in high schools or junior high schools, the exclusion of dropouts and absentees from the study may result in more conservative results, as many absent youth are likely to be at higher risk to use and abuse drugs (Johnston, 1973; Kandel, 1975b).

For approximately the past two decades, the source of much of the data on adolescent substance use patterns has been the NIDA sponsored National High School Senior Survey (Johnston, O'Malley, & Bachman, 1991), the National Household Survey on Drug Abuse, and the Drug Abuse Warning Network (DAWN) (Oetting & Beauvais, 1990). The National Senior Survey (NSS) administered by Johnston and associates at the Institute for Social Research at the University of Michigan collects information from over 16,000 public and private high school seniors in approximately 130 high schools. The sample is representative of seniors and the survey is standardized. Its annual administration since 1975 and its longitudinal study of subgroups from each class allow monitoring of both secular trends over time and developmental factors within cohorts. The NSS often includes questions about the availability of substances, student attitudes, and perceived dangerousness of substances. The NSS is limited by its failure to include dropouts and absentees.

The National Household Survey on Drug Abuse is a general population survey of a random sample of all U.S. households, stratified by geographic location and population density. The survey includes household members at and above the age of 12 and has been administered every two to three years since 1971. The survey also often includes a variety of questions on substance use beyond quantity and frequency. Limitations of the household survey include the exclusion of those living in institutions (prisons, military bases, hospitals, and residential settings) and administration of the interview in the household where an adolescent may feel inhibited in providing an accurate report of substance use.

The Drug Abuse Warning Network (DAWN) is a report of emergency room episodes for substance use-related problems and medical examiner cases for substance use-related fatalities. DAWN data reports and monitors the health consequences and substance abuse trends.

The following discussion involves data taken predominantly from the National Senior Survey (Monitoring the Future Survey) and the National Household Survey. Data from the NSS consists of the prevalence of the use of specific substances by 12th graders, 10th graders, and 8th graders (Johnston, O'Malley, & Bachman, 1991, 1993; University of Michigan, 1994). (See Tables 3.1, 3.3, 3.4,

TABLE 3.1.   Trends in the Lifetime Prevalence of Substance Use for High
School Seniors*

	Percent Who Ever Used				
Substance	Class of 1975	Class of 1980	Class of 1985	Class of 1990	Class of 1993
Alcohol	90.4	93.2	92.2	89.5	87.0
Cigarettes	73.6	71.0	68.8	64.4	61.9
Any Illicit Drug	55.2	65.4	60.6	47.9	42.9
Any Illicit Drug (except marijuana)	36.2	38.7	39.7	29.4	26.7
Marijuana	47.3	60.3	54.2	40.7	35.3
Cocaine	9.0	15.7	17.3	9.4	6.1
crack	—	—	—	3.5	2.6
Heroin	2.2	1.1	1.2	1.3	1.1
Other Opiates	9.0	9.8	10.2	8.3	6.4
Stimulants	22.3	26.4	26.2	17.5	15.1
Hallucinogens	16.3	13.3	10.3	9.4	10.9
LSD	11.3	9.3	7.5	8.7	10.3
Sedatives	18.2	14.9	11.8	5.3	6.4
Inhalants	—	17.3	18.1	18.0	17.4
Steroids	—	—	—	2.9	2.0

* From Johnston, O'Malley, and Bachman, 1993; University of Michigan, 1994.

and 3.5.) The National Household Survey reports substance use by 12- to 17-
year-olds as a single group (Department of Health and Human Services, 1991).

Alcohol

The drinking of alcoholic beverages has continued since antiquity. Currently, alcohol consumption remains a popular and generally accepted social activity in
most countries of the world. As previously noted, prior to the 1960s, alcohol
use by adolescents was the only use of a psychoactive substance that was not
considered a significant deviant behavior. This pattern follows as alcohol remains the most frequently used substance among adolescents. Despite the fact
that alcohol is illegal for adolescents, experience with alcohol is almost universal among youth. Data from the late 1960s shows that over 80 percent of high
school students reported at least some experience with alcohol (Johnston, 1973).
Findings from the National High School Senior Survey since 1975 consistently
show approximately 9 out of 10 seniors reporting some lifetime experience with
alcohol. Although there has been a very modest decrease in the lifetime prevalence in alcohol use among high school seniors from a peak of 93.2 percent in

TABLE 3.2.   Problems Associated with Alcohol Use Reported during the Past Year, Adolescents, Age 12 to 17*

Type of Problem	Percent Reporting Problem
Aggressive or cross while drinking	21.0
Heated arguments while drinking	14.0
Stayed away from school or work	5.9
High on job or at school	12.7
Partner told me I should cut down	9.3
Relative told me I should cut down	6.2
Friend told me I should cut down	7.5
Drank fast to get effect	24.8
Afraid I might be or become an alcoholic	15.2
Stayed drunk for more than one day	5.1
Difficult for me to stop drinking	11.7
Unable to remember what happened	25.2
Quick drink when no one was looking	20.3
Drink first thing in the morning	2.1
Got high while drinking alone	12.5
Kept on drinking after promising myself not to	8.0

* From National Household Survey, DHHS, 1991.

1980 to 87.0 percent in 1993, lifetime prevalence of alcohol use has not shown the dramatic declines recently noted during the past decade in the lifetime prevalence of substances such as marijuana and cocaine.

Data from the National Household Survey from 1974 to 1990 (U.S. Department of Health and Human Services (DHHS), 1991) estimated lifetime prevalence for alcohol use by adolescents between 12 and 17 years of age. While lifetime prevalence for the entire 12- to 17-year age range peaked at 70.3 percent in 1979, the figure has remained at least at approximately 50 percent during the last 15 years. Most recently, in 1990, 48.2 percent of 12- to 17-year-olds reported some lifetime experience with alcohol.

While at least some experience with alcohol is all but universal among adolescents, more frequent use is also quite common. During the past 16 years, the National Senior Surveys (Johnston, O'Malley, & Bachman, 1991, 1993; University of Michigan 1994) have found that over 50 percent of senior students report having had alcohol during the preceding 30-day period (one month prevalence). As early as the late 1960s, over 50 percent of adolescents were reporting monthly use of alcohol (Johnston, 1973). However, the monthly prevalence of alcohol use among high school seniors has gradually declined from a peak of 72 percent in 1980 to 54 percent in 1991. Among the range of 12- to 17-year-olds, the monthly prevalence rate of alcohol use peaked at 37.2 percent in 1979

TABLE 3.3.   Trends in the Thirty-Day Prevalence of Substance Use for High School Seniors*

Substance	Percent Who Used in Last 30 Days				
	Class of 1975	Class of 1980	Class of 1985	Class of 1990	Class of 1993
Alcohol	68.2	72.0	65.9	57.1	51.0
Cigarettes	36.7	30.5	30.1	29.4	29.9
Any Illicit Drug	30.7	37.2	29.7	17.2	18.3
Any Illicit Drug (except marijuana)	15.4	18.4	14.9	8.0	7.9
Marijuana	27.1	33.7	25.7	14.0	15.5
Cocaine	1.9	5.2	6.7	1.9	1.3
crack	—	—	0.7	0.7	0.7
Heroin	0.4	0.2	0.3	0.2	0.2
Other Opiates	2.1	2.4	2.3	1.5	1.3
Stimulants	8.5	12.1	6.8	3.7	3.7
Hallucinogens	4.7	3.7	2.5	2.2	2.7
LSD	2.3	2.3	1.6	1.9	2.4
Sedatives	5.4	4.8	2.4	1.0	1.3
Inhalants	—	1.4	2.2	2.7	2.5
Steroids	—	—	—	1.0	0.7

* From Johnston, O'Malley, and Bachman, 1993; University of Michigan, 1994.

TABLE 3.4.   Trends in the Prevalence of Daily Substance Use for High School Seniors*

Substance	Percent Who Used Daily in the Last 30 Days				
	Class of 1975	Class of 1980	Class of 1985	Class of 1990	Class of 1993
Alcohol	5.7	6.0	5.0	3.7	2.5
5 drinks in a row/ last 2 weeks	36.8	41.4	36.7	32.7	27.5
Cigarettes	26.9	21.3	19.5	19.1	19.0
Marijuana	6.0	9.1	4.9	2.2	2.4
Cocaine	0.1	0.2	0.4	2.2	2.4
Heroin	0.1	0.0	0.0	0.0	0.0
Stimulants	0.5	0.7	0.4	0.2	0.2
Hallucinogens	0.1	0.1	0.1	0.1	0.1
Sedatives	0.3	0.2	0.1	0.0	0.1
Inhalants	—	0.1	0.2	0.3	0.1
Steroids	—	—	—	0.2	0.1

* From Johnston, O'Malley, and Bachman, 1993; University of Michigan, 1994.

**TABLE 3.5.   Lifetime and Thirty-Day Prevalence in Use of
Various Types of Substances by 8th and 10th Grade Students 1993**

	8th Grade	10th Grade
Marijuana		
lifetime	12.6	24.4
thirty-day	5.1	10.9
Inhalants		
lifetime	19.4	17.5
thirty-day	5.4	3.3
Hallucinogens		
lifetime	3.9	6.8
thirty-day	1.2	1.9
LSD		
lifetime	3.5	6.2
thirty-day	1.0	1.6
Cocaine		
liftime	2.9	3.6
thirty-day	0.7	0.9
Heroin		
lifetime	1.4	1.3
thirty-day	0.4	0.3
Stimulants		
lifetime	11.8	14.9
thirty-day	3.6	4.3
Steroids		
lifetime	1.6	1.7
thirty-day	0.5	0.5
Cigarettes		
lifetime	45.3	56.3
thirty-day	16.7	24.7
daily	8.3	14.2
Smokeless Tobacco		
lifetime	18.7	28.1
thirty-day	6.6	10.4

* Adapted from data: University of Michigan, 1994.

and declined to 24.5 percent in 1990 (DHHS, 1991). Trends in the daily use of alcohol by adolescents have also shown a decline. As early as the late 1960s, 6.4 percent of high school students were reporting daily alcohol use (Johnston, 1973). Among high school seniors, daily use of alcohol peaked at 6.9 percent in 1979 and has declined to 2.5 percent in 1993 (University of Michigan, 1994).

The reported use of alcohol is a very crude measure which does not specify quantity of alcohol use or the consequences of use, including intoxication. The frequency of drinking to intoxication may be at least an indirect measure of heavy or problem drinking. The National Senior Survey has collected data from seniors reporting five or more drinks in a row at least once in the prior two-week period. Since 1975, the percent age of seniors reporting this level of use has remained above one-third. However, recently this statistic has declined from a peak of 41.4 percent of seniors in 1981 to 27.5 percent in 1993 (University of Michigan, 1994).

During the last three years of the National Senior Survey, each grade surveyed reported the prevalence of being drunk. Over 60 percent of seniors reported having ever been drunk (62.5 percent in 1993). Approximately 30 percent of seniors (28.9 percent in 1993) reported having been drunk sometime in the preceding 30 days and 0.9 percent reported being drunk on a daily basis during the 30 days preceding the survey in 1993. Among 8th graders in 1993, 26.4 percent reported being drunk at some point in their young lives, 7.8 percent reported being drunk sometime during the preceding 30 days, and 0.2 percent reported being drunk daily. In 1993, tenth graders reported intermediate levels of drunkenness with lifetime, 30-day, and daily prevalence of being drunk at 47.9 percent, 19.8 percent and 0.4 percent, respectively.

Alcohol use is more prevalent and frequent among high school seniors than among lower classmen, and the prevalence in the 12- to 17-year age group reflects an average. The National Adolescent Student Health Survey (NASHS) in 1987 found that 75.9 percent of 8th graders reported a lifetime prevalence of alcohol use (Windle, 1991). Lifetime prevalence of alcohol use among 10th graders was 87.3 percent. During the 30 days preceding the survey, two-thirds of 8th graders reported no alcohol use and the majority of those using reported infrequent use. Among 10th graders, over one-half of the adolescents used alcohol during the prior 30 days, with 13 percent reporting frequent use. Using the definition of heavy drinking in the National Senior Survey, data from the National Adolescent Student Health Survey (NASHS) found that 23.7 percent of drinking 8th graders reported consuming five or more drinks in a row at least once during the preceding two weeks. Over one-third (36.6 percent) of drinking 10th graders reported a similar pattern of heavy drinking (Windle, 1991).

In a national survey of adolescent drinking behavior in 1972, Rachel and associates (1976) classified adolescent drinkers according to quantity and frequent data, and determined problem-drinker status according to reported drunkenness four or more times in the past year and/or reporting two or more areas of negative consequences of drinking behavior. Designation of a moderate-heavy drinker or as a heavy drinker required drinking at least two to four drinks at least once a week or an average of five or more drinks three to four times a month. Based on these definitions, over 24 percent of adolescents could be defined as moderate-heavy or heavy drinkers while 27.8 percent of adolescents were considered "problem drinkers." Although overall, the prevalence of rates of alcohol use have changed relatively little, a long-term decline in episodes of heavy drinking among 12th graders appears to have decelerated (University of Michigan, 1994).

Unfortunately, no data exists measuring the prevalence of a standard definition of alcohol abuse or dependence among a large general population and representative sample of adolescents. In the National Household Survey (U.S. DHHS, 1991), the percent age of adolescents, age 12 to 17, reported problems associated with alcohol use during the past year. In this general population sample, 21.0 percent reported being aggressive while drinking, 14.0 percent having a heated argument while drinking, 24.8 percent drinking fast to hasten the effects, and 25.2 percent as having had blackouts. Another 20.3 percent reported taking a quick drink when no one was looking. Other common problems are noted in Table 3.2. Students endorsed cognitive or psychological consequences much less frequently than behavioral consequences of drinking.

Marijuana

Other than alcohol, and perhaps tobacco, marijuana currently remains the most widely used illicit drug among youth. The lifetime prevalence in the use of marijuana by high school seniors peaked in 1979 at 50.8 percent and subsequently declined to 32.6 percent in 1993 before increasing to 35.3 percent in 1993 (University of Michigan, 1994). The National Household Survey (U.S. DHHS, 1991) reported a similar pattern of lifetime experience with marijuana by adolescents age 12 to 17 years old. In 1972, 14 percent of this age group reported lifetime use of marijuana. The lifetime prevalence peaked in 1979 at 30.9 percent and declined to 14.8 percent in 1990. Monthly prevalence of marijuana use showed a similar peak at 37.1 percent of high school seniors in 1978 with a similar decline to a 16-year low of 11.9 percent in 1992 before increasing to 15.5 percent in 1993. The National Household Survey shows monthly prevalence at 7.0 percent of 12- to 17-year-olds in 1972, peaking at 16.7 percent in 1979, and declining to 5.2 percent in 1990. Daily use by high school seniors peaked at 10.7 percent in 1978, showing a precipitous decline in the late 1980s to 1.9 percent in 1991 (University of Michigan, 1994).

Data from the Centers for Disease Control (DHHS, 1991b) shows lifetime prevalence of marijuana use at 20.6 percent for a sample of 9th graders in 1990. This figure increases steadily through the 10th and 11th grades to 42.2 percent for high school seniors. Monthly prevalence of marijuana use shows a similar increase with 9.5 percent of 9th graders reporting use within the preceding month and increasing to 18.5 percent in the 12th grade. In the 1993 National Senior Survey, 12.6 percent of 8th graders reported lifetime marijuana use while 5.1 percent reported use within the last month. For 10th graders in 1993, lifetime and 30-day prevalence for marijuana use was 24.4 percent and 10.9 percent, respectively. The proportion of younger adolescents using marijuana is increasing faster than older groups of youth. During the past two years, students from all three grades have reported a reduction in the perceived harmfulness of marijuana use, either on an occasional basis or on a regular basis

(University of Michigan, 1994). While most youth continue to perceive marijuana use as harmful, this trend may portend future increases in actual use.

Cocaine

Similar to marijuana, cocaine use by adolescents appears to be declining from a peak in the late 1980s. Lifetime prevalence of cocaine use among high school seniors was 9.0 percent in 1975. After a progressive increase during the late 1970s and early 1980s, the lifetime prevalence peaked at 17.3 percent of seniors in 1985 before dramatic declines from 1988 to 1992. In 1992 and 1993, 6.1 percent of high school seniors reported using cocaine at least once during their lifetime. Among the range of adolescents, age 12 to 17, the National Household Survey (DHHS, 1991) reported a lifetime prevalence of 1.5 percent in 1972. This figure increased steadily to a peak of 6.5 percent in 1982 with subsequent declines to 6.5 percent in 1990. By grade, only 3.6 percent of 9th graders report lifetime use of cocaine while 5.8 percent, 7.6 percent, and 9.3 percent of 10th, 11th, and 12th graders, respectively, reported lifetime cocaine use in 1990 (CDC, 1991). According to the Monitoring the Future Survey in 1993, few students have tried cocaine or crack by the 8th grade (2.9 percent and 1.7 percent lifetime prevalence, respectively) or by the 10th grade (3.6 percent and 1.8 percent lifetime prevalence, respectively).

Lifetime "crack" cocaine use has been surveyed by the National Senior Survey since 1987. In 1987, 5.4 percent of high school seniors reported lifetime crack use. Lifetime "crack" use has subsequently declined to 2.6 percent in 1993 (University of Michigan, 1994).

For the monthly prevalence of cocaine use, 1.3 percent of high school seniors reported cocaine use in the prior month in 1993. Monthly prevalence peaked for seniors in 1985 when 6.7 percent reported cocaine use. Again, this figure declined to 0.7 percent in 1993. For the range of adolescents, age 12 to 17, 0.6 percent of adolescents reported use in the preceding month in 1972 (DHHS, 1991). After peaking at 2.6 percent in 1982, the monthly prevalence for cocaine use declined to 1.0 percent in 1990. By grade in 1990, only 1.1 percent of 9th graders reported use of cocaine in the prior month. Monthly prevalence jumps to 2.4 percent for 10th graders with a similar number of 11th and 12th graders endorsing cocaine use in the preceding month. Monitoring the Future Survey data shows month prevalence rates in 1991 for both 8th and 10th graders to be well below 1 percent of students who were surveyed. The monthly prevalence of "crack" use for high school seniors was 1.3 percent in 1987 with steady declines to 0.7 percent in 1991. According to the National Household Survey in 1990 (DHHS, 1991), only 0.1 percent of adolescents, age 12 to 17, reported crack use in the prior month.

The daily use of cocaine as reported by high school seniors has remained at very low levels. Starting with 0.1 percent of seniors reporting daily use of cocaine in 1975, daily use rose to a peak of 0.4 percent in 1986, and subsequently declined to a level of 0.1 percent in 1993 (University of Michigan, 1994).

Inhalants

Inhalants are one of the few classes of substances failing to show significant declines in use by adolescents during the past two decades. Trends in the lifetime prevalence of inhalant use among high school seniors has shown a gradual increase during the past 16 years. In 1976, 10.3 percent of high school seniors reported lifetime inhalant use. The lifetime prevalence has gradually increased to a level of 18.0 percent in 1990 and 17.4 percent in 1993, although adjustment for likely under-reporting of amyl and butyl nitrates boosted lifetime prevalence figures to a peak of 20.1 percent in 1986 and 18.5 percent and 18.0 percent in 1990 and 1993, respectively. Monthly prevalence rates for high school seniors are relatively low. From a monthly prevalence of 0.9 percent in 1976, this figure has gradually increased to a peak of 2.8 (3.5 percent adjusted) percent in 1987 and 2.5 (2.6 percent adjusted) percent in 1993.

The rather large differences between lifetime and monthly prevalence is likely a result of inhalant being primarily a substance used by younger adolescents rather than seniors. Monitoring the Future Survey data in 1993 shows that 19.4 percent of 8th graders and 17.4 percent of 10th graders report lifetime inhalant use. In the National Household Survey, adolescents, aged 12 to 17, had a lifetime prevalence of 6.4 percent in 1972. Although reaching a peak of 9.8 percent in 1979, lifetime prevalence was 7.8 percent in 1990. Monthly prevalence among this group of adolescents for inhalant use was 1.0 percent in 1972, reaching a peak of 3.4 percent in 1985, before declining to the most recent level of 2.2 percent in 1990.

Hallucinogens

The National Senior or Monitoring the Future Survey reports lifetime prevalence of total hallucinogen use at 10.9 percent of surveyed high school seniors. The peak for lifetime prevalence comes quite early as the senior classes of 1975 and 1976 reported prevalence rates of 16.3 percent and 15.1 percent, respectively, with subsequent gradual declines to the present. Most recently, LSD makes up a majority of hallucinogen use with a lifetime prevalence of 10.3 percent in 1993. Reported PCP lifetime prevalence was 2.9 percent in 1993. In 1979, the lifetime adjusted prevalence of LSD use was 9.5 percent while 12.8 percent of seniors reported lifetime PCP use or 72 percent of the total hallucinogen use reported by seniors in 1979. In 1993, 8th graders reported a lifetime prevalence of 3.9 percent for hallucinogens and a monthly prevalence of 1.2 percent. Tenth graders reported a lifetime prevalence of 6.8 percent and a monthly prevalence of 1.9 percent. Students from both grades indicated little, if any, daily hallucinogen use. The National Household Survey found a lifetime prevalence of 3.3 percent for adolescents, age 12 to 17, in 1990. This represents a decline from previous years with a peak of 7.1 percent in 1979.

As with illicit drugs, other than alcohol or marijuana, the prevalence of daily use of hallucinogens including LSD or PCP as reported by high school seniors, is quite low with a range of 0.1 to 0.3 percent and daily use reported by only 0.1 percent of 1993 seniors.

Overall, LSD has been increasing gradually at all three grade levels during the past several years according to the Monitoring the Future Survey. This increase is despite a history of past declines, a response in part to perceived danger or risk attributed to LSD use (University of Michigan, 1994).

Heroin and Other Opiates

For the Monitoring the Future Survey, only a small proportion of high school seniors report lifetime heroin or other opiate lifetime use. From a peak of 2.2 percent of senior reporting lifetime use in 1975, the lifetime prevalence has declined to 0.9 percent in 1991, before increasing to 1.1 percent in 1993. The biggest portion of this decline occurred in the late 1970s. The use of other opiates is more common among students. Following a stable period with a range of lifetime prevalence between 9.0 and 10.3 percent, the lifetime prevalence of other opiate use declined from 1988 to 1993 to a level of 6.4 percent.

For adolescents in the National Household Survey, age 12 to 17, less than 1 percent (0.7) report lifetime heroin use in 1990 while 6.5 percent report nonmedical use of analgesics (DHHS, 1991).

Monthly prevalence patterns of heroin use show similar patterns to lifetime use with a seemingly stable range of 0.2 to 0.4 percent of seniors reporting monthly use. Other opiate use during the prior month is reported by 1.3 percent of seniors in 1993 with a peak in monthly prevalence during the late 1970s.

The daily use of both heroin and other opiates is reported at almost insignificant levels by less than 0.1 percent of high school seniors in 1993.

According to the Monitoring the Future Survey, 8th graders in 1993 reported a lifetime prevalence for heroin use of 1.4 percent and a monthly prevalence of 0.4 percent. Tenth graders reported a lifetime prevalence of 1.3 percent and a monthly prevalence of 0.3 percent in 1993.

Stimulants

A significant proportion of high school seniors report lifetime stimulant use (including amphetamines). In 1993, 15.1 percent of seniors reported using stimulants at some point in their lives. This figure represents a steady decline from an adjusted figure of 27.9 percent in 1882 when there was a likely peak in use during the early 1980s. For adolescents, age 12 to 17, the lifetime prevalence has been fairly stable with a peak level of 5.2 percent in 1977 and the most recent report of 4.5 percent in 1990 (DHHS, 1991).

The Monitoring the Future Survey reported the monthly prevalence by high school seniors as 3.7 percent in 1993. Similar to data from lifetime use of both stimulants and other illicit substances, the monthly prevalence of stimulant use has declined since the early 1980s from an adjusted peak of 10.7 percent. The monthly prevalence of stimulant use by adolescents, age 12 to 17, was 1.0 percent in 1990, following a peak of 2.6 percent in 1982 (DHHS, 1991). Daily use, as reported by high school seniors, has also declined since the early 1980s with a 1993 prevalence of 0.2 percent.

For younger adolescents, 8th graders in 1993 reported a lifetime prevalence of 11.8 percent and a monthly prevalence of 3.6 percent, while 10th graders reported a lifetime prevalence of 14.9 percent and monthly prevalence of 4.3 percent. Despite a significant decline from the early 1980s, stimulant use has risen at all three grade levels during the past one to two years.

Sedatives and Tranquilizers

Although almost all surveys separate sedative and tranquilizer use, both classes of agents are CNS depressants. Among high school seniors, the lifetime use of sedatives has shown a steady decline since the mid- and late 1970s. Following a peak lifetime prevalence of 18.2 percent in 1975, lifetime sedative use declined to a low of 6.1 percent in 1992, before increasing to 6.4 percent in 1993. Barbiturate use occupies most of the sedative use by seniors with a similar pattern of decline in the report of lifetime use. Methaqualone (Quaalude) lifetime use peaked at 10.7 percent in 1982 with subsequent, significant declines in use to 0.8 percent in 1993. Lifetime tranquilizer use shows a similar pattern with a peak of 18.0 percent in 1977 and a steady decline to a low of 6.0 percent in 1992 before increasing to 6.4 percent in 1993. For the wider range of adolescents, age 12 to 17, the lifetime prevalence appears more stable with a peak of 5.8 percent reporting sedative use in 1982 and 3.3 percent reporting lifetime use in 1990. Tranquilizer use parallels sedative use with a peak of 4.9 percent in 1982 and 2.7 percent in 1990.

Monthly prevalence of both sedative and tranquilizer use mirror the pattern of decline noted in lifetime use. From peaks in the late 1970s, declines in the monthly prevalence of both sedative and tranquilizer use were reported by high school seniors. In 1993, 1.3 percent of seniors, respectively, reported sedative and tranquilizer use in the preceding month. Recent levels of reported daily use were less than 0.1 percent for both types of substances in 1993.

Steroids

The Monitoring the Future Survey has only recently begun to survey high school seniors for the use of steroids. In 1989, when questions about steroid use were first included, 3.0 percent of seniors reported lifetime use. In 1993, 2.0 percent of seniors reported use. Monthly prevalence was reported by 0.7 percent of seniors in 1993. Daily use was reported by 0.1 percent or less in 1989 and 1993. Eighth graders report a lifetime prevalence of 1.9 percent and 10th graders report a lifetime prevalence of 1.8 percent.

Cigarettes and Tobacco

The lifetime prevalence of cigarette use among high school seniors has shown a gradual decline from 1977 when 75.7 percent of seniors reported lifetime cigarette use. Following a steady decline, a low of 61.9 percent of seniors reported lifetime cigarette use in 1993. Monthly prevalence among seniors appears more stable with a peak of 38.8 percent in 1976 and a low of 27.8 percent in 1992, increasing to 29.9 percent in 1993. Daily use has followed a pattern of steady decline from a peak of 19.4 percent of seniors reporting daily cigarette use in 1977 to 18.1 and 19.0 percent of seniors reporting daily use in 1988 and 1991, respectively. Of those seniors who smoke daily, almost 60 percent smoke a half a pack of cigarettes or more per day (University of Michigan, 1994; Johnston, O'Malley, & Bachman, 1991).

In 1993, 8th graders report a lifetime prevalence of 45.0 percent and daily use by 8.3 percent of students, with almost half of smokers reporting smoking a half a pack or more per day. Tenth graders report a lifetime prevalence of 56.3 percent and daily use by 14.2 percent of students. Almost half of all 8th and 10th grade students who smoke daily report smoking a half a pack or more per day.

Cohort and Secular Trends

The data reporting the prevalence in the use of individual classes of substances by most adolescents clearly demonstrates a trend of long-term gradual declines in the use of any illicit substance until the past several years, with gradual increases in use since that time. Although the rates of declines and the timing of the peaks for individual classes of substances differ, the decline is clearly present for almost all agents at all levels of use during the late 1980s and early 1990s. The recent increases are more prominent for marijuana, LSD, inhalants, and stimulants.

The past declines in substance use by adolescents during the 1980s are especially prominent in the lifetime prevalence or how many adolescent ever try a particular substance. This includes time periods of peak lifetime prevalence and the percent age decline of use of each substance from peak to 1991 level. Overall, the use of any illicit substance peaked in approximately the early 1980s with a subsequent 32 percent decline to 1991. While the lifetime prevalence of cocaine, opiates, marijuana, stimulants, sedatives, and tranquilizers showed significant declines over the past decade, declines in alcohol, inhalants, and cigarette use are less impressive. These substances represent the most available substances.

Declines from peak monthly prevalence and heavy drinking status for alcohol appear more impressive. Monthly prevalence for senior alcohol use has declined 25 percent since the late 1970s. Heavy drinking status, defined as the use of five or more drinks in a row in the prior two week period declined 28 percent during the same time interval. Declines in the monthly prevalence of use of other individual substances parallels the significant declines noted in lifetime prevalence. As past declines were attributed to changes in the perceived risks, harmfulness, and disapproval associated with specific substance use, the recent increases in the use of some substances may be due, in part, to a decrease in the perceived risks and other negative changes in attitudes and beliefs in the past several years (University of Michigan, 1994). Access to substances is likely a small factor, at best, as high school seniors' reports of availability have remained stable—and high—over the past tow decades.

Before assuming an optimistic outlook in predicting a decrease in substance use among adolescents, one should remember that most surveys tend to under-sample high-risk adolescents. In data from Canada, while large declines in drinking levels were found, no decreases were noted for the most serious problems (Smart, Adlof, & Walsh, 1994). This finding indicates that there may be a relatively unchanging proportion of problem-drinking adolescents. Changes in overall rates of substance use do not portend similar changes in the rate of substance *abuse* among adolescents. Other studies have reported secular increases in the rates of substance abuse from past years with most of the increased numbers coming from more high-risk individuals being affected (Reich, Cloninger, Van Eerdewegh, Rice, & Mullaney, 1988).

Relationships with Later Substance Use

The Monitoring the Future Surveys also provide follow-ups of annual cohorts into early adulthood. An examination of substance use patterns following adolescence can provide clues as to the continuity of substance use behaviors.

Although most of the initiation of substance use is started before or during adolescence, the substantial proportion of youth who have at least tried any illicit substance (other than alcohol or cigarettes) continues to grow larger through their early and mid-twenties. Although lifetime prevalence for most drugs becomes higher in older age groups, active illicit substance use remains at levels similar to those reported by high school seniors. Active use, as defined by annual or monthly prevalence or daily use, is similar for any illicit substance use and marijuana use, but young adults have lower annual prevalence with inhalants, LSD, sedatives, heroin, and other opiates. Active cocaine use continues to increase until the mid-twenties.

Age

The initiation into substance use and the progression into use of other substances appears to follow a usual order of acquisition. Substances that are legal for adults—alcohol and cigarettes—are almost always the "gateway" substances marking initiation into substance use. In 1990, high school seniors reported that 19 percent of them had at least one cigarette by the 6th grade, 32 percent in grades 7 to 9 and another 14 percent reported having their first cigarette in high school. Regular daily smoking was started by 12 percent before the 10th grade and by 10 percent during the remainder of high school. For alcohol, 1990 seniors reported that 10.8 percent had their first drink by the 6th grade, 26.9 percent in grades 7 and 8, 22.3 percent in the 9th grade, and 29.4 percent during the remaining years of high school. Thus, middle school and the first year in high school are the most likely periods for initiation into substance use by adolescents. Almost 40 percent of adolescents have tried alcohol before entry into high school. By the end of the 9th grade, over half of 1990 seniors reporting lifetime alcohol intoxication have had their first experience with "getting drunk."

Inhalants are another group of substances commonly used before or during early adolescence. Approximately two thirds of the onset of inhalant use was prior to the 10th grade. Other substances generally have a later onset of use. Over 30 percent of eventual senior lifetime marijuana users report an onset of use prior to the 9th grade.

Gender

In general, higher proportions of males than females use illicit drugs, especially at higher levels of use (Johnston, O'Malley, & Bachman, 1991). For alcohol use among high school seniors in 1990, lifetime prevalence of use is nearly equal between males and females, at approximately 90 percent. However, males are more likely to report drinking larger quantities with 39 percent of males drinking five or more drinks within the preceding two weeks while only 24 percent of females reported this pattern. Daily use of alcohol was reported by 5.2 percent of males versus 1.9 percent of females. Similarly, lifetime marijuana use is only slightly higher in males although daily use is three times higher for males than for females. Lifetime use of an illicit drug other than marijuana is reported by 19 percent of males and 16 percent of females, while annual prevalence rates are much higher for males in all illicit drugs except for tranquilizers and methaqualone where rates are nearly equal for each gender.

For cigarettes, there is little difference between males and females. Slightly more males (11.6 percent) than females (10.8 percent) smoke a half-pack or more per day, although there is no difference in any daily smoking.

Over the past decade and a half of the Monitoring the Future Survey, sex differences for types of substances have generally remained unchanged with trends in use running parallel for both genders. Sex differences in marijuana, tranquilizers, and alcohol have narrowed somewhat in recent years.

Findings from the National Adolescent Health Survey (Windle, 1991) also show that gender differences among students who drink are declining, although more males are frequent drinkers. There were minimal differences between sexes in the number of heavy drinkers (i.e., five or more drinks consecutively within the preceding two-week period) in the 8th grade. However, by the 10th grade, more males (40 percent) reported heavy drinking than females (33 percent). This gender difference continued into the 12th grade when 45 percent of males endorsed heavy drinking compared with 28.1 percent of females.

Race and Ethnicity

Early studies of African-American youth in the 1970s revealed no significant differences in drinking patterns by race in rural populations, although African-American youth have slightly lower rates of drinkers and heavy drinkers (Dawkins, 1976; Globetti, 1970). Later studies of multiethnic adolescent populations found modest but significant differences in the frequency of substance use between African-Americans, Hispanics, Caucasians, and Asians (Maddahian, Newcomb, & Bentler, 1986, 1988; Newcomb & Bentler, 1986). Caucasians and Hispanics used alcohol and "hard" drugs more frequently than African-Americans and Asians. Caucasians also used marijuana most frequently followed by African-Americans, Hispanics, and Asians.

Monitoring the Future study results show similar trends (Bachman et al., 1991). Native Americans had the highest prevalence rates for cigarettes, alcohol, and most illicit drugs. For most drugs, white students consistently had higher rates than Hispanic students, African-American students, or Asian students who had the lowest rates. African-American students had consistently lower rates than white students.

The lower levels of alcohol use by African-American youth is further illustrated by findings showing African-American students representing the largest percent age of abstainers from alcohol use across grade levels and gender groups (Windle, 1991). Hispanic students are more likely to be frequent drinkers. Consistent with prevalence data, African-American youth appear to have fewer risk factors for alcohol abuse than white or Hispanic adolescents who have similar levels of risk (Maddahian, Newcomb, & Bentler, 1988).

As demonstrated by general secular trends, patterns of use of specific substances by specific groups of adolescents can rapidly change. For example, the explosive growth of crack cocaine use among young, urban African-Americans during the past decade may have contributed to changes within the families and communities of African-American adolescents. Given these significant changes, the decade-old studies previously mentioned may not be currently accurate.

Regional Differences

There appear to be differential patterns of substance use by students in different parts of the United States. According to the Monitoring the Future Survey, the highest annual prevalence of illicit drug use is in the Northeast where 36 percent of high school seniors report use in the past year. The South has the lowest annual prevalence at 28 percent; the North Central and West follow close behind the Northeast at 34 percent. The West ranks highest in the annual prevalence of use of any illicit drug other than marijuana. This appears due to regional differences in annual cocaine use. In 1990, the annual prevalence was 6.6 percent in the West, 6.5 percent in the Northeast, 4.8 percent in the South, and 4.1 percent in the North Central states. Similarly, the annual prevalence of crack, hallucinogens, and ice is also highest in the West. Alcohol use, especially the rate of occasional heavy drinking, is higher in the Northeast and North Central than the West or the South.

In terms of trends over time, regional differences appear to have been minimal except for cocaine use. In the mid-1970s, there was relatively little variation in the lifetime prevalence of cocaine use among high school seniors. Into the 1980s, as the epidemic of cocaine use grew, lifetime use in the West and Northeast tripled while doubling in the North Central section and only increasing by about 30 percent in the South. As the epidemic subsided, regional differences have been reduced.

SUMMARY

The past quarter of a century has witnessed a dramatic increase in adolescent use of a variety of psychoactive substances of abuse. Despite recent decreases in the lifetime and annual prevalence of substance use, the adolescents in the United States show a significant level of involvement with substances. Most of this involvement is best characterized as occasional use, sometimes to high quantity levels in the case of alcohol. Almost one out of three adolescents probably drink to intoxication within any two-week period and many of these adolescents will meet diagnostic criteria for alcohol abuse at sometime prior to adulthood.

Rates of specific substances differ across age, gender, and ethnic status. These rates can also change across generations or succeeding cohorts of adolescents. Knowledge of the demographic differences in the epidemiology of adolescent substance use and abuse allows an understanding of the variability of risk for substance use and abuse across different subgroups of adolescents.

CHAPTER 4

Development, Risk, and Consequences

Although the origination and subsequent institutionalization of our current concept of adolescence is a relatively recent phenomenon, adolescence as a distinct stage of life development is firmly entrenched in Western society and culture (Aries, 1962). A high prevalence of substance use among youth in modern Western society is an even more recent phenomenon. Unlike previous periods of widespread substance use (for example, alcohol in colonial America), substance use by youth is not sanctioned but rather overtly condemned and discouraged by society and its agents of social control. Yet, as the current seeming epidemic of overall substance use by adolescents continues through an entire generation and into the next, society must consider whether at least a certain level of substance use is actually endemic and has been incorporated, like alternative styles of dress and hairstyles, into a begrudgingly tolerated social and psychological concept of adolescence. How does substance use by adolescents fit into a broad scheme of normal or abnormal development? For the purposes of understanding problems related to substance use, how is substance abuse by adolescents explained by problems with adolescent development?

"NORMAL" ADOLESCENT DEVELOPMENT

Besides birth and death, the onset of adolescence is identified by the most distinct of developmental markers, puberty. Puberty is characterized by a host of physical changes including a period of accelerated growth and differing patterns of growth along gender lines (Tanner, 1962). These patterns of growth are controlled largely through the changes in gonadotrophic hormone excretion during adolescence (Tanner, 1962). As the developing adolescent increases in size and shape, he or she becomes both quantitatively and qualitatively different than their younger, prepubertal peers. The change in physical identity produces explicit evidence that the adolescent is no longer a child and becomes manifest to both the adolescent and to most adults, including parents. Hormones, especially androgens, have behavior effects, including a pronounced increase in sexual drive and energy. Changes in the levels of gonadal hormones, although poorly understood, likely have behavioral and emotional effects, including aggression (Rutter, 1979). Accumulating evidence points to post-puberty being associated with a significant increase in the onset of major psychiatric disorders (Burke, Burke, Reiger, & Rae, 1990).

The changes in physical and secondary sexual characteristics open the adolescent to changes in social relations, especially the increased focus on opposite gender peers and heterosexual interests. Social changes and expectations may be further reinforced by changes in the pubescent adolescent's social environment, including transfer from elementary to middle or secondary school and increased exposure to "mature," older adolescents. Masturbation, and subsequently other forms of sexual activity including intercourse, become increasingly more prevalent through adolescence (Brooks-Gunn & Furstenberg, 1989).

Adolescence is a critical period of cognitive development with eventual progress to adult capacities. Although the timing of cognitive changes during adolescence and the universality of various models coupled with the effects of environment on cognitive development remain less than firmly established, there are definite changes in the adolescent's ability to assimilate data and understand the world and its phenomena. With the emergence of what Piaget called formal operational thinking (Piaget, 1969), post-pubertal youth become able to formulate and examine hypotheses about phenomena in the world and become able to make deductions and think about abstract concepts. Although the ability of adolescents over a wide range of backgrounds to achieve sufficient levels of formal operations varies significantly, adolescents are generally increasingly able to think in a theoretical mode, over a wide time scale, and to critically reflect on personal thoughts. However, the cognitive and social changes of adolescence are not distinct like the clearly visible physical changes of puberty. Social and cognitive changes are often gradual, discontinuous, and likely not universal among all groups of adolescents within our society.

DEVELOPMENTAL TASKS OF ADOLESCENCE

Beyond the basic biological, physical imperative of achieving adult physical maturity and physiological functional development, social and cognitive development has traditionally been divided into stages. Completion of certain characteristic tasks with each stage is required to progress successfully to a succeeding stage of development. Within the cognitive-social sphere, there are specific developmental tasks for adolescents. A summary of these developmental tasks concludes: Successful adolescents are able to achieve a separate identity, independence from their parents, and prepare themselves for appropriate societal and individual relations to achieve the adult developmental tasks of job, marriage, and family.

TABLE 4.1. Adolescent Developmental Behaviors Which
Promote Substance Use

Establishing independence and a separate identity from parents
Experimentation with alternative attitudes, lifestyles, and behavior
Increase in peer-oriented attitudes and behaviors
Desire for adult status and perceived adult behaviors

Within the context of these tasks, in their search for independence and a separate identity from their parents, adolescents experiment with a wide range and variety of attitudes and behaviors. Not only do these activities reflect a desire for an identity separate from their parents, but also their desire to be considered autonomous individuals, that is, adults. While many adults find current adolescent fashions and behavior somewhat distasteful, objectionable, or even bizarre at times, adolescents are often modeling adult behavior or what they perceive to be adult behavior.

Substance use is but one of many "adult" behaviors which are adopted by youth. More often, substance use is an expression of independence and autonomy. The choice of experimental use or regular use of substances by adolescents is governed by a host of other developmental factors, especially the increasing importance of peer attitudes and behavior on the adolescent (see Table 4.1). Prominent examples are peer and individual attitudes emphasizing independence from parents and adults, minimizing adult influence, and making one's own decisions.

Given the widespread prevalence of the use of alcohol and even other illicit drug use among adolescents in this and the previous generations of adolescents, experimental use of substances, especially those substances legal and available to adults in our society, should be considered within the normative range of behaviors. Despite the illicit nature of alcohol and other drug use, substance use should not automatically be equated with abuse, at least in the pathological sense. This acknowledgment of the reality of substance use among adolescents is not a statement of the desirability of substance use among adolescents. Society should discourage even experimental use of all psychoactive substances, even among adults.

DEVELOPMENTAL STAGES OF
ADOLESCENT SUBSTANCE USE

Abstinence and experimental use are two points on one side of a continuum of substance use that continues to abuse and dependence which are indicative of patterns of problem use. This continuum potentially offers much confusion for parents, clinicians, and researchers alike. How can adolescent substance use be understood within a developmental context? As an individual adolescent ages and matures, there are likely developmental forces which pull him or her toward more conventional, socially-approved attitudes and behaviors, and other forces which pull the adolescent toward inappropriate attitudes and behaviors, such as substance abuse and dependence. These latter forces can be considered risk factors or perhaps causal factors for substance use, abuse, and dependence. Because these forces are acting on or within the developing adolescent, they are best understood within the developmental process of an adolescent or specific populations of adolescents.

In viewing adolescence as a stage of development, we can now consider how adolescents, and even children, initiate the use of alcohol and other drugs of abuse and progress to more serious levels of substance use. Kandel and associates' (Kandel, 1975b; Yamaguchi & Kandel, 1984) longitudinal studies have reported a fairly consistent sequential pattern of involvement in alcohol and other drugs. Data from other longitudinal and cross-section studies has confirmed this sequence among other populations of adolescents (Brook, Whiteman, & Gordon, 1982; Donovan & Jessor, 1983; Huba & Bentler, 1982; Welte & Barnes, 1985).

In this sequence (Table 4.2), adolescents first try substances that are legal for adults—alcohol (beer and wine) and cigarettes. Beer and wine precede the use of hard liquor or spirits. The use of alcoholic beverages precedes the use of marijuana, followed by other illicit or "hard" drugs, such as opiates and stimulants. Adolescents are unlikely to initiate marijuana or hard drug use without prior use or experimentation with alcohol and/or cigarettes. Based on these studies, alcohol and cigarettes, legal and accessible drugs for adults, are established as "gateway" drugs. Almost all adolescents enter at the earliest stages of this sequence with progressively fewer adolescents eventually advancing to later stages. As adolescents advance through this sequence of substance use, they continue to use "gateway" drugs, adding the other drugs to an expanding repertoire, as opposed to replacing the "gateway" drugs (Mills & Noyes, 1984).

Further studies have modified the original drug use sequence. Despite the rise, and eventual fall, of cocaine use prevalence among adolescents during the 1980s, cocaine use precedes the onset of hard drug use other than pills, and follows marijuana use, rather than being another "gateway" drug (Ellickson, Hays, & Bell, 1992). Problem drinking or regular alcohol use also follows marijuana use and precedes the use of all other illicit drugs (Donovan & Jessor, 1983; Ellickson, Hays, & Bell, 1992). In extending their analyses into young adulthood, Yamaguchi and Kandel (1984), established a later stage of substance use involving the use of medically prescribed drugs.

The progression along this sequence may have important modifications or alternatives along gender lines. While progression to illicit drugs among men is dependent upon prior use of alcohol, among women either cigarettes or alcohol

TABLE 4.2. Developmental Stages of Adolescent Drug Involvement*

Stage	Antecedents (Predictors of initiation)
1. Beer/wine	—Greater peer involvement —Greater exposure to peer and parent models —Minor delinquent activities
2. Cigarettes or hard liquor	
2.a. Problem drinking	Acceptance of beliefs and values favorable to use and in opposition to adult standards
	Minor delinquent activity Exposure to peer use
3. Marijuana	—Psychological distress —Poor parental relations —Exposure to models —Heavy marijuana use —Nonconforming attitude —More deviant personal characteristics
4. Other illicit drugs	

*Data from Kandel, 1975a.

is a sufficient condition for progression to marijuana (Kandel, Yamaguchi, & Chien, 1992). Other variations from the standard sequence may exist for certain ethnic groups. For Asian youth, regular or weekly alcohol use follows rather than precedes the use of hard drugs, whereas Hispanic, African-American, and Caucasian youth follow the sequence of regular alcohol use preceding hard drug use (Ellickson, Hays, & Bell, 1992).

While the order of the substance involvement sequence is consistent, the age of entry into the sequence and the time of progression or time spent in each stage is highly variant between groups of adolescents with differing characteristics. The age of onset into a particular stage of substance use and the frequency of use of substances at an earlier stage are strong predictors of further progression to later stages (Kandel, Yamaguchi, & Chien, 1992).

Given the variation between groups of adolescents in terms of age of entry into stages of the developmental sequence of substance use, speed of progression, and extent of progression into various stages of the sequence, the identification of antecedents or risk factors for the initiation, maintenance, and progression of substance use may allow an improved understanding of the role of substance use in adolescent development. There is strong evidence for stage-specific antecedents, predictors, or risk factors and adolescent substance use. Many risk factors associated with substance use at one point or at one stage may not be as important or predictive at other stages (Kandel, 1982; Kandel, Kessler, & Margulies, 1978). At the earliest stage of substance involvement, use of gateway drugs—beer and wine—is predicted by engagement in minor delinquent or deviant activities, high levels of peer sociability, and peer and parent drinking models. Environmental influences, in the form of pro-drug messages and models from peers, parents, and the media appear most important at the initiation of substance use (Ellickson & Hays, 1991). Later in the sequence, the use of marijuana is preceded by acceptance of beliefs and values (usually deviant) that are favorable to marijuana use, involvement with marijuana-using peers, and participation in deviant behaviors. Finally, the use of other illicit drugs is predicted by poor relationships with parents, by exposure to peer and parent drug-use models, by psychological distress, by heavy marijuana use, and by increasingly more deviant behaviors than in preceding stages.

Although examination of risk factors or antecedents in a stage-specific of development framework is potentially useful, several broad classes of risk factors for substance use and abuse in adolescents deserve attention. These types of risk factors include: (a) peer factors, (b) parent factors, (c) individual factors, (d) biological factors, and (e) community/social/cultural factors.

Peer Factors

As peer influences play a central role in adolescent development, these influences likewise play a critical role in adolescent substance use, especially in the earliest stages of substance involvement (see Table 4.3). There is a strong relationship between an individual adolescent's substance use and the substance use and other behaviors of his or her peers (Kandel, Kessler, & Margulies, 1978). Peer influences are especially prominent in predicting initiation and continuation of the use of marijuana (Kandel, Kessler, & Margulies, 1978). Adolescents who frequently use marijuana appear to be more oriented to friends than to parents and have more peer use models. High levels of sociability and involvement with peers, rather than alcohol or other drug involvement per se, predict initiation into the use of beer and wine (Kandel, Kessler, & Margulies, 1978). More participation in peer-centered social settings, such as dating and parties, favorable to substance use may both reinforce and

TABLE 4.3. Peer-Related Risk Factors

Peer substance use
Peer attitudes about substance use
Greater orientation (attachment) to peers
Perception(s) of peer substance use/attitudes

increase the risk to use substances (Kandel, Kessler, & Margulies, 1978). Peer influences appear greater for females than males (Jessor & Jessor, 1977; Margulies, Kessler, & Kandel, 1977).

Not only is actual peer use an important antecedent or risk factor for adolescent substance use, but an adolescent's perception of peer use and peer support for use are also strong predictors of use, especially for marijuana use (Jessor & Jessor, 1977; Kandel, Kessler, & Margulies, 1978)—but also for alcohol use (Wechsler & Thum, 1973).

Peer influences likely change during later stages of the substance sequence. Exposure to peer models for the use of illicit drugs other than marijuana is only one of several antecedents to illicit substance use (Kandel, 1982; Kandel, Kessler, & Margulies, 1978).

The mechanisms of peer influences in affecting the initiation of substance use in several stages of adolescent use are likely influenced by other risk factors, particularly parent factors. Adolescents with greater susceptibility to peer influences are those with greater peer attachment versus parent attachment (Brook, Linkoff, & Whiteman, 1980; Kandel, Kessler, & Margulies, 1978). Strong bonds to parents and family decrease the likelihood of association with substance using and deviant peers (Elliot, Huizinga, & Ageton, 1982). The strength of an adolescent's bonding to his parents and family is probably determined prior to adolescence and exposure to substances and peer substance use. Assortative or selective pairing with like-behaving and, presumably, like-thinking peers may be a peer factor in addition to the influence of peers and the greater socialization seen during adolescence. Data from Kandel's work also supports the observation that peer influences may be relatively short-lived in comparison to parent and other factors (Kandel, 1982).

Parent/Family Factors

As with other types of antecedents or predictors, parent factors (see Table 4.4) vary in importance at different stages of the substance involvement sequence. For initiation into alcohol use, parent role-modeling of alcohol use and single parent homes are factors (Kandel, Kessler, & Margulies, 1978; Wechsler & Thum, 1973). Parental use and modeling of hard liquor predicts adolescent use

TABLE 4.4.   Parent/Family Risk Factors

Parent substance use
Parent beliefs/attitudes about substance use
Parent tolerance of substance use/deviant behavior
Lack of closeness/attachment with parents
Lack of parental involvement in child's life
Lack of appropriate supervision/discipline

of hard liquor and illicit drugs other than marijuana (Kandel, Kessler, & Margulies, 1978). Parental beliefs and attitudes about substances, especially attitudes of tolerance and beliefs in the harmlessness of substances, predict subsequent drug use (Kandel, Kessler, & Margulies, 1978). Among additional maternal characteristics predicting the initiation of marijuana use are absence of closeness, maternal passivity, lack of involvement in their children's activity, and low educational aspirations (Brook, Linkoff, & Whiteman, 1980; Jessor & Jessor, 1977). Adolescent initiation into the use of illicit drugs other than marijuana is predicted by poor relationship with parents and parental use of a variety of legal and illicit drugs (Kandel, 1982; Kandel, Kessler, & Margulies, 1978). In considering general parental antecedents or predictive factors of adolescent drug use, Kandel suggests three basic types of parental factors: (1) parent substance use, (2) parent attitudes, and (3) parent-child interactions.

A number of studies have found that parental self-reports of their own substance use are related to initiation of use of alcohol and other substances by their teenage children (Kandel, Kessler, & Margulies, 1978; Zucker, 1979). Although the most likely mechanism for the effect of parent use upon adolescent use is parental modeling, a contribution of genetic effects cannot be dismissed.

Offspring of alcoholics and other substance abusers are at increased risk for the development of alcohol and other substance use disorders (Cotton, 1979). In search for a mechanism of this transmission of risk, investigators have identified a number of differences among children of alcoholics or substance abusers (COAs or COSAs). These differences include: greater alcohol or other substance involvement, greater consequences associated with substance use, greater behavioral undercontrol, greater psychiatric distress, and lower verbal abilities and academic achievement (Sher, Walitzer, Wood, & Brent, 1991). Although acknowledging the likely existence of multiple pathways between parental and offspring alcoholism, Sher and colleagues advanced the following causal ordering: (1) family history of alcoholism: (2) personality traits, especially behavioral undercontrol, negative affectivity; and lower verbal ability; (3) alcohol expectancies; and (4) alcohol involvement.

The elevated risk for substance abuse among children of substance abusers may have more to do with the other characteristics of substance-abusing parents and the home environment that they provide. For example, regardless of parental history of alcoholism, poor parent monitoring predicted early adolescent substance use (Molina, Chassin, & Curran, 1994). Thus, poor parent management may allow increased exposure to substance-using peers and a high-risk environment. The effects of parental substance abuse in increasing the risk of adolescent substance use may be due to both general parental impairment and poor role-functioning, and a more specific effect through a history of parental substance abuse (Chassin, Rogosch, & Barrera, 1991).

Parental attitudes about substance use and parent-child interactions are closely related. The belief in the lack of harmfulness of substances and tolerance of use and deviant behavior are strong predictors of adolescent use. As for parent-child interactions, lack of closeness and lack of involvement in the adolescent's activities were previously noted to be antecedent to adolescent use. Parenting styles are also implicated as predictors with lack of conventionality, family disruption, negative communication patterns, lack of or inconsistent behavioral limits, and lack of anger control as characteristics of families with adolescent substance users (Baumrind, 1983; Reilly, 1979). Single-parent or non-intact families also appear to predict later adolescent substance use (Robins, 1980; Wechsler & Thum, 1973). The observation of an increased prevalence of physical and sexual abuse among adolescent substance abusers suggests a role for these types of family-related trauma as a risk for adolescent substance use and abuse (Van Hasselt et al., 1993). Although a history of physical or sexual abuse likely has a significant influence on subsequent adolescent behavior, the mechanism of effect or causal role is difficult to ascertain, as abusive families are usually loaded with a variety of other risk factors for substance use and abuse.

If adolescent substance use is considered along with a larger constellation or even a syndrome of deviant behavior, a number of parental characteristics predict deviance or delinquency in adolescents. Among the family predictors of deviant behavior are parent management style and techniques, including poor monitoring and inconsistency of structure and limit-setting (Baumrind, 1983; Dishion & Loeber, 1985; Patterson, 1982), and parent antisocial behavior (Loeber & Dishion, 1983).

Parent factors may also be protective against the development of substance use and abuse. Positive parent-child relationships, parent involvement with children's activities, and strong child-parent attachment appear to limit or even discourage adolescent initiation into substance use (Wechsler & Thum, 1973; Jessor & Jessor, 1977).

Individual Factors

Individual factors constitute a relatively broad category of antecedents or risk factors for adolescent substance use that are intrinsic to the individual adolescent (see Table 4.5). Individual factors include: (a) early childhood characteristics,

TABLE 4.5. Individual Risk Factors

Early childhood characteristics
 Early conduct problems, aggression
 Poor academic performance/school failure
Early onset of substance use
Adolescent attitudes/beliefs about substance use
Risk taking behaviors

(b) age of onset of substance exposure and use, (c) substance use patterns, (d) academic factors, (e) psychological factors, (f) cognitive factors, and (g) deviant behavior. Several predictive factors for adolescent substance use can be identified in early childhood. These factors include aggressive behavior and shyness (Kellam, Simon, & Ensminger, 1980) and rebelliousness (Smith & Fogg, 1978). Early conduct problems are often continuous into adolescence and predict adolescent substance use (Kandel, Kessler, & Margulies, 1978; Robins, 1978; Wechsler & Thum, 1973). Antisocial behavior usually precedes the onset of substance use (Elliot, Hiuzinga, & Ageton, 1982).

Early substance abuse is an independent predictor of later substance abuse (Robins & McEvoy, 1990). Both early drunkenness and the early use of illicit drugs, especially prior to 15 years of age, predict later progression to substance use, particularly at a more severe level (Robins & McEvoy, 1990; Robins & Przybeck, 1985). A variety of studies show that earlier onset of initiation into substance use is associated with increased risk, increased subsequent abuse of that substance, and an increased probability of use of more serious drugs (Brunswick & Boyle, 1979; Mills & Noyes, 1984; Kleinman, 1978). Age commonly interacts with other predictors, such as conduct problems, to further affect substance use patterns and related deviant behaviors. Early onset of substance use is associated with later alcoholism and antisocial personality (Robins & Przybeck, 1985); the earlier the onset of use, the greater subsequent risk of a variety of other psychiatric disorders. For adolescents using illicit substances, the more deviant the behaviors, the earlier use begins with early use as an independent predictor of later substance abuse (Robins & McEvoy, 1990).

Poor academic performance is a common predictor or antecedent of substance use initiation by adolescents (Jessor & Jessor, 1977; Kandel, Kessler, & Margulies, 1978) with school failure as a predictor of substance abuse (Robins, 1980; Brook, Linkoff, & Whiteman, 1977). It is not certain whether school performance itself or factors leading to poor academic achievement is the real predictor of later substance use. These academic factors can include low IQ, learning disabilities, attention-deficit hyperactivity disorder, or poor socialization.

The use of hard drugs is predicted by psychological distress (Kandel, Kessler, & Margulies, 1978). Kellum and associates (1980) found that aggression with or without shyness is an early childhood predictor of later substance abuse. Depression and anxiety among adolescents also appear to increase the risk of subsequent substance abuse (Christie et al., 1988; Deykin, Levy, & Wells, 1987). As previously mentioned, psychopathology in the form of childhood and adolescent conduct problems is perhaps the most robust predictor of adolescent substance abuse.

Poor attitudes and a lack of commitment toward education and other socially sanctioned or pro-social activities characterize adolescents who are more likely to use substances (Robins, 1980; Brook, Linkoff, & Whiteman, 1977). Adolescent substance users are more often truant than nonusers (Brook,

Linkoff, & Whiteman, 1977; Kandel, 1982). A series of individual attitudes and beliefs predict adolescent substance use. The use of marijuana is predicted by adolescent acceptance of beliefs and attitudes favorable to marijuana use and in opposition to adult standards (Kandel, Kessler, & Margulies, 1978; Jessor & Jessor, 1977) These findings suggest several cognitive factors associated with adolescent substance use, including nonconformity to traditional values, high tolerance of deviance, a strong desire for independence. Lower self-esteem, external locus of control, and increased alienation also characterize adolescent substance users (Jessor & Jessor, 1977). Generally, these attitudes and beliefs demonstrated a lack of conformity and social bonding with conventional society (Hawkins, Lishner, & Catalano, 1986). Actually, the adolescent's perception of peer attitudes and behavior, as much as actual peer behavior and attitudes, influences substance use. In the case of a more deviant peer group, the adolescent perceives his or her peer's attitudes and behaviors as deviant and follows along.

The adolescent's expectancies of the behavioral and social effects of alcohol and other drugs can predict the onset of alcohol use and the eventual progression to abuse (Christiansen, Goldman, & Brown, 1985). Knowledge about alcohol and other drugs is available to children from a very young age through media exposure and modeling of parents and others in the environment (Christiansen, Goldman, & Inn, 1982). Common adolescent alcohol expectancies include its enhancement or impeding of social behavior, its ability to both improve and hinder one's cognitive and motor abilities, its ability to enhance sexual performance, increase physiological arousal, and promote relaxation and/or tension reduction (Christiansen, Goldman, & Inn, 1982). The more the adolescent expects alcohol to produce positive effects—especially improving social interactions and performance—the greater probability that the adolescent will begin drinking and subsequently drink in an abusive manner.

As previously mentioned, both deviant attitudes and behaviors are very sturdy predictors of adolescent substance use and abuse. In addition to specifically antisocial behaviors such as aggression, a number of other behaviors are associated with adolescent substance use. A variety of risk-taking behaviors are more common among adolescent substance users (Jessor, 1984). Among the more prominent risk-taking behaviors are driving while drinking or intoxicated, driving without using seat belts, and motorcycle operation with the use of a helmet. Although the 1960s and 1970s saw a liberalization of legal age for drinking laws, the forced return of these laws to 21 years has resulted in greatly reduced rates of adolescent motor vehicle fatalities as well as lower levels of alcohol use among high school seniors (O'Malley & Wagenaar, 1991).

Sexual behavior, like drinking and the subsequent use of other drugs, is associated with early association with peers. Today, with the specter of HIV infection and disease and other sexually transmitted diseases (STDs), sexual activity is also risk-taking behavior. Past studies have shown that about one half of adolescents do not use contraception the first time that they have sexual relations (Zelnik & Shah, 1983). Minority adolescents are especially at risk due to high rates of sexual activity, lower rates of contraceptive use, having less knowledge about the risk of infection and the protection offered by condom use, and perceived lower vulnerability to infection (DiClemente, Boyer, & Morales, 1988; DiClemente, Zorn, & Temoshok, 1986). Although adolescent substance use and precocious sexual behavior appear to be highly correlated behaviors, alcohol and other drug use may contribute more directly to adolescent sexual activity. In a telephone survey of adolescents, aged 16 to 19, 49 percent of sexually active teenagers reported than they were more likely to have sex if they or their partner had been drinking and 17 percent used condoms less often after drinking. After drug use, 32 percent of sexually active youth stated that they would be more likely to have sex with 10 percent less likely to use condoms (Strunin & Hingson, 1992).

Biological Factors

The presence of biologic or constitutional factors as a predictor of adolescent substance use or abuse has received less attention than the previously discussed risk factors due largely to technical and methodological limitations. In a search for mechanisms of etiology and risk, we inevitably need to examine the relative contribution of "nature" versus "nurture," or genes and constitutional factors versus environmental factors. Clinicians have long observed that some families show a disproportionate amount of substance abuse. Researchers have demonstrated that substance use disorders, particularly alcoholism, aggregate within families (Cotton, 1979). In attempting to establish a genetic mode of transmission for alcoholism, researchers have used twin and adoption studies (Dinwiddie & Cloninger, 1991).

In twin studies, the concordance or agreement of alcoholism among monozygotic (identical) twins who share identical genetic makeup is compared with concordance for alcoholism among dizygotic (nonidentical) twins who share only, on an average, half their genes. A genetic influence would be indicated by an excess concordance among dizygotic twins. Indeed, twin research has consistently demonstrated higher concordance for alcoholism in identical twins.

Adoption studies compare adoptees raised by nonbiologically related parents, thus attempts to separate pre- and post-natal influences. More agreement between adoptee and biological parents than between adoptee and adoptive parents would support genetic factors. Most adoption studies show an increased risk for alcoholism among adopted-away children of alcoholics (Goodwin et al., 1974) and for substance abuse other than alcoholism (Cadoret, Troughton, O'Gorman, & Heywood, 1986). Alcohol abuse by adoptive parents does not appear to increase the risk for alcohol abuse in their adoptive children, thus suggesting less of a contribution for such environmental influences as modeling (Cloninger, Bohman, Sigvadsson, & Von Knorring, 1985)

Given some role for genetic inheritance in substance abuse, many researchers have embarked on studies to establish the mechanism of this genetic inheritance. While single-gene or Mendelian transmission does not appear to fit available family data, polygenetic theories continue to be advanced to explain genetic transmission of substance abuse. Recent studies in human molecular genetics have linked an increased risk for alcoholism (Blum et al., 1990) and multiple substance abuse/dependence (Comings, Muhlman, Ahn, Gysin, & Flanagan, 1994) to a specific gene, the D2 dopamine receptor gene, although this finding remains controversial (Conneally, 1991; Cloninger, 1991).

There are two basic types of biologic risk factors which may differentiate family history positive (FHP) or high-risk individuals from family history negative (FHN) or low-risk individuals. The first type are biologic markers which are biologic measures without any obvious or specific role in the etiology of alcohol or other substance abuse, but which are increased in individuals with substance abuse. The second type of biologic risk factors are biologic characteristics which may have a potentially more specific role in the vulnerability to and etiology of substance use in a high-risk individual. The biological markers of today may later be implicated in the vulnerability or etiology of substance abuse.

Proposed biological "markers" include differences in blood enzymes such as monoamine oxidase and adenylate cyclase (Tabakoff et al., 1988), electrophysiological measures such as evoked potentials, and cortical electroencephalogram (EEG) differences (Begleiter & Porjesz, 1988); neurologic abnormalities such as tremor and static ataxia (Hill, Steinhauser, & Zubin, 1987).

Biologic risk characteristics with a potential role in the specific etiologic mechanism of substance abuse include physiologic response(s) to substances (especially alcohol), preexisting neuropsychological deficits, and a variety of psychological characteristics or traits which may predispose to substance use and eventual abuse. At-risk individuals may be less sensitive to the effects of alcohol (Schuckit, 1985a, 1994) in terms of subjects' feelings of intoxication (Schuckit, 1988), or in terms of objective measures such as change in body sway or latency of P_3 component of evoked potentials (Porjesz & Begleiter, 1990; Hill, Steinhauser, & Zubin, 1987). High-risk populations may display differences in their ability to metabolize alcohol (Grant, 1988), or in the development of more rapid tolerance to alcohol than in low-risk populations, although these findings have not been consistent (Wilson & Nagoshi, 1988). High-risk individuals may also have reduced expectation of the effects from drinking or intoxication, although this finding appears to be unreliable (Wilson & Crowe, 1991). Recently, investigators have attempted to identify potential differences in the responsivity of serotonin systems between high- and low-risk individuals.

Tarter, Alterman, and Edwards (1985), among others, have proposed a role for behavioral traits as risk factors. Certain temperamental traits which have a biologic, heritable basis, may lead to vulnerability to a number of psychiatric or behavioral disorders, including substance abuse. The interaction of a certain aggregation of traits and various environmental factors would determine the type, and perhaps severity, of the disorder. Substance-abusing adolescents appear to be distinguishable from normals on a variety of temperamental dimensions, although only behavioral activity regulation appears to be associated with the severity of substance use (Tarter, Laird, Mostefa, Bukstein, & Kaminer, 1990). Similarly, Cloninger (1987) has proposed neurogenetic mechanisms for the vulnerability to alcoholism. These mechanisms differ in their heritability and resulting behavioral constellations or personality dimensions. Although originally proposed to explain differing patterns of inheritance (Cloninger, Bohman, & Sigvardsson, 1981), Type 1 and Type 2 alcoholics were further characterized in terms of personality dimensions and even associated with specific brain neurotransmitter systems (Cloninger, 1987).

Biologic vulnerability to substance abuse may depend not only on specific factors which have a specific genetic origin, but also on more general constitutional factors such as personality or temperament. Personality and temperament are subject to a significant amount of environmental modification. The expression of biologic vulnerability is dependent upon such environmental factors as exposure to substance and can be modified by such environmental/social factors as cultural attitudes, price, supply, and availability (Dinwiddie & Reich, 1992).

Community/Social/Cultural Factors

Different adolescent racial and ethnic groups appear to have varying degrees of risk for the development of substance use and abuse. Previous research has found generally lower rates of substance use among African-American youth than among Hispanic and particularly white adolescents (Barnes & Welte, 1986; Newcomb & Bentler, 1986a, 1986b). However, minority groups may experience more negative social consequences than white youth (Barnes & Welte, 1986; Harper, 1979; Trimble, Padilla, & Bell, 1987). Differential rates of use of specific substances may be found with minority populations usually showing higher rates of heroin and cocaine use (Kandel, Single, & Kessler, 1976).

Community or neighborhood characteristics such as low socioeconomic status, high population density, low population mobility, physical deterioration, and high crime are associated with greater substance use in adolescence (Brook, Whiteman, Gordan, & Brook, 1990). Communities or neighborhoods with high rates of unemployment and other economic problems offer few resources for youth. Deviant norms are provided in these communities, condoning the use and abuse of substances. Crime and violence are associated with similar community characteristics. Youth become less bonded to nondeviant social norms, become more rebellious, less attached, and more alienated (Kumpfer, 1989). In many central urban neighborhoods, formal and informal control systems have broken down.

Risk Factors and Developmental Theories of Adolescent Substance Use

Rarely, if ever, are individual risk factors alone sufficient to account for developmental progression into stages of substance use or, ultimately, abuse. Rather, a number of risk factors, producing a variety of interactions with each other and the environment, place the child and adolescent on a trajectory toward substance use and/or abuse. Although some risk factors may be more powerful predictors, especially at given stages of development, no specific risk factor or specific grouping of risk factors necessarily leads to a substance use or abuse outcome in an individual adolescent. In fact, predictive studies suggest that the number of risk factors predicts adolescent substance use better than any particular set of risk factors (Bry, 1983).

Starting from a developmental paradigm, researchers have advanced several theories to explain the interactions of multiple risk factors through child and adolescent development to produce either abstinence, the initiation or maintenance of substance use, the progression to different substances and to substance abuse and dependence, and the eventual advancement into nonpathologic patterns of legal substances in young adults. Jessor and associates (Donovan & Jessor, 1978; Jessor & Jessor, 1977) suggest the concept of "proneness" to describe the tendency of risk factors to promote or discourage the occurrence of problem behaviors which include substance use.

The perspective of the *problem-behavior theory* is one of learned behavior within a psychosocial framework—as opposed to a biologic or genetic-based theory. Risk factors operate within three systems of psychosocial influence: (1) the perceived environment system, (2) the personality system, and (3) the behavior system. The characteristics of an adolescent through the relevant dimensions of these three systems determine whether substance use specifically, or a problem behavior syndrome in general, occurs. Proneness toward problem behavior is represented in the three systems by risk factors including unconventional attitudes, greater involvement with peers than parents, and more involvement in deviant behaviors.

The concepts advanced in problem-behavior theory are useful within a developmental context, as the risk factors which predict proneness to problem behavior are tied conceptually to explain their effects on the developing adolescent in a stage of transition when the three systems of psychosocial influence exert an optimal effect toward or away from deviance. Even with problem behaviors such as substance use, adolescents will be motivated to engage in these behaviors if they perceive them as functional and helping the adolescent achieve desired goals. Often, adolescents who have, or are perceived as having, limited conventional options for behavior are at greatest risk for engaging in deviant behaviors such as substance abuse. While the *Jessor problem-behavior theory model* helps to account for the interplay of multiple environmental attitudinal and behavioral risk factors which may lead to substance use, abuse, or other deviant behaviors, it does not account for the contribution of genetic/biological risk factors in influencing the adolescent's environment and, ultimately, a substance use/abuse outcome.

Other developmental theories have attempted to account for a genetic/biological contribution. Tarter's *developmental behavior genetic theory* (Tarter, Alterman, & Edward, 1985) accounts for a biologic predisposition which interacts with environmental risk factors to produce a given outcome. If the biologic vulnerability and the environmental risk factors alone or together are sufficient, the outcome will be negative; that is, substance abuse or a possibly related psychiatric disorder, depending on the interaction between type of genetic vulnerability and type of environmental risk factor. Cloninger's *neurogenetic model* (1987) emphasizes genetic factors in the etiology of early onset of alcoholism. Cloninger hypothesizes three dimensions of personality that may reflect individual differences or genetic differences in brain or neurotransmitter systems which control the individual's specific response not only to alcohol, but also to other environmental stimuli. Unfortunately, the interaction of these genetic factors with environmental factors receives minimal attention in Cloninger's explanation of this theory.

DEVELOPMENTAL CONSEQUENCES OF ADOLESCENT SUBSTANCE USE

Newcomb and Bentler (1986) and their colleagues have studied and documented the effects and consequences of regular adolescent substances use. Like other researchers, they found that substance use rarely occurs in isolation but is integrated and consistent with other attitudes and behaviors of the adolescent. The most common pattern is one of low social conformity and high deviance. However, there are many possible patterns. Adolescent substance use appears to be associated with early involvement in family creation, including marriage and having children, although use also predicted divorce and increased unhappiness in these relationships. Use reduced college involvement and the use of hard drugs lowered the chances of graduating from high school. Adolescent substance users appear to enter the work force earlier than nonusers and, thus, earn more money into early adulthood. Eventually, nonusers surpass their using peers in income, suggesting that the earlier educational limitations imposed by substance use may limit later income potential. Similarly, adolescent substance use is predictive of lower job stability.

While general substance use by adolescents appeared to increase involvement in drug crimes, users showed lower levels of violent crime except for substances such as cocaine. Substance use had no general influence on mood or affective states, although the use of hard drugs (especially stimulants, hypnotics, inhalants, and narcotics) predicted increased suicidal ideation and other self-destructive thoughts as well as reduced social support and increased loneliness in young adulthood. The use of hard drugs also appears to lead to unusual beliefs, bizarre thoughts, and disorganized thinking.

Despite these obviously negative effects of substance use on adolescent developmental tasks, the use of specific agents may actually have beneficial effects. The use of alcohol predicts decreased relationship problems, decreased loneliness, increased social support and an increased positive effect. Newcomb and Bentler's results suggest that the adolescent's use of alcohol, the most commonly used psychoactive agent by our society, can have a positive, adaptive function in improving social interactions among adolescents. Within a developmental context, adolescent alcohol use, as opposed to abuse, may prepare the adolescent for adult social interactions where alcohol is commonly used as a social lubricant. It should be noted that the Newcomb and Bentler data reflects the consequences of adolescence substance use rather than abuse. By definition, abuse and dependence require negative consequences or impaired functioning within one or more areas of an adolescent's life.

Consistent with past theories on the effects of adolescent substance use, Newcomb and Bentler's results predict that substance use by adolescents can seriously disrupt the ability of adolescents to adequately handle developmental tasks. Often, this involves a premature involvement into many areas, such as work and families, prior to the adolescents developing the ability to handle these developmental tasks. Baumrind and Moselle (1985) proposed that adolescent substance use inhibits maturation by affecting several processes essential to achieving such developmental tasks, such as identity formation.

NATURAL HISTORY OF ADOLESCENT SUBSTANCE ABUSE

A majority of adolescents experiment with substances, especially alcohol. A number of these adolescents progress to problem use—again, usually involving alcohol. Although adolescent problem drinkers may form the core of those ultimately developing alcohol abuse or dependence in adulthood (Zucker, 1979), there is substantial evidence that for most adolescents, problem use peaks between ages 18 and 20, and declines thereafter (Yamaguchi & Kandel, 1984).

Research shows evidence of discontinuity of problem-drinker status between adolescence and young adulthood (Jessor, 1984). In examining two of the most common patterns of alcohol use in adolescence, "social-appropriate" drinking and problem drinking, many alcohol-related problems in the latter group appear to differ little from the problems seen in adult problem drinkers (Hughes, Power, & Francis, 1992). Presumably, within the context of normal adolescent experimentation, "socially appropriate" adolescent drinkers do not experience the same consequences of use despite often high levels of frequency and quantity of consumption. Similarly, patterns of involvement with marijuana and other illicit drugs peak in late adolescence (Kandel & Logan, 1984). Advanced drinking habits in mid-adolescence are neither necessary nor sufficient conditions for the later development of alcohol abuse in early adulthood (Andersson & Magnusson, 1988).

This lack of continuity between adolescent and adult use patterns suggests a maturational process. With increasing access to substances, especially alcohol, and declining supervision following high school, it is not surprising that the 18-to-20 age period is the time of peak substance consumption (Yamaguchi & Kandel, 1984). As most adolescents and young adults discover, they cannot successfully fulfill the developmental roles of young adulthood, that is, higher education, stable vocation, sustained relationships, and, ultimately, family while maintaining a pattern of heavy or problem substance use. Life events such as marriage, parenthood, and moving away from the adolescent subculture increase the likelihood of decreasing and discontinuation of substance use (Esbensen & Elliot, 1994).

Further affecting these developmental maturation effects are cohort or period effects, that is, changes in overall drug use patterns between generations or even between groups of adolescents living in successive time periods, regardless of the age of the substance user. The overall rise in adolescent substance use beginning in the late 1960s and the subsequent declines in adolescent marijuana and cocaine use from the late 1970s and mid-1980s, respectively, are examples of these period or cohort effects (O'Malley, Bachman, & Johnston, 1988). Despite the seemingly favorable direction in the decline of substance use among adolescents (University of Michigan, 1994), this news is tempered by data suggesting a declining age of onset for alcoholism (Reich et al., 1988).

Which adolescent substance users or abusers go on to continue their abusive pattern or to develop more severe problems with substance use in adulthood? Examining the list of risk factors, those who do not recover from substance abuse in adolescence are those with a greater number of risk factors, especially several salient risk factors such as early age of onset of substance use and/or conduct problems, coexisting severe conduct problems, poor academic performance, lower levels of parental attachment, and a family history of substance abuse or dependence. While substance abuse or dependence is possible in any adolescent, it is obvious that the risk of substance abuse is not evenly distributed among all adolescents. Multiple risk factors and multiple contexts for risk suggest multiple pathways for the development of substance abuse. Using a developmental perspective, Zucker (1994) suggests multiple types of alcoholism based on the presence or absence of various risk factors. *Antisocial alcoholism and developmentally-limited alcoholism* are both characterized by deviant behaviors and presence during adolescence, although developmentally-limited is marked by a lower risk factor load and lack of continuity into adulthood. In another type of alcoholism, *primary alcoholism,* individuals develop alcohol problems without continuity and without significant comorbidity and due to alcoholic-specific variation. Yet another type, *negative affect alcoholism,* involves depression and anxiety, may also be seen in adolescents. The identification of valid subtypes of adolescent substance abusers should ultimately assist the identification of specific risk factors and consequences for each subtype. This might facilitate targeted interventions to specific subtypes or populations of adolescents.

SUMMARY

Why do adolescents begin to use psychoactive substances and why do some adolescents, and not others, progress to abuse of or dependence on specific substances? To answer these questions, substance use and abuse by adolescents must be considered within a developmental context given the social, cognitive tasks of adolescence and the drive toward maturation and adulthood. In this transition between childhood and adulthood, the adolescent may be initially at risk due to constitutional or temperamental characteristics which have a biologic or genetic origin. The adolescent is then exposed to parent, adult, and peer models and attitudes, popular culture, and media messages promoting and encouraging substance use or, in some cases, discouraging use. As the adolescent attempts to achieve independence from parents, he or she experiments with a variety of perceived adult behaviors such as substance use. However, their limited cognitive development and judgment places them at risk for certain problems or consequences of substance use. These consequences may, in fact, inhibit further maturation or development and successful transition into young adulthood. Other developmentally specific factors may also place the adolescent at risk for substance abuse. These factors include the increased frequency of psychiatric disorders, especially conduct disorder and aggression, in adolescents and the stresses of achieving competence in social and especially intimate relationships, and achieving educational and ultimately vocational competence. Characteristics of the adolescents, their peers, families, and their social milieu appear to be predicative of further substance abuse problems in young adulthood and beyond.

The distribution of risk factors among certain populations of adolescents and the developmental context of risk factors have important implications for the prevention, screening, assessment and ultimately the treatment of substance abuse and dependence in adolescence. Understanding and identifying these characteristics and their effects on the successful development of adolescents will determine whether society and clinicians are successful in the prevention and treatment of adolescent substance abuse.

CHAPTER 5

Coexisting Psychiatric Disorders

The importance of psychiatric disorders coexisting with substance abuse is well-documented in adults. In a large epidemiological study of adult mental health problems, 37 percent of adults having either an alcohol or other drug disorder had a comorbid or coexisting psychiatric disorder (Regier et al., 1990). Among those with a psychiatric disorder, there was a 2.7 times greater risk of having some addictive disorder with a lifetime prevalence of about 29 percent. Adults in clinical settings have even a higher risk of having comorbid disorders. For adults with alcohol use disorders, the highest specific disorder comorbidity rates are for affective disorder, especially Bipolar Disorder, anxiety disorder, and antisocial personality disorder. Among persons with other drug disorders, over 50 percent have other mental health diagnoses including high rates of affective disorder (26 percent), anxiety disorder (28 percent), and antisocial personality disorder (18 percent).

Unfortunately, there are no large-scale general population studies of the prevalence of coexisting psychiatric and substance use disorders in adolescents. In fact, the existing studies of adolescent comorbidity in clinical populations suffer from significant methodological problems which question the validity of the data and the ability to generalize these findings to other adolescent populations. Nevertheless, it is likely that comorbid psychiatric disorder and substance use problems are as important in adolescent populations as in adults.

There are several obstacles blocking serious research into adolescent comorbidity. The lack of a valid, reliable nosology and specific criteria for substance use disorders in adolescents prevents a true understanding of coexisting behavioral and emotional symptoms. As an alternative to categorical classification, dimensional measures have rarely been used in comparing adolescents with other forms of psychopathology.

The definition of psychopathology coexistent with substance abuse presents a host of additional methodological problems. Differences in the rates of comorbidity obtained in previous studies may be due to differences in the samples studied, the type and methods of assessment, the mental status of the informants, and the timing of the assessment.

RELATIONSHIPS BETWEEN COEXISTING
SUBSTANCE ABUSE AND PSYCHOPATHOLOGY

Although a number of possible relationships exist between coexisting substance abuse and psychopathology, several specific relationships are suggested by Meyer (1986). These relationships include: (a) psychiatric symptoms or disorders developing as a consequence of substance use or abuse, (b) psychiatric disorders altering the course of substance abuse, (c) substance abuse altering the course of psychiatric disorders, (d) psychopathology, both in the individuals and their families, as a risk factor for the development of substance abuse, and (e) substance abuse and psychopathology originating from a common vulnerability. Beyond documenting the prevalence of comorbidity among specific adolescent populations, much of the research involving comorbidity has attempted to elucidate these relationships.

The use of the primary-secondary paradigm (Winokur et al., 1970) or a hierarchical approach are two proposed solutions to classification of psychopathology and its relationship to addictions or substance use disorders. The primary-secondary classification refers to ordering the diagnoses according to their chronological appearance: The diagnosis whose specific signs and symptoms appeared first is considered primary and the later-appearing diagnoses are considered secondary. As originally conceived by the Washington University group (Winokur, Reich, Rimmer, & Pitts, 1970), this paradigm does not assume a direction of causality or an etiology. Several studies have examined the value of the primary-secondary distinction and have found that it appears to reduce diagnostic heterogeneity by distinguishing groups in terms of differing

TABLE 5.1.   Common Comorbid Psychiatric
Disorders

Conduct Disorder, especially aggressive type
Attention Deficit Hyperactivity Disorder (ADHD)
Mood Disorders
   Major Depression
   Dysthymia
   Bipolar Disorder
   Cyclothymia
Anxiety Disorders
   Social Phobia
   Post Traumatic Stress Disorder (PTSD)
   Generalized Anxiety Disorder
Bulimia Nervosa
Schizophrenia
Borderline Personality Disorder

---

onset, course, prognosis (Schuckit, 1985b), family history, and prevalence of coexisting psychiatric disorder (Guze, Woodruff, & Clayton, 1971).

Interestingly, within the drug and alcohol treatment community and its literature, addiction is often called a "primary" disorder or disease. Although exactly what defines "primary" is not often clear, a "primary" disorder is assumed to be the underlying disorder which requires first and perhaps foremost attention and treatment prior to treatment of the coexisting disorder(s) (MacDonald, 1984). In truth, the direction of influence is often bi-directional; that is, substance use/abuse and psychiatric disorders influence each other. The co-occurrence of both types of problems produces a third entity, often called "dual diagnosis." Identification of "dual diagnosis" and optimal treatment involves a knowledge of both the psychiatric disorders and substance abuse disorders in adolescents. There are a number of psychiatric disorders that commonly occur with substance abuse in adolescents (see Table 5.1).

Deviant Behavior, Conduct Disorder, and Antisocial Personality Disorder

Deviant behavior, conduct disorder, and later antisocial personality disorder have long been associated with substance abuse. Because substance use, and certainly abuse, by adolescents is considered to be a deviant behavior, the association may be, in part, a tautology.

In epidemiologic studies of the general population, adult antisocial personality disorder is the psychiatric condition most commonly associated with substance abuse. The Epidemiologic Catchment Area (ECA) study found that 83.6 percent of individuals with antisocial personality disorder also met criteria for some form of substance abuse (Regier et al., 1990). ECA data shows that a family history of risk for substance abuse among individuals having a history of either conduct disorder or antisocial personality increased the probability of having alcoholism (Lewis, Rice, & Helzer, 1987).

Several investigators have observed that childhood antisocial behavior, including aggressiveness, predicted adult alcohol and drug problems (Kellam, Stevenson, & Rubin, 1983; McCord & McCord, 1960; Robins, 1966). Most evidence suggests that deviant behavior and conduct disorder precede substance abuse (Gittleman, Mannuzza, Shenker, & Bongura, 1985; Huizinga & Elliot, 1981). Such factors as an earlier onset and greater variety of early conduct problems, aggressive behavior, and the presence of attention-deficit hyperactivity disorder (ADHD) may increase not only the risk for later antisocial behavior, but also for later substance abuse (Loeber, 1988). Early onset of conduct problems is associated with a higher frequency and greater variety of antisocial behavior which includes substance abuse.

Loeber (1988) hypothesized three paths of development to explain differential outcomes among deviant children. The first path, the *aggressive versatile path,* is characterized by an early onset of conduct problems, aggressive behavior, greater rates of ADHD, poor social skills and peer relations, male predominance, and a low remission rate. The aggressive versatile path is more likely to show early onset of substance use and abuse. A *nonaggressive antisocial path* is described as having a later onset, few problems with attention, impulsivity, social skills, peer relations, and aggression and a higher remission rate. Although nonaggressive deviant behaviors may be more predictive of later substance use or abuse, aggression may be a more robust predictor of poly substance use (Loeber, 1990, 1991). Several studies have found that aggression in adolescence, rather than in childhood, may be a better predictive of stage of substance abuse or negative consequences of use (Brook et al., 1986). A third pathway, the *exclusive substance abuse path,* is characterized by the development of alcohol and/or other drug abuse in middle to late adolescence without significant antecedent deviant behavior. Perhaps a majority of later heavy substance abusers were not significantly antisocial during childhood. The onset of substance use and subsequent abuse is generally later than in the more deviant pathway groups.

There appear to be significant interactive effects between conduct disorder and substance use and abuse. Among adolescents who have an early onset of substance use, there is a greater likelihood of continued substance use, continuation of antisocial behavior, and more substance abuse related symptoms (Fleming, Kellam, & Brown, 1982; Mills & Noyes, 1984; Robins & Przybeck, 1985).

Aggression

Aggressive behaviors are present in a large number of adolescents who have conduct problems or deviant behavior and who also abuse substances (Milan et al., 1991). The pharmacologic effects of various substances of abuse can explain some of the violent behavior found in substance-abusing youth. Consumption of certain substances such as alcohol, amphetamines, and phencyclidine increase the likelihood of subsequent aggressive behavior (Tuchfeld, Clayton, & Logan, 1982). The direct pharmacologic effects resulting in aggression may be mediated by disinhibition, attention deficits, poor judgment as well as by environmental context. Pharmacologically produced aggression may be further exacerbated by the relative inexperience of adolescents with some agents, the use of multiple agents simultaneously, or the presence of preexisting psychopathology, such as bipolar disorder, or neurologic disorders, such as temporal lobe epilepsy.

Acute pharmacologic effects do not explain the entire relationship between substance abuse and aggression. When viewed from a developmental perspective, chronic aggressive behavior among adolescents is associated with other concurrent antisocial behaviors in an aggressive form of conduct disorder (Loeber, 1991). Conduct disorder or delinquency almost always precedes substance use (Loeber, 1990). Such aggressive behavior patterns can be noted early in males, with aggressiveness in grade 1 being predictive of substance use 10 years later (Kellam, Brown, Rubin, & Emsminger, 1983). Youth who display a high frequency or early onset of aggressive behavior are more likely to persist into later years. As previously noted, early aggressive behavior predicts subsequent substance abuse (Robins, 1966). The more serious interpersonal aggressive behavior before drug use, the more serious the subsequent involvement with drugs (Johnston, O'Malley, & Eveland, 1978). Other findings indicate that early aggressive behavior leads to later increases in alcohol use and alcohol-related aggression, but that levels of alcohol use are not related to later aggressive behavior (White, Brick, & Hansell, 1993). While nonaggressive antisocial behavior appears to be more predictive of later substance use or abuse, aggressive antisocial behavior is more predictive of polydrug abuse, especially in males (Loeber, 1990). Childhood aggressive behavior appears to be a better predictor than antisocial personality disorder of increases in anger and aggression when drinking (Jaffe, Babor, & Fishbein, 1988).

Adolescents committing violent crimes and behavior are often noted to have characteristic drug abuse histories (i.e., heavy use of several types of "hard" illicit drugs during adolescence; Chaiken & Chaiken, 1984). Generally, the more serious the substance use, the higher likelihood of more serious forms of delinquency (Bohman, Cloninger, Sigrardisson, & Von Korring, 1982; Dishion & Loeber, 1985). Among all substance abusers, adolescents and young adults may be more prone to violent behavior. Data from the Epidemiologic Catchment Area (ECA) study indicates that those reporting violent behavior within the preceding year tended to be young, male, from lower socioeconomic classes, and have engaged in alcohol or drug abuse (Swanson, Holzer, Ganju, & Tsutomu, 1990). Early onset of alcoholism (less than 20 years old) appears to differentiate groups of alcoholics. The early onset group has more violent criminal behavior, parental alcoholism, more depression, and four times more suicide attempts than the older onset group (Buydens-Branchey, Branchey, Noumair, & Lieber, 1989). Other studies have reported similar results in addition to the younger onset group having more bipolar and panic disorder (Roy et al., 1991).

In attempting to explain early aggressive behavior among youth who abuse substances, one finds increased rates of comorbid psychiatric disorders such as attention-deficit hyperactivity disorder (ADHD), learning disabilities, or mood disorders among this population (Bukstein, Brent, & Kaminer, 1989). In ADHD, the frequent occurrence of comorbid conduct disorder is likely a critical variable in that aggressivity, not ADHD alone, appears to predict later substance use (August, Stewart, & Holmes, 1983; Halikas, Meile, Morese, & Lyttle, 1990).

On a biochemical level, several studies have identified serotonin metabolism as having a possible role in both aggressive and suicidal behavior (Asberg, Traskman, & Thoren, 1976; Branchey, Shaw, & Lieber, 1984). Linnoila and colleagues (Linnoila, DeJong, & Virkkunen, 1989) found a 97 percent rate of alcohol abuse among a population of adult violent offenders and impulsive fire setters. Among the 60 percent of this group with alcoholic fathers, lower CSF 5-HIAA and higher impulsivity scores were found. Similarly, in a group of children and adolescents, externalizing, hostility, and aggressive behavior scores were inversely correlated with low central serotonergic activity (Birmacher et al., 1990). Thus, youth at risk for early onset of substance use and abuse are characterized by early onset of conduct problems and aggressive behavior, and go on to manifest a variety of psychopathology. Many of these problems may be caused or mediated by deficits or abnormalities in brain neurotransmitter systems. Cloninger attempted to explain subtypes of alcoholics not only by their differing age of onset, male predominance, and accompanying psychopathology, but also by a proposed deficit in a specific neurotransmitter system (Cloninger, 1987).

Attention-Deficit Hyperactivity Disorder

Attention-deficit hyperactivity disorder (ADHD) has been hypothesized as an antecedent or risk factor for later substance use and abuse in either adolescence or adulthood. A number of retrospective studies (Alterman, Tarter, Baughman, Schneider, 1985; Tarter, McBride, Buonpane, & Schneider, 1977) reported a greater frequency of childhood histories of hyperactivity or minimal brain dysfunction, as the disorder was formerly known, among adult substance abusers. Several other studies observed an increased occurrence of both alcohol and other drug abuse among adolescents with histories of attention-deficit disorder (ADD), as the disorder was known under the DSM-III diagnostic classification system (Blouin, Bornstein, & Trites, 1978). The increased prevalence of drug use only by adolescents with a history of ADD was reported by several retrospective studies (Gittleman et al., 1985; Weiss & Hechtman, 1986). In Weiss and Hechtman prospective study of ADD children with follow-up at 10 and 15 years, more ADD subjects than control subjects had a history of marijuana use at the 10-year follow-up and fell into heavy use categories at the point of maximum use. In another prospective study of adolescents with histories of ADD, Barkley and colleagues (Barkley, Fischer, Edelbrock, & Smallish, 1990) found that only hyperactive adolescents reported high use levels of only cigarettes and alcohol.

Investigators have also used family-genetic studies in an attempt to explain the possible relationships between substance abuse and ADHD/hyperactivity. Family studies have found high rates of alcoholism and antisocial personality disorder in the parents of hyperactive children (Cantwell, 1972; Morrison & Stewart, 1978).

Unfortunately, the literature showing higher rates of substance use and abuse in ADHD children and their families may obscure the true relationship between ADHD and substance abuse. Alterman and Tarter (1986), in a review of the literature of hyperactivity as a risk factor for alcoholism, concluded that conduct disorder, rather than hyperactivity, places individuals at risk for alcoholism. The observed association between hyperactivity and alcoholism is due to the high rate of comorbidity between hyperactivity and conduct disorder. Indeed, a closer examination of the literature appears to confirm this association. Barkley and associates (1990) divided their ADHD group into an ADHD group with conduct disorder and one without conduct disorder. Upon prospective follow-up, the ADHD-only group did not have higher use levels than normal controls, while the ADHD plus conduct disorder group had rates of alcohol and cigarette use two to five times more than normal controls. Similarly, in studies of family history, childhood aggression and resistance to discipline were associated more closely with parental antisocial personality disorder and alcoholism than with parental hyperactivity (Stewart, DeBlois, & Cummings, 1980). Aggressive, antisocial boys were more likely to have antisocial, alcoholic fathers, whereas fathers of hyperactive probands displayed no higher rates of diagnoses of alcoholism or antisocial personality disorder. This is consistent with the findings of Tarter, Hegedus, and Gavaler (1985) who observed no differences in hyperactivity between delinquent sons of alcoholics and delinquent sons of nonalcoholics. Thus, in family studies, the greater incidence of antisocial behavior and alcoholism in the families of ADHD children is primarily associated with the presence of conduct problems among ADHD children (August, Stewart, & Holmes, 1983).

The relationship between conduct disorder, ADHD, and substance abuse may point to interesting interactional effects. The combination of ADHD and conduct disorder appears to be a more robust risk factor for later substance abuse then conduct disorder alone. Lahey and colleagues (Lahey et al., 1988) found the highest rates of alcohol and drug abuse among the parents of children with ADHD plus conduct disorder. Parents of children with conduct disorder alone had lower rates of alcohol and drug abuse than the parents of the conduct plus ADHD group. The parents in both of these groups had higher rates of substance abuse than parents of children with ADHD alone.

The suggested relationship is between the severity of deviant and aggressive behavior in ADHD children and the degree of antisocial behavior and substance abuse in parents and other family members. Children with ADHD plus conduct disorder are more likely to have parents with high rates of psychopathology and are, themselves, at higher risk for the eventual development of substance abuse than their peers with either diagnosis alone.

With regard to the possible role of ADHD to the development of substance abuse in conduct disorder children, several possible mechanisms might be involved. The added impulsivity noted in ADHD youth may produce poorer social choices in terms of both behavior and the selection of peers, as well as poor problem solving. Substance use might serve a type of self-medication function in ADHD youth. Finally, ADHD may reflect a type of brain functioning with a high level of reinforcement from certain psychoactive agents. Although it has been suggested that the use of stimulants, the primary drug for the treatment of ADHD in children, may increase the risk for later substance abuse, there is currently no evidence associating the long-term treatment of ADHD children with stimulants and higher rates of substance abuse (Barkley et al., 1990; Weiss & Hechtman, 1986).

Mood Disorders

Mood or affective disorders are perhaps the most studied psychiatric problems coexisting with substance abuse. The high prevalence of depressive disorders and depressive symptoms in adult substance abusers is well established. Among treatment populations of adult substance abusers, studies show high rates of depressive symptoms in alcoholics (Weissman et al., 1987) as well as mood or affective disorders in a community sample of alcoholics (Weissman & Meyer, 1980), among inpatient drug abusers and among both outpatients and inpatients receiving treatment for cocaine abuse (Rounsaville, Kosten, Weissman, & Kleber, 1986).

The study of mood symptoms and disorders in adolescents is much less extensive. Several studies have identified depression from a larger list of psychosocial and personality correlates of drug use or risk factors in the initiation and maintenance of drug use.

A number of studies of various clinical populations of adolescents have observed high rates of substance abuse and mood disorders. In a study of adolescents seen for emergency evaluation in a general hospital emergency room, almost half of those with elevated blood alcohol levels (17 percent of the total sample) had at least one additional psychiatric diagnosis and that the most common diagnosis was depression (Reichler, Clement, & Dunner, 1983). Interviews with 100 adolescent substance abusers in a drop-in counseling center for youth found that 16 percent showed evidence of double depression, that is, a major depression superimposed on dysthymia (Kashani, Keller, Solomon, Reid, & Mazzola, 1985). Other studies of clinical populations have reported significant percentages of adolescent substance abusers as having mood disorders. These percentages usually are greater than 50 percent of the studied population (Bukstein, Glancy, & Kaminer, 1992; Stowell, 1991). In a more representative community sample, the adolescent users of illicit drugs other than marijuana were more depressed than nonusers or users of marijuana only (Paton, Kessler, & Kandel, 1977). In this sample, while the onset of illicit drug use was associated with increased depressed mood, the continued use of multiple illicit substances is actually associated with reduced depressed mood.

In a study of college freshman, Deykin and associates (Deykin, Levy, & Wells, 1987) found that alcohol abuse was associated with major depression only while drug abuse was associated with major depression as well as other diagnoses. In another study of adolescents in residential drug and alcohol treatment, Deykin and colleagues (Deykin, Buka, & Zeena, 1992) observed a high rate of depression (24.7 percent), although only 8.1 percent had primary depression. Female adolescents with paternal psychopathology and a history of physical abuse were more likely to have major depression, especially primary depression. As in the adult literature, females were generally more likely to have primary depression and an earlier age of onset of depression. Secondary depression was predicted by school failure, drug problems in siblings, and alcohol problems in family members.

In a study of symptom frequency and severity in depressed adolescents, Ryan and colleagues (Ryan et al., 1987) reported that the excessive use of alcohol was associated with the psychotic subtype, a suicidal plan or attempt, phobia with avoidance, and conduct problems and disorder. The use of other illicit drugs was associated with the psychotic subtype of depression as well as with conduct problems and disorder. The existence of multiple comorbid diagnosis, usually substance abuse conduct disorder *and* depression is also common (Bukstein, Glancy, & Kaminer, 1992; Stowell, 1991).

Hovens, Cantwell, and Kiriakos (1994) found that hospitalized adolescent substance abusers had higher rates of comorbidity, in general, and specifically more dysthymmia, major depression, and social phobia than nonsubstance abusing adolescents with conduct/or oppositional defiant disorder.

Explaining the Relationship between Mood Disorders and Substance Abuse

There are several potential mechanisms for the relationship between substance abuse and mood symptoms and disorders in adolescents. Alcohol has primarily depressant pharmacological effects; although with acute use, alcohol is often initially perceived as a stimulant with a euphoric effect. However, as the blood level drops, euphoria can change to irritability and dysphoria (Mayfield, 1968). There may be individual differences in the perception of depressed or dysphoric mood following acute alcohol use or intoxication. Given the disinhibition and altered level of judgement produced by acute intoxication, especially in the more inexperienced adolescent user, this dysphoria may lead to unfortunate results in terms of violence toward self or others.

After chronic alcohol use, the development of more persistent mood symptoms is common. These depressive symptoms are likely to clear within several days or weeks of abstinence alone (Schuckit, 1986), although there may be a significant subgroup of patients who display serious, dysfunctional symptoms even after relatively long periods of abstinence (Behar, Winokur, & Berg, 1984).

Pharmacological effects are not the only mechanism for depression in substance abusers. An abusive or pathologic pattern of substance use may produce a number of social consequences such as academic and vocational failure, loss and disruption in interpersonal relationships, family conflict,and medical problems. Certainly, the existence of multiple social problems and/or stressors can contribute to or precipitate depressed mood.

The presence of mood symptoms may adversely affect the course of substance abuse adversely. Alcoholics with depression have been found to become alcoholic at an earlier age and have a more rapid course to problem drinking than alcoholics without additional psychopathology (Hesselbrock, Meyer, & Keener, 1985). McLellan and colleagues (McLellan, Childress, & Woody, 1985) found that the severity of the comorbid psychiatric condition, regardless of the diagnosis, was the best single predictor of treatment response in an adult inpatient population. However, subgroups of substance abusers may be affected differently than other subgroups. In follow-up studies of adult alcoholics and opiate addicts, coexisting psychiatric diagnoses, including depression, predicted poorer treatment outcome in male alcoholics and opiate addicts, although female alcoholics with major depression had better outcomes than those without depression (Rounsaville, Dolinsky, Babor, Kranzler, & Kadden, 1993). A better prognosis has been observed in alcoholics with primary mood disorders than those with primary alcoholism (Schuckit, 1985b, 1986).

Few studies have examined the natural history or treatment response of adolescents with comorbid depression and substance abuse. Hovens, Cantwell, and Kiriakos (1994) reported that among hospitalized adolescent substance abusers, psychopathology preceded or coincided with substance abuse except for major depression. However, dysthymia preceded substance abuse in a majority of the cases. This suggests a prior vulnerability toward mood disorder. Bukstein, Glancy, and Kaminer (1992) found that the primary-secondary distinction did not predict acute remission of depressive symptoms in a clinical population. In other words, it may not matter which came first, depression or substance abuse, in predicting the short-term course of depressive symptoms in adolescents.

Vulnerability and Risk

The existing literature supports consideration of mood disorder, particularly depression, as a risk factor for substance abuse. Psychopathology as a direct risk factor for the subsequent development of a substance abuse disorder in individual adolescents is only one aspect of risk. Another approach to examining the risk of comorbidity of substance abuse and affective disorder is via family-genetic studies. The existence of psychopathology in the families of adolescents raises the possibility of a familial or genetic risk factor to substance abuse disorder. For example, there is evidence that offspring of depressed probands have an increased risk of substance abuse disorders (Schuckit, 1983; Winokur, 1979). In adult family studies, the families of probands with "reactive depression" or depressive spectrum disease show an increased risk of alcoholism and affective disorder (Van Valkenburg, Winokur, Lowry, Behar, & Van Valkenburg, 1983). In family studies of bipolar patients, increased rates of alcoholism are found in the families of bipolar patients (Helzer & Winokur, 1974). These findings suggest the existence of a depressive spectrum or a broader, shared genetic vulnerability to various forms of psychopathology, with the underlying genetic or familial risk manifested in different disorders, alcoholism, or affective disorder, mostly along gender differences.

However, Weissman and coworkers (Weissman, Leckman, Merikangas, Gammon, & Prusoff, 1984) found no increase in alcoholism among relatives of depressed patients when compared with normal controls, although other studies support the finding that probands with alcoholism secondary to affective disorder have fewer alcoholic relatives and more depressed relatives than primary alcoholics (Woodruff, Guze, & Clayton, 1971). Merikangas and associates (Merikangas, Leckman, Prusoff, Pauls, & Weissman, 1985a) further demonstrated the independent transmission of alcohol abuse and depression in adults and in examining familial risk factors in adolescents and children, Merikangas (Merikangas, Weissman, Prusoff, Pauls, & Leckman, 1985b) observed no increased risk of depression in children of secondary alcoholics when compared with children of depression-only probands. Several other studies also found an absence of aggregation of alcoholism and affective disorders in families (Cloninger, Reich, & Wetzel, 1979; Grove et al., 1987; Schuckit, 1985a). Additional data (Merikangas, Prusoff, & Weissman, 1988) supports that maternal alcoholism gives an increased risk of depression to offspring beyond the increased risk of maternal depression and anxiety. As Merikangas and associates note, maternal alcoholism was always found with depression and/or anxiety disorder. The maternal alcoholism may constitute an indicator of severity of affective disorder rather than demonstrating a transmissible vulnerability to alcoholism. In family studies of bipolar patients, several studies show no increased risk of alcoholism in family members of bipolar patients when compared with families of controls (Dunner, Hensel, & Fieve, 1979; Morrison, 1974).

Merikangas and associates (1985a) commented that the frequently observed association of these disorders may be due to familial clustering of social risk factors that are related to the development of major depression, alcoholism, and other disorders. An alternative explanation is that familial depression might increase the risk of social problems or behaviors such as substance use.

Suicidal Behavior

The adult literature has established a significant relationship between the use of alcohol and other psychoactive substances and an increased risk for suicide (Flavin, Franklin, & Francis, 1990). Increasing research in adolescent suicide reveals a similar relationship between substance abuse and suicidal behavior. Suicide is currently the second leading cause of death among youth (Centers for

Disease Control, 1985). The suicide rate among 15- to 19-year-olds has risen since 1950. Accumulating evidence suggests that much of the increase in the adolescent and young adult suicide rate is related to substance use and abuse (Brent, Perper, & Allman, 1987; Rich, Young, & Fowler, 1986a).

A variety of studies support substance abuse as a risk factor for suicidal behavior, including ideation, and attempted and completed suicide (Crumley, 1990). In a study of completed suicides in Allegheny County, Pennsylvania, from 1960 to 1983, Brent and associates (1987) found a marked increase in the suicide rate among youth, particularly among white males aged 15 to 19 years old. The proportion of suicide victims having detectable alcohol levels rose 3.6-fold to 46 percent in 1978 to 1983. Suicide victims who used firearms were 4.9 times more likely to have been drinking than those using less lethal methods of suicide. Both the increased use of alcohol and the availability of firearms may have significantly contributed to the increased rate of suicide among adolescents. In a study of completed suicides in San Diego, 53 percent of 133 consecutive young suicides (less than 40 years old) had a principal diagnosis of substance abuse (Rich, Young, & Fowler, 1986b). Sixty-six percent of young suicides in the same study group were substance abusers (Rich et al., 1986b). Eleven percent of the substance abusing group committed suicide before age 20.

In other studies of adolescent suicide completers, significant percentages of victims were substance abusers. Shaffer and colleagues (Shaffer, Garland, Gould, Fischer, & Trautman, 1988) found substance abuse to be associated with 37 percent of male and 5 percent of female suicides. Twenty-two percent of the victims were determined to be substance abusers. Other studies show ranges of substance abuse in suicide completers from 27.6 percent (Poteet, 1987) to 70 percent (Shaffi, Carrigan, Whittinghill, & Derrick, 1985). The increased risk of completed suicide among adolescent substance abusers is further supported by Benson and Holmberg (1984) in a 10-year follow-up of two groups of adolescents. When compared with a group from the general population, adolescents with a prior history of substance abuse had a two to eight times greater death rate, with one half of the deaths due to suicide.

It is not clear whether substance use or abuse is more common in adolescent suicide completers than suicide attempters. Brent and associates (1988) found that the diagnosis of substance abuse was not significantly different between groups of adolescent completers versus attempters and ideators with a lethal plan. A number of studies show high rates of substance abuse among adolescent suicide attempters. Studies of hospitalized adolescent attempters reported substance abuse rates from 23 percent (Stevenson et al., 1972) to 50 percent (Crumley, 1979; Pfeffer, Plutchik, Mizruchi, & Lipkens, 1986). In a study of 340 outpatient adolescent substance abusers, suicide attempts were three times more likely among substance abusing youth than a group of normal matched controls (Schwartz & Berman, 1990). Adolescent suicide attempters with a diagnosis of substance abuse may have more serious or potentially lethal attempts

(Brent et al., 1986; Pfeffer, Plutchik, & Mizruchi, 1983). Substance abuse in depressed adolescents appears to increase both the risk of multiple attempts and the medical seriousness of the attempts (Robbins & Alessi, 1985).

Substance abuse may distinguish attempters from ideators (Kosky, Siburn, & Zubrik, 1990), although substance abuse has been identified as a risk factor for suicidal ideation among college students (Levy & Deykin, 1989). Like completers, a male predominance among adolescent substance abusers with suicidal attempts and ideation is noted (Kotila & Lonnggvist, 1988; Levy & Deykin, 1989). In attempting to answer the question of why adolescent substance abusers have a high risk for suicidal behavior, one can examine several possible mechanisms, including acute and chronic effects of substance use or abuse. Adolescent suicide victims are frequently using alcohol or other drugs at the time of suicide (Brent, Perper, & Allman, 1987; Friedman, 1985). The acute use of substances may produce a transient but intense dysphoric state, disinhibition, impaired judgment, and increased levels of impulsivity. The acute use of alcohol or other drugs may exacerbate preexisting psychopathology, including depression and anxiety (Schuckit, 1986). Adolescents often have less tolerance for extreme mood states and limited judgment and behavioral controls when compared with adults. Therefore, the acute effects of substances on behavior may have more potentially severe effects on adolescents. In fact, drugs are often the method for the suicidal act (Garfinkel, Froese, & Hood, 1982).

Chronic effects of substance abuse include pharmacologic effects such as depression (Mayfield, 1968), serotonegic depletion (Ballanger, Goodwin, Major, & Brown, 1979), or social effects including disruption of peer and family relationships. Youth experiencing an acute stressor involving a social loss or a blow to self-esteem are at greater risk for suicidal behavior (Hoberman & Garfinkel, 1988). As noted in studies of adult populations, alcoholics with hopelessness and interpersonal losses are at increased risk for suicide (Beck, Weissman, & Kovacs, 1976; Murphy, Armstrong, Hermele, Fischer, & Clendenin, 1979). As many adolescent substance abusers have dysfunctional families with parents who also abuse substances (Kandel, 1974), environmental stress may be further increased. Runeson (1990), in a report of 58 consecutive suicides by adolescents and young adults, reported that exposure to parental substance abuse, early parental divorce, and suicide attempts in the family were more frequent in the 47 percent of the sample diagnosed with substance abuse.

The association of adolescent substance abuse with other forms of psychopathology may also mediate both the acute and chronic effects previously noted in suicidal behavior in this population. Substance abuse in adolescents is often evident concurrently with a number of other psychiatric disorders, including mood disorders, anxiety disorders, bulimia nervosa, schizophrenia, and conduct disorder (Bukstein, Brent, & Kaminer, 1989; Greenbaum et al., 1991). Each of these disorders confers an increased risk of suicidal behavior in adolescents (Brent & Kolko, 1990) as well as an increased risk of substance abuse

(Bukstein, Brent, & Kaminer, 1989). However, comorbidity, especially mood disorders with other nonmood disorders including substance abuse, is one of several putative risk factors for completed suicide (Brent et al., 1988).

In a study of adolescents with a lifetime diagnosis of substance abuse, 23 suicide victims were compared with community controls also having a lifetime diagnosis of substance abuse (Bukstein et al., 1993). Suicide victims were more likely than controls to have active substance abuse, comorbid major depression, prior suicidal ideation, a family history of depression and substance abuse, legal problems, and the availability of a handgun in the home. Depression and substance abuse often appear together in a variety of additional psychiatric disorders. Borderline personality disorder, particularly when comorbid with mood disorders, often leads to suicidal behavior, including completions (Runeson, 1990) and attempts (Crumley, 1979; McManus, Lerner, Robbins, & Barbour, 1984). Similarly, schizophrenia has high rates of suicidal behavior and comorbid mood disorders (Runeson, 1990).

As previously discussed, conduct disorder is observed, more often than not, as being comorbid with substance abuse. A diagnosis of conduct disorder is often noted in adolescents with suicidal behavior (Shaffer, 1974; Shaffi et al., 1985). Although conduct disorder is also commonly comorbid with mood disorders (Ryan et al., 1987), many adolescents with substance abuse and conduct disorder manifest suicidal behavior without the presence of mood disorder (Apter, Bleich, Plutnik, Mendelsohn, & Tyano, 1988). Aggression and impulsivity, both common in conduct disorders, may be important factors in the risk for suicidal behavior in substance abusing adolescents (Apter et al., 1988).

The study of impulsivity and aggression as risk factors for suicidality may reflect underlying cognitive, problem-solving styles or underlying neurobiology rather than discrete diagnosis as the true risk factors (see Table 5.2). Adolescents with high rates of the aggressive type of conduct disorder and attention-deficit hyperactivity disorder are more likely to engage in substance abuse than youth with ADHD alone or nonaggressive conduct disorder (Milan et al., 1991). Youths displaying explosive, aggressive outbursts appear to be at greatest risk for repetitive suicidal behavior (Pfeffer, Newcorn, Kaplan, Mizruchi, &

TABLE 5.2.   Dimensional Comorbidity Behavioral and Emotional Characteristics Commonly Seen in Adolescent Substance Abusers

Impulsivity
Irritability/Mood Instability
Aggression
Suicidality
Poor Social/Problem-Solving Skills
Learning Problems/Disabilities
Alienation

Plutchik, 1988). Also, research linking low serotonergic states with suicidal and aggressive behavior in substance abusing adults (Roy & Linnoila, 1986) is now being applied to adolescents. Impulsivity and aggression may be as important as depression in the etiology of suicidal behavior as evidenced by adolescents with conduct disorder having higher suicidality scores than adolescents with major depression (Apter et al., 1988).

In summary, substance-abusing adolescents appear to be at increased risk for suicidal behavior across the continuum from ideation to completion. This increased risk is mediated by both the acute and chronic effects of substance abuse. Adding to the risk of suicidal behavior are comorbid psychiatric disorders or personality characteristics such as depression and impulsivity which are commonly noted in both suicidal or substance-abusing adolescents.

Anxiety Disorders

Data from the ECA study show a lifetime prevalence of substance use disorders in 23.7 percent of individuals reporting any anxiety disorder diagnosis, reflecting an increased risk of 1.7 times greater than those not having an anxiety disorder. However, there is a substance abuse rate of 35.8 percent for panic disorder and a rate of 32.8 percent for obsessive-compulsive disorder. For individuals having an anxiety disorder, the risk of having any drug disorder diagnosis (other than alcohol) is even higher. For those with any alcohol use disorder, 19.4 percent have an anxiety disorder diagnosis, a rate similar to that found in the general population. Among those with other drug use disorders (other than alcohol), 28.3 percent report an anxiety disorder, representing a 2.5 times increased risk of having an anxiety disorder.

A number of studies of adults in clinical populations describe high rates of anxiety disorders, including agoraphobia and other phobic disorders, among substance abusers (Kushner, Sher, & Beitman, 1990). In family studies, the risk of substance abuse disorders is increased among relatives of individuals with panic disorder or agoraphobia (Leckman, Weissman, Merikangas, et al., 1983; Weissman et al., 1984). Merikangas and associates (1985a) observed a greater risk of anxiety disorders in the relatives of individuals with alcoholism, although this was specifically attributed to the presence of alcoholism plus an anxiety disorder in the individual. Among young adults with an anxiety disorder, age 18 to 30 years old, there was an increased risk of developing a substance use disorder of 1.7 times above that seen for those without anxiety disorders (Christie et al., 1988). Most reported the onset of anxiety disorder prior to the onset of the substance use disorder.

In one of the few studies examining anxiety disorders in adolescent substance abusers, Clark and Jacob (1992) found that anxiety disorders were common among an adolescent treatment population with early-onset alcoholism. Fifty percent of this sample had at least one lifetime anxiety disorder diagnosis with post-traumatic stress disorder as the most common anxiety disorder diagnosis (25 percent of total sample). Even substance-abusing adolescents without anxiety disorder diagnoses had higher anxiety levels than a normal control group. Not surprising, adolescents with comorbid substance abuse, conduct disorder, and anxiety disorder had more depressive symptoms and suicidal behavior than normal controls, although the comorbid group did not differ on these variables from a similar group without anxiety disorder. The comorbid group with anxiety disorders was less impaired in terms of substance abuse behavior, school problems, peer relations, and overall problem density than the comorbid group without anxiety disorders. In a comparison of young male alcoholics with abstainers, Rydelius (1983a, 1983b) found that the heavy alcohol users were more likely to report anxiety symptoms and interpersonal difficulties due to shyness.

In clinical populations of adolescents with comorbid anxiety and alcohol abuse, Clark and Jacob (1992) found that a substantial proportion (85 percent) had the onset of the anxiety disorder prior to onset of alcohol abuse. The order of appearance of comorbid disorders appears to be variable, depending on the specific anxiety disorder. Social phobia and agoraphobia usually precede alcohol abuse while panic disorder and generalized anxiety disorder tend to follow the onset of alcohol abuse (Kushner, Sher, & Beitman, 1990).

Obviously, the pharmacologic effects of alcohol and other substances may account for much of the relationship between substance use and abuse and anxiety disorders. Although alcohol, for example, has direct anxiolytic properties, the expectation or belief that alcohol will reduce anxiety may often promote alcohol use, despite the real effects of alcohol in reducing anxiety (Clark & Sayette, 1993). In support of such theories as the tension-reduction theory or self-medication, the early onset of phobic disorders suggests attempts at self-medication. The later appearance of panic and generalized anxiety disorders may be due to preexisting excessive consumption and/or withdrawal states (Kushner, Sher, & Beitman, 1990).

The reasons for use and continued use by adolescents in the earliest states of alcohol use may hold clues as to the possible role of anxiety in eventually leading to anxiety disorders. Forty-one percent of U.S. high school seniors reported "to relax or relieve tension" as a reason for their drug use; 64 percent of barbiturate users, 69 percent of tranquilizer users, and 40 percent and 41 percent of alcohol and marijuana users, respectively, mentioned tension reduction as a reason for their substance use (Johnston & O'Malley, 1986). As with adults, many adolescents view alcohol and other substances as social lubricants which may allow them to be more social in often anxiety-provoking social situations found during adolescence. For those adolescents with clinically significant anxiety symptoms, the expectancies of alcohol along with the anxiolytic pharmacologic properties may further reinforce alcohol use. In some cases, the exacerbation of anxiety symptoms by alcohol use may bring anxiety symptoms to clinical levels. McKay, Murphy, Maisto, and Rivinus (1992) found that alcohol-abusing adolescents with high problem severity were more likely than those with low problem severity to report believing that alcohol enhances social behavior. This finding is consistent with the Christiansen, Smith, Roehling, and Goldman (1989) report that the expectancy of alcohol as enhancing social behavior was the strongest predictor of drinking severity and drinking-related problems.

Schizophrenia and Psychotic Symptoms

Drug-induced psychotic symptoms in adults have been associated with the use of hallucinogens, stimulants, phencyclidine, and cannabis (Castellani, Petrie, & Ellinwood, 1985). Sustained use of stimulants can produce a classic paranoid psychosis; this pharmacologic parallel provides a useful model for schizophrenia (Castellani, Petrie, & Ellinwood, 1985). The pattern-specific drug use behavior by schizophrenics may provide clues to underlying neuropathologic mechanisms in the development and maintenance of schizophrenia.

The acute alcohol withdrawal syndromes of alcohol hallucinosis and delirium tremens can be manifested by hallucinations and agitation seen in a psychotic state. While these withdrawal syndromes are usually noted in chronic alcohol users, it is uncertain what quantity and pattern of alcohol intake are sufficient to elicit physiological symptoms in adolescents or how often withdrawal states occur in adolescents. Actual physiological dependence or severe withdrawal symptoms in adolescents appears to be rare, as noted by Vingelis and Smart (1981).

Eating Disorders

Eating disorders are another group of psychiatric disorders often associated with substance abuse. Several studies point to a high incidence of substance abuse among bulimic patients as opposed to those with restrictive anorexia nervosa (Bulik, Sullivan, Epstein, Weltzin, & Kaye, 1992; Hatsukami, Eckert, Mitchell, & Pyle, 1984). Several studies report high rates of substance abuse among relatives of bulimic women (Bulik, 1987; Hudson, Pope, Jonas, Yurgelun-Todd, & Frankenburg, 1987; Kassett, Gershon, & Maxwell, 1989). Kaye and associates (Kaye, Gwertsman, Weiss, & Jimerson, 1986) suggest that reports of decreased tension and anxiety after binging as well as reports of a "giddy, silly, or somewhat intoxicated" mood upon termination of binging and vomiting compare with substance abuse as tolerance can develop to the tension reduction or intoxicating effects. Bulimic behavior is then continued to maintain the reduction of adverse affective states rather than to get high.

The increased prevalence of substance use and abuse among the bulimic subtype suggests shared characteristics. The observed comorbidity of eating disorders and affective disorders may explain much of the comorbidity of eating disorders and substance abuse. Another alternative is that bulimia, alone or in combination with other addictions, represents an alternate expression of a shared vulnerability or genetic predisposition. Bulik (1987) suggests that the expression of this vulnerability may be shaped by individual biological factors and environmental-social factors such as cultural restrictions on female drinking and drug use. In another study, Bulik and colleagues (Bulik, Sullivan, McKee, Weltzen, & Kaye, 1994) found that bulimic women with alcohol abuse differed from bulimic women without alcohol abuse by having higher novelty-seeking temperaments. High novelty-seeking has been implicated as characteristic in specific subtypes of alcoholics.

Comorbidity and the Development of Substance Abuse in Adolescence

There is ever-increasing support for specific psychiatric disorders influencing the risk, onset, and course of substance abuse disorders in adolescents. This relationship may also be nonspecific in terms of psychopathology adding to other social stressors or risk factors for substance abuse. The relationship between substance abuse and pathology is likely not a simple one. The term "dual diagnosis" commonly used to describe comorbidity in clinical settings is somewhat of a misnomer as adolescents are more commonly "multiple diagnosed" with a variety of both internalizing and externalizing psychiatric disorders in addition to substance abuse. Whether they receive discrete psychiatric diagnoses, many substance-abusing adolescents appear to have higher levels of psychiatric symptoms including mood and anxiety symptoms (Bukstein, Brent, & Kaminer, 1989). For example, I observe adolescents with conduct disorder and substance abuse commonly as having affect regulation problems manifesting as labile, irritable, and highly reactive mood states.

Tarter, Alterman, and Edwards (1985) reviewed the psychological and biological characteristics associated with the vulnerability to alcoholism and suggested that vulnerability could be explained in terms of empirically established temperamental traits such as strength and speed of response, quality of prevailing mood, and lability of prevailing mood. Clarification of temperamental traits may be useful for identifying characteristics which distinguish alcoholic individuals or those at risk for alcoholism with such traits from those without these traits. Temperamental traits may be the basis for a common diathesis for alcoholism and antisocial personality and/or other psychiatric disorders.

In a similar fashion, Cloninger (1987) proposed that clinical subgroups differing in patterns of abuse, personality traits, neurophysiological characteristics, and inheritance result from various response biases or neurogenetic adaptive mechanisms that medicate an individual's adaptation to experiences, including the response to the use of substances. Cloninger's Type I and Type

II alcoholics reflect various combinations of these adaptive mechanisms that result in substance-seeking behavior and later dependence after initial or early exposure. Dimensional characteristics of adolescents, including aggression and behavioral disinhibition, may be even more important than categorical comorbid diagnoses in subtyping adolescent substance abusers according to natural history, prognosis, and treatment response. A cluster analysis by Mezzich and associates (1993) found that adolescent alcohol abusers formed two clusters. The majority of adolescents from a clinical population was characterized by behavioral disinhibition and hypophoria, whereas the other group was characterized primarily by negative affect. The first group had an earlier age of onset, more substance abuse involvement, and greater severity of psychiatric disorder and behavioral disturbance.

Substance use as self-medication of coexistent psychiatric symptoms continues to be an hypothesis worth exploring both in the clinic and in the laboratory. On the basis of psychodynamic and other clinical findings, Khantzian (1985) suggests that the specific psychotropic effects of illicit drugs, especially cocaine and heroin, interact with psychiatric disturbances and "painful affect states" to predispose to addictive disorder. Addicts' drug choice is the result of an interaction between the psychopharmacologic properties of the drug and the primary feeling state experienced by the addict. However, as others have observed Khantzian and the literature that he cites fail to distinguish between psychiatrically-induced addictive disorder and substance-induced psychopathology. Several sources support the theory of use of alcohol and other drugs by adolescents in response to distress and negative affective status. Kandel (1978) found that psychological distress predicted the use of hard or illicit drugs other than marijuana. McKay and colleagues (1992) observed that the alcohol-abusing adolescents with high problem severity reported a greater propensity of drinking in response to unpleasant emotions.

The observation that the use of alcohol and tobacco, as well as illicit substance use, peaks during the 18 to 34 age group while highest rates for prescribed psychoactive medications peak after age 26 suggest that both use patterns have similar social and psychological functions. In a review of longitudinal studies of both high school and college students, Kandel (1978) reported that many of behaviors and psychological symptoms thought to be consequent to drug use actually predate substance use. Dilsaver (1987) suggests that cholinergic and aminergic neurotransmitter systems influence mood and affect and psychomotor status. Abnormal interaction of these systems, as well as supersensitivity of muscarinic cholingeric systems, form the basis for pathophysiology of affective disorders. Both drugs of abuse and medications prescribed for affective disorders have common neurochemical effects which presumably treat the abnormality. Self-medication of psychiatric symptoms may be the common denominator in explaining the relationship between various psychiatric disorders coexisting with pathologic substance use. Investigators have identified psychological distress as a contributing factor or explanation for relapse in alcoholic and opiate-dependent populations (Bradley, Phillips, Green, & Gossop, 1989; Ludwig, 1989). Consistent with classical conditioning models, negative affective states (for example, depression or anger) appear to be able to directly trigger craving and possibly precipitate relapse (Childress, McLellan, & O'Brien, 1992).

Substance abusers may have abnormal brain-reward mechanisms and may find it difficult or impossible to experience reward or pleasure from normal, everyday life; they depend on the psychoactive effects of substances to stimulate brain-reward centers (Gawin & Kleber, 1984).

Clinical Implications of Comorbidity

It is critical that clinicians recognize the importance of comorbid psychiatric disorders in the assessment and treatment of adolescents with substance abuse disorders. In clinical settings, there is a substantially increased risk of encountering coexisting problems. As discussed in Chapters 6 through 9, comorbid psychiatric disorders will influence the symptoms and behaviors displayed by the adolescent, the course of the component disorders, as well as the approach and response to treatment.

Through the further identification of subtypes of accompanying risk factors, more specific identification of populations at risk could be helpful in prevention, treatment, and follow-up. Prevention efforts or early intervention may prevent not only the occurrence or morbidity of either the substance use disorder or psychiatric disorder, but also potentially the comorbid presentation which is usually associated with poorer treatment response and outcome. Due to the implications of additional diagnoses toward treatment and prognosis, evaluation of adolescents would be more thorough, whether the primary problem is identified as either substance abuse or other psychopathology. Increased effort would be made in obtaining a thorough family history and chronology of symptom onset. Following such a complete evaluation and differentiation of individuals into subgroups, each subgroup would likely benefit from a specific, individualized program or set of interventions; for example, tricyclic antidepressants for those in whom alcohol abuse was secondary to depressive symptoms. In order to ensure inclusion into the appropriate subgroup, ongoing evaluation of patient symptoms, behavior, and response to treatment would be continued.

As improved treatment methods are developed for psychiatric disorders in adolescents, these improvements can be potentially modified and applied to the comorbid group of adolescents. A further discussion of the importance of comorbidity in assessment, treatment, and prevention is presented in Chapters 7, 8, and 10.

SUMMARY

The frequent comorbidity of substance abuse and other psychiatric disorders in adolescents is a critical fact that has important implications for the prevention, assessment, and treatment of adolescents. A knowledge of the types of comorbid presentation will assist the clinician and researher in developing more effective interventions as well as understanding the etiology of the component comorbid disorders.

CHAPTER 6

Assessment

Assessment is the cornerstone of clinical management. Assessment should not only provide for identification of a case or a problem needing treatment, but also measure the severity and range of problems associated with adolescent substance abuse so the effect of treatment interventions may be later evaluated. For adolescent substance abuse, assessment at its simplest level becomes: Does the adolescent *use* alcohol or other illicit drugs? What effect does this use have on the adolescent's functioning in his or her environment? At its most complex level, assessment utilizes instrumentation and researched-based methodology to provide quantitative and qualitative information measuring a variety of variables related to substance use, its consequences, antecedents, and related behaviors in adolescents.

In this chapter, I will begin with consideration of screening for substance use and abuse in adolescence and proceed through a review of practical elements of interviewing adolescents, other methods and sources of gathering clinical information, what areas to assess, and, finally, consideration of the use of assessment instruments.

SCREENING

Screening refers to the initial, and usually brief, assessment of individuals or groups to identify the likely presence or absence of a given problem. Individuals so identified are then referred for or are given a more detailed, comprehensive assessment. As illustrated by the Chapter 3 discussion on epidemiology and substance use patterns in adolescence, one can expect significant numbers of adolescents to report at least occasional use of substances. An overwhelming majority of adolescents will report some exposure to alcohol. Considering quantity and frequency information is also problematic. Use data will probably serve to identify a large population of adolescents to whom administering a more comprehensive evaluation would be impractical. In keeping with a useful definition of substance abuse, screening should inquire of dysfunction and/or distress associated with levels of substance use.

With the exception of epidemiological studies or other research projects, screening should be targeted to a population of adolescents at risk. While a primary care physician or other healthcare worker should briefly inquire about substance use and associated problems during a routine visit, time constraints may limit both the extent of the inquiry and the reliability of the adolescent's response, especially when no other informant or additional information is available. School staff, especially counselors or senior administrative staff, mental health clinicians and social agency staff should be acquainted with psychoactive substance use/abuse screening questions and procedures. There should be a reason for screening an individual adolescent or a particular group of adolescents unless they have been previously identified as high risk.

The method of screening depends largely upon the setting and the purpose for screening. In general clinical settings, several questions in a clinical interview format are the most common method. These questions should include types of substances used, quantity, and frequency, as well as a general screen for negative consequences of use. The use of specific screening instruments is becoming an increasingly more common method. Screening instruments will be presented in a later section of this chapter.

Are Adolescent Self-Reports Valid and Reliable?

The astute clinician should always question whether any self-report about substance use or other deviant or antisocial behavior is truthful. The adult literature appears to support the validity and reliability of self-reports from alcoholics and drug abusers (Sobell & Sobell, 1990). There is considerably less information about the validity of adolescent self-reports. In surveys of substance use among nonclinical groups of adolescents, there is no objective validation of self-report data (Johnston, Bachman, & O'Malley, 1985), although the investigators point to evidence of construct validity, low nonresponse rates, large affirmative response rates, and consistency of findings across more than a decade of surveys as evidence for validity. Winters and associates (1991) found that the great majority of drug clinic and school adolescents gave temporally consistent reports of substance use with only a small portion having extreme response-bias tendencies. Although self-reports appear to be reliable in some populations (Barnea, Rahav, & Teichman, 1987), specific populations, especially extremely antisocial youth, have much higher responses of "faking good" than drug clinic samples (Winters, 1990).

INTERVIEWING: GUIDELINES AND TECHNIQUES

Substance use by adolescents is usually a covert behavior, hidden from parents and other authority figures. The clinician's knowledge of an adolescent's involvement with alcohol or other drugs may range from no knowledge or vague suspicion to awareness of significant levels of use and abuse confirmed by both the adolescent and other informants. However, for any adolescent presenting with a problem, psychosocial dysfunction, or high-risk status, the clinician should exercise some level of suspicion of substance abuse regardless of the chief complaint or nature of the presenting problem.

Because of the covert and often deviant nature of adolescent substance use, adolescents rarely self-refer for evaluation and treatment. With the exception of emergency medical settings, the adolescent will rarely appear intoxicated or high at assessment. Therefore, the clinician must depend on the adolescent's self-report about substance use and associated behaviors, informant reports, and the ability to synthesize information about lifestyle, behaviors, and attitudes consistent with substance abuse.

Engaging the Adolescent

Assuming the appropriately skeptical clinician and the typical guarded adolescent, beginning an assessment interview with a less confrontational approach often serves to engage the adolescent while providing useful information as well. A suggested tactic is an initial inquiry about the adolescent's current life circumstances. Asking about where the adolescent lives, school attended, academic progress, home composition, relationships, friends, and preferred activities allows the clinician to pass through objective data and gradually engage the adolescent. The clinician should be honest with the adolescent and display genuine interest and concern as an independent person while withholding any display of criticism or judgment. In identifying the behavioral patterns and environmental milieu of the adolescent, the clinician can determine whether the adolescent fits into a high-risk profile. If an adolescent indeed fits into such a profile, the clinician may be less dependent upon the adolescent's self-report to be at a reasonable level of suspicion that the adolescent may be abusing alcohol and/or other drugs.

Adolescents may also be willing to share information about anonymous friends, including the friends' alcohol and drug use. If the adolescent reports numerous friends using and/or abusing alcohol and other drugs, attending parties where use is present, and fits into other "high-risk" characteristics, the clinician's level of suspicion should be raised even further.

The purpose for an initial visit for assessment is to obtain as much information as possible; therefore, the clinician should avoid any unnecessary confrontation that may compromise accurate, reliable reporting. Inconsistencies should initially be gently probed. For example, when an adolescent states that she has tried beer only twice, both times at friends' parties, the clinician may ask, "I'm a little confused. You told me before that you never went to a party where there was alcohol or other drugs." Later, when the clinician provides the adolescent and his or her family with feedback, a more pointed, direct confrontational approach is often both necessary and effective. When a more substantial history of alcohol or other drug use is suspected, the clinician should calmly state the suspicions, and offer help and understanding if the adolescent chooses to be honest with the interviewer.

The clinician should be honest and clear about the extent of confidentiality. While the clinician may feel that the specifics of the adolescent's behavior may be held in confidence, the clinician is often obliged to provide verbal and/or written summaries of the evaluation to third parties such as parents, child welfare staff, and juvenile justice personnel, such as a judge or probation officer. The clinician should inform the adolescent that such a report will be made and what information is likely to be contained in such a report. Dealing with dangerous behavior such as suicidality or homicidal ideation with a plan necessitates an obvious exception to confidentially, but should be revealed to the adolescent at the outset of the interview.

As with any clinical interview with youth, identifying the adolescent's developmental and cognitive level is critical in order to ask questions in an appropriate manner and to understand the adolescent's answers. Given the high frequency of developmental and learning disabilities and delays in adolescents with substance abuse, an individual adolescent's facility with expressive and receptive language may lag considerably behind his or her chronological age.

COMPREHENSIVE ASSESSMENT: THE DOMAIN MODEL

Given the multiple risk factors, frequent comorbidity and multiple areas of possible dysfunction related to alcohol and other drug abuse, the comprehensive assessment of substance abuse and related problems in adolescents requires evaluation of many areas of functioning in areas of the adolescent's life and possible psychopathology. Tarter (1990) describes a multilevel evaluation procedure for adolescents with suspected substance abuse. Following the identification of areas of dysfunction through the use of a comprehensive screening interview or instrument, each domain (Table 6.1) is then more thoroughly

TABLE 6.1. Evaluation of Adolescent Substance Abuse: The Domain Model

1. Substance use behavior
2. Psychiatric and behavioral problems
3. School and/or vocational functioning
4. Family functioning
5. Social competency and peer relations
6. Leisure and recreation

assessed by use of more detailed questions or by the use of standardized instruments which are designed to assess that specific domain.

Substance Use Behavior

For the detailed assessment of substance use and related behaviors, questions should inquire about four major areas: (1) patterns of use, (2) negative consequences, (3) context of use, and (4) control of use (see Table 6.2). Patterns of substance use includes information about the types of agents used and the age of onset of use for each substance. In addition to age of first exposure and initial use, the clinician should ask about the progression of use and age of regular use. While quantity and frequency data are essential to any complete assessment, the variability in adolescent substance use is often great. Therefore, the adolescent may report periods of abstinence as well as periods of rapid acceleration of use and heavy use of particular agents. A time-line drug chart is often useful to allow the adolescent to report quantity, frequency, and variability data across time with important dates, holidays, and other time cues as a guide.

TABLE 6.2.   Substance Use Behavior

1. *Patterns of Use*
   Onset: Age and progression of use
   Quantity
   Frequency
   Variability
   Types of agents used

2. *Negative Consequences*
   School/vocational
   Social
   Family
   Psychological/psychiatric
   Physical, including withdrawal

3. *Context of Use*
   Time/place of use
   Peer use levels/attitudes/pressure
   Mood antecedents/consequences
   Expectancies
   Overall social milieu

4. *Control of Use*
   Use view of problem
   Attempts to decrease or stop use
   More time spent obtaining/using
   Inability to control use episode
   Give up activities/responsibilities to use

Although reports of heavy alcohol or other drug use may be suggestive of a diagnosis of psychoactive substance abuse or dependence, an account of the negative consequences of use is the cardinal sign of pathology. The clinician should be careful to inquire about directly related effects or negative consequences of use and not to assume that all problems in an adolescent's life are due to substance use.

Context of use constitutes: the time and place of use; with whom use occurs; peer use levels, attitudes, and pressure; and who acquires the substance(s) to be used. The adolescent's mood and attitude both prior and subsequent to use and his or her expectancies from use are also important elements in determining the overall social or substance-consuming milieu. Along with attitudes and beliefs, specifically about substance use, the clinician should also inquire about the adolescent's values and attitudes in general. Does the adolescent have nonconforming values, alienation from society, or sense of hopelessness about the world and his or her future in it? Assessment of substance use behavior may follow a functional analysis of use to determine usual antecedents to use and consequences of use. Such an analysis will allow a more specific targeting of relevant antecedents during treatment.

Inquiry into control of use generally follows DSM-IV criteria for psychoactive substance dependence. Does the adolescent view his or her use as a problem and have efforts been made to control or stop use? Does the adolescent spend longer than planned obtaining, using, and recovering from the effects of the substance? Does the teenager take more than planned? Does the adolescent get drunk or high when expected to fulfill role obligations such as school or work? Has the adolescent given up previous important and favored activities in order to use? Has use continued despite repeated negative consequences? Despite the lower prevalence of physical sequelae of substance use and the rarity of overt physiological withdrawal symptoms, questions about these features are essential and, if answered in the affirmative, indicate a severe level of substance dependency for the adolescent.

Questions should be substance-specific. If use of a particular substance is endorsed, the clinician should proceed with a more detailed inquiry about the negative consequences, context, and control of use for each specific substance.

Toxicological testing of urine for the presence of one or more illicit substances is useful to confirm the presence of the substance(s). What urine or similar toxicological measurements of bodily fluids cannot do is make a diagnosis of abuse or dependence. The threat (with parent backup) of urine testing is often sufficient to convince the adolescent to reliably report the substances that he or she has used. The clinician should advise the patient and parents that a refusal to give a sample should be considered as if the sample was positive. A more detailed discussion of toxological testing is contained in Chapter 7.

Making a Diagnosis of Substance Abuse or Dependency

Substance dependence represents one level of substance "abuse," consisting of a core of negative consequences in addition to signs, symptoms, or behaviors indicating physical dependence and/or compulsive use. *Psychoactive substance abuse* represents a lower level of abuse indicating the presence of direct negative consequences of use. Understanding how to use these criteria in assessing an adolescent's involvement in substance use is a essential skill.

Substance Use

Although any level of substance use by adolescents should be cause for concern, the regular use of alcohol and/or experimental use of other agents in the absence of negative consequences of use, psychosocial impairment, compulsive use, or preoccupation with use does not warrant a diagnosis of a psychoactive substance use disorder. Such an adolescent user is at high risk for developing such a disorder and may benefit from prevention and other interventions designed to control substance use behaviors.

Psychoactive Substance Abuse

Under both DSM-III-R and DSM-IV, substance abuse was intended to be a milder, prodromal condition to dependence. Criteria consist of continued use despite having a recurrent social, occupational, psychological, or physical problem that is caused or exacerbated by substance use or recurrent use in hazardous situations over a period of at least one month. The emphasis is on recurrent negative consequences of use. The clinician must attempt to distinguish problems caused by substance use from problems caused by coexisting psychiatric disorders or family dysfunction. Consequences should also be developmentally appropriate.

Substance Dependence

A review of the dependence criteria (applicable to DSM-IV) allows us to point to assessment aspects relevant to adolescents and to suggest possible questions to assess specific diagnostic criteria.

1. *Tolerance*
   - Did you ever feel that you needed more alcohol or other drugs for same effect?
2. *Withdrawal*
   - Have you ever had withdrawal symptoms after you stopped or cut down use (that is, felt sick)? Hallucinations? Fits or seizures?
   - Have you ever drank (or took drugs) to avoid withdrawal symptoms (or to avoid feeling sick)?

3. *Substance often taken in larger amounts or over a longer period than the person intended.*
   - Did you ever find that once you started using (alcohol or other drugs):
     You ended up using much more than you had planned to?
     You found you were spending much more time using than you planned?
     You kept using when you promised yourself not to?
     Do you ever have trouble turning down alcohol or drugs when offered to you?
     Do you ever go on binges?
     Do you ever feel an irresistible compulsion (urge) to use?

4. *Persistent desire or one or more unsuccessful efforts to cut down or control substance use.*
   - Do you want to quit using (alcohol or other drugs)?
     For how long have you wanted to quit?
     Have you ever felt you had a problem with alcohol or other drugs?
     Have you ever really tried to quit using?

5. *Much time spent in activities necessary to get the substance, taking the substance, or recovering from its effects.*
   - Did you ever spend a lot of time thinking about using or getting drunk or high?
     Were there times when you couldn't think or keep your mind on your work because you needed to use alcohol or other drugs?
     Did you ever spend a lot of time getting alcohol or other drugs?
     Does the sight, thought or mention of alcohol or other drugs trigger urges and cravings to use?

6. *Important social, occupational, or recreational activities given up or reduced because of substance use.*
   - Have you ever . . .
     Spent less time with family because of using (alcohol or other drugs)?
     Spent less time with friends because of using?
     Spent less time at school because of using?
     Spent less time at work because of using?
     Missed out on other things because you spent too much money on alcohol or other drugs?

7. *Continued substance use despite knowledge of having a persistent or recurrent social, psychological, or physical problem that is caused or worsened by the use of the substance.*

- Have you ever . . .

Continued use despite a physical problem?

Continued use despite increase in depression and/or anxiety caused by alcohol or other drugs?

Continued use despite arguments with family or friends about use?

Substance Abuse

Questions should focus on the presence of problems which are attributable to substance use by the adolescent.

1. *Recurrent use resulting in inability or failure to meet major role obligations at work, school, or home.*
   - While using, have you not gone to school or not returned to school?
   - While using, have you been unable to work at a job or mess up on the job, leave early, or not shown up for work at all?
   - While drunk or high or while recovering from being drunk or high have you ever:

   Not been able to do homework?

   Went to school high or drunk?

   Drank or got high *at* school?

   Neglected your responsibilities (chores/work at home)?

   Missed a day (or part of a day) at school?

   Missed a day (or part of a day) at work?

   Lost a job due to using?

2. *Recurrent use in physically hazardous situations.*
   - While using, have you driven a car, motorcycle, or bicycle?
   - While using, have you ever operated a machine?
   - While using, have you ever been in a caretaker role?

   for example, babysitting?

3. *Recurrent substance use-related legal problems.*
   - While using (or due to use), have you ever been arrested?
   - Have you ever been in trouble due to use or a positive drug screen?

4. *Continued use despite continuing or recurrent social or interpersonal problems caused or worsened by the effects of the substance.*
   - Have you ever had problems with friends, girl- or boyfriend, family members due to use (for example, complaining about your use)?
   - While using, have you ever done something to or with someone else that you would not have done while high (for example, had sex, got into a fight)?

Psychiatric and Behavioral Problems

In view of the significant comorbidity of adolescent substance abuse with other behavioral and emotional problems, screening and eventual detailed assessment of coexisting psychopathology is essential. Screening questions about depression, suicidal ideation and behavior, anxiety, aggressive behavior, and current and past mental health treatment should be made. Inquiry should include whether the symptoms or behaviors are present during both substance use or intoxication and abstinence. Chronology of symptoms and behaviors relative to the onset of specific substance use behaviors—for example, onset of first use, regular use, and pathologic use—should be established. Do the symptoms or behaviors exist independently of substance use or intoxication and even well into significant periods of abstinence?

Obtaining a family history of psychiatric disorder can often give clues to untangling a confusing set of symptoms and behaviors. Not only should past treatment history and established psychiatric diagnoses of family members be queried, but also whether similar, but undiagnosed comorbid symptom patterns exist in other family members.

In choosing the level of inquiry into psychopathology, the clinician is usually guided by the setting and the purpose of the assessment. Several screening questions into depression, suicidality, aggression, psychosis, and treatment history may be sufficient in order to augment other information in determining where an adolescent should be referred for a more detailed, comprehensive psychiatric evaluation. In such a thorough assessment, either in an inpatient or outpatient setting, questions about psychiatric and behavior problems should cover, in detail if necessary, every major diagnostic group.

To augment the clinical interview, the clinician may wish to use one of a number of diagnostic or dimensional instruments to assess the severity of psychopathology and to obtain psychiatric diagnoses. A more detailed discussion on the use of instrumentation is provided in a later section of this chapter.

School and/or Vocational Functioning

Most adolescents are enrolled in school which constitutes the primary "job" of adolescence. Regular attendance and satisfactory progress in school require many of the same functional skills required of adults in obtaining, performing, and maintaining adequate employment. Satisfactory performance in the school setting requires interpersonal and cognitive skills, behavioral controls and at least a minimal level of achievement orientation. Not only can school failure promote substance use and abuse, but academic failure and poor school behavior often identify the adolescent substance abuser.

Although the adolescent's report of school performance and behavior, attitude toward school and achievement are important, objective information including grades, attendance records, and past psychoeducational testing (e.g., IQ and achievement test scores) have a higher level of reliability. Teacher and school administration reports and observations complement the objective record and the adolescent's own report.

The academic environment is often very useful in fully understanding the context of the adolescent's substance abuse. Beginning at home, what are the parents' attitudes about school achievement and behavior? Do they hold the adolescent responsible for problems at school or do they blame the school? Do the parents encourage or demean school achievement—or are they ambivalent? Factors influencing the school environment include the availability of alcohol or other drugs, the level of supervision of adolescents, the school administration's attitude about substance use, and the larger social context, for example, urban schools with high dropout rates and surrounded by rampant hard drug use are different contexts than suburban or rural schools.

For those adolescents not in school, the clinician should inquire about their school history and the circumstances of their leaving, for example, academic failure, expulsion or "dropping out." What are the adolescent's future plans regarding future education or vocation? Is the adolescent employed and, if so, what is his or her employment record regarding attendance, advancement, and/or number of jobs?

Family Functioning

In view of the research and clinical experience pointing to a number of family factors as predictors of childhood and adolescent psychosocial functioning and level of substance involvement, it is not surprising to find a number of family variables as the targets of assessment. Family organization, communication, and social values will greatly influence the adolescent's behavior despite the increasing importance of the adolescent's autonomy from the family and the increasing influence by peers.

Assessment of family functioning proceeds on several levels. First, who are members of the adolescent's family? In addition to nuclear family members, it is important to count influential extended family members—or even nonfamilial adults who may reside with the adolescent. The clinician should inquire about the quality of family relationships in terms of communication styles, conflicts and possible abusive relationships. Questions about parent management of adolescent behavior should include parent attitudes about limit-setting and the success or failure of past and current efforts.

The clinician should inquire about overt parent behaviors. How much does each of the adolescent's parents use alcohol or other drugs. Is there a history of substance abuse or dependence in the past and, if so, was treatment obtained? If a history of parental substance abuse is noted, how did the parent's behavior affect the family and the adolescent? Similarly, family histories of substance abuse should be obtained for all primary and secondary family members.

Although overt substance use behavior provides a significant influence on current and later adolescent behavior, parental and family attitudes are also important. Do the parents clearly discourage substance use by their child and provide appropriate consequences for violations of their prohibition? Do the parents ignore both subtle and obvious evidence of substance use or dismiss use as an inevitable developmental stage?

An examination of stressors upon the family and individual members assists the clinician in determining the family context. Are family members overwhelmed by other problems, including unemployment, financial difficulties, and illness including psychopathology. Not only is identification of family stressors important, but also evaluation of the family's adaptive and problem-solving skills points to the family's ability to meet the challenges of stressors.

Social Competency and Peer Relations

Social competency refers to the ability of the adolescent to function adequately with both peers and adults. Included within the larger concept of social competency are communication skills, anger control, relaxation skills, and problem-solving skills. The clinician should be careful to evaluate social competency of the adolescent across settings and include school, family, and peer competence. Peer relations are especially critical given the developmentally appropriate transfer of interest and influence from family and parents to the adolescent's peer group. As previously emphasized, the clinician should question the adolescent about his or her peer relations. Does the adolescent have friends? A best friend? What activities does the peer group prefer? What are their attitudes, especially about deviant behavior in general and about substance use in particular?

Within a peer group, does the adolescent feel accepted and comfortable? Inquiry about social avoidance and possible social phobia may point to anxiety disorder or poorly developed social and communication skills. How does the adolescent handle conflict with peers? Is there a level of sustained attachment and loyalty to a particular peer group?

Leisure and Recreation

The adolescent's availability and use of leisure time may determine the adolescent's engagement in deviant behavior and substance use. The clinician should not only catalog the adolescent's current leisure-time attitudes, interests, and activities, but also ask about past activities, either prosocial or deviant. In addition to interest or disinterest in various activities, does the adolescent have the minimal physical capability to participate? Does the adolescent have any special talents which have yet to be identified or, if known, cannot be displayed due to various environmental circumstances such as lack of access?

Community and Social Context of the Adolescent

This category has received little attention as a target for evaluation. The social context of the adolescent is critical to understanding both the prospects for treatment and the type of treatment and interventions necessary for a particular substance-abusing adolescent. What is the adolescent's economic and legal status? What other agencies, such as child welfare and juvenile justice, are involved with the adolescent and his or her family? Where does the adolescent live? Is there gang involvement? Is the neighborhood economicallty depressed with rampant violence and substance involvement?

The differing types of social environments may greatly influence the adolescent's risk for, initiation, and maintenance of substance use and abuse as well as the level of risk for relapse. A nonsupportive environment may require a very different treatment approach than a supportive one.

INSTRUMENTS FOR ASSESSMENT IN ADOLESCENT SUBSTANCE ABUSE

The need for more thorough and complete assessment in the area of adolescent substance abuse in a variety of clinical and nonclinical settings has resulted in a veritable cottage industry in the creation of a wide range of instruments. The varied uses of such instruments include the diagnosis of substance abuse and dependence and other psychiatric disorders, rating the severity of substance use and related behaviors, and assessment of many other specific domains related to adolescent substance use and psychopathology.

Justification for the use of instruments covers both clinical and research needs. The need for standardized assessment in research has proved to be the primary motivation for developing instruments. In a developing and still basically scientifically naive area such as adolescent substance abuse, the need for standardized, rigorous methodology, quantifiable data, and intelligibility in the scientific literature has produced a number of instruments. Research needs require a higher standard than routine clinical use, including the establishment of psychometric properties such as validity and reliability.

The value of instruments to the clinician is similar and includes the ability of instruments to obtain more consistent, reliable information, to obtain serial measures at regular intervals, and to define more homogenous patient populations to determine treatment needs. Instruments can assist in determining relevant outcome variables, adjunct clinical judgment, and potentially allow the user a more inexpensive, efficient method of assessment. Whether the user is a researcher or a clinician, or both, the attributes of a good instrument are the same: the instrument should be valid; that is, it should measure the concept it purports to measure. The instrument should be reliable, that is, consistent in its results across time and across users. The instrument should also be practical, not demanding too much time, effort, or cost for the amount and type of information that it provides.

There are several major types of instruments used in the assessment of adolescents with suspected or confirmed problems with substance use. During the remainder of this chapter, we will discuss the types of assessment instruments and briefly mention specific instruments. While we have attempted to be as complete as possible, the dynamic nature of instrument development and the inevitable lag between drafting and ultimate publication will likely cause omission of newer instruments and more recent versions of more established instruments.

Screening Instruments

Screening instruments are used by both clinicians and nonclinicians to identify adolescents at risk for substance abuse, those with substance abuse, and those meeting a minimum threshold of problematic behavior and requiring further, more detailed assessment to determine their substance use status. In fact, except for the value of some screening instruments in large-scale surveys, screening instruments are designed to be the gatekeeper for more comprehensive assessment. Within a fairly large group of screening instruments, there are instruments which are unidomain and multidomain. Unidomain instruments measure a specific area, most likely substance use and directly related behaviors. Multidomain instruments assess a wider range of variables including behaviors, psychiatric symptoms, family and school functioning, and attitudes.

Unidomain Screening Instruments

The most common single domain is substance use behavior. The *Michigan Alcohol Screening Test* or MAST (Selzer, 1971) is designed for adults and assesses the consequences related to pathological adult use. No norms or validation among adolescent populations have been published. The *Adolescent Alcohol Involvement Scale* or AAIS (Mayer & Filstead, 1979) is a brief 14-item instrument designed for screening for pathological levels of alcohol use. Winters (1990) lists several recently developed instruments including tools for screening, self-report, and interview. Although many have good face validity, they are often limited by lack of construct validity and published psychometric data, and may be based on out-of-date diagnostic criteria (DSM-III).

Multidomain Screening Instruments

Given the need for multidimensional or multidomain assessment of adolescent substance abuse, multidomain instruments are likely more useful to both clinician and researcher. In addition to information about substance use, multidomain instruments assess other areas of adolescent functioning which may be affected by the adolescent's substance use. As a result of a National Institute of Drug Abuse (NIDA) project to develop improved methods of substance abuse assessment in adolescents, the *Drug Use Screening Inventory* (DUSI) (Tarter, 1990) was designed to screen multiple domains and identify youth in need of further assessment in each domain or area where problems appear to exist. The DUSI is a self-report, self-administered instrument available in paper and pencil and/or computer-assisted versions.

There are several multidomain instruments available in an interview format. The *Addiction Severity Index* (ASI) by McLellan, Luborsky, Woody, and O'Brien, (1980) represents a standard for adult assessment and has been used by McLellan and others in longitudinal research. Based on the ASI, are several ASI "clones" with a similar structure based on the assessment of multiple domains of adolescent functioning as well as substance use behavior. The *Adolescent Problem Severity Index* (Metzger, Kushner, & McLellan, 1991), the *Adolescent Drug Abuse Diagnosis Instrument* (Friedman & Utada, 1989) and the *Teen Addiction Severity Index* (Kaminer, Wagner, Plummer, & Seifer, 1993) are each structured interviews which require a measure of interviewer training for use. These interviews are broad in their reach of multiple domains and more comprehensive than other screening instruments. However, these instruments are screens and the clinician will likely wish to explore some domains in much greater detail.

Comprehensive Instruments

The use of multiple instruments for the assessment of adolescents is not always practical for clinical programs. The search for a single comprehensive instrument or group of complementary instruments to assess adolescent substance use/abuse and related problems has led to the development of several such instruments. The *Chemical Dependency Adolescent Assessment Project* (CDAAP) was begun in the early 1980s to assist clinicians to identify, refer, and treat adolescents with substance abuse problems (CDAAP, 1988; Winters & Henly, 1988). Actually, CDAAP has three component instruments, each examining a content area. The personal experience screening questionnaire (PESQ) is a 38-item self-report screening instrument which indicates whether the adolescent is in need of a more thorough, comprehensive assessment. Content areas of the PESQ include chemical use problem severity, drug use frequency, other

mental health/behavioral problems, defensiveness (faking good), and infre-
quency (faking bad).

The personal experience inventory (PEI) (Winters & Henly, 1988) is a 300-
item self-report instrument available in both paper and pencil and computer-
assisted versions. In addition to providing detailed information about the level
of substance abuse involvement in adolescents, the PEI also identifies personal
risk factors that may precipitate or sustain substance abuse. The PEI has two
component sections. The first is a problem severity section which has five basic
scales, five clinical scales, three validity scales, and questions about substance
use onset and frequency. The second section, the psychosocial section, has
eight personal adjustment scales, four family and peer environment scales, and
two validity scales.

The last component of the CDAAP is a diagnostic interview to obtain
sociodemographic information, severity of psychosocial stressors, alcohol
and marijuana use, screen for other psychiatric disorders and determine level
of functioning. This allows the clinician to determine axes I through V of
DSM-III-R. Extensive data on normative and clinical population indicates
good reliability and validity of the scaled scores (CDAAP, 1988).

The National Institute on Drug Abuse (NIDA) developed a manual to provide a model to guide the assessment of adolescents with substance abuse problems (Tarter, 1990). The model consists of four steps: (1) early identification,
(2) comprehensive assessment, (3) treatment matching, and (4) referral. At the
screening or early identification level, 10 domains are assessed for possible
dysfunction. The DUSI is used to evaluate each of these 10 domains. For each
domain identified by the DUSI as being an area for concern, a more comprehensive assessment is performed on that area through the use of a number of
recommended instruments. Unfortunately, the NIDA assessment and referral
model may be too time-consuming and perhaps outdated in the belief that the
results of such a comprehensive assessment will alone determine appropriate referral and treatment.

Other Instruments

The clinician or researcher should consider the use of other instruments to
augment substance abuse assessment procedures. For comprehensive diagnostic assessment of psychopathology in adolescents, the use of structured
interviews such as the DISC (Costello, Edelbrock, Dulcan, Kalas, & Klaric,
1984) or a semi-structured instrument such as the *Childhood Schedule for
Schizophrenia and Affective Disorders* or Kiddies-SADS (K-SADS) (Puig-Antich
& Chambers, 1978) can provide DSM-III-R diagnoses, including psychoactive
substance use disorders. The use of self-report instruments such as the *Beck
Depression Inventory* (Beck, Ward, Mendelsohn, Mock, & Erbaugh, 1961) allows baseline and follow-up assessment for depression, a problem common in

substance abusers. The *Child Behavior Checklist* (CBCL) measures behavior problems and provides information on somatic complaints, schizoid traits, communication, maturity, delinquency, aggression, withdrawal, and hyperactivity (Achenbach & Edelbrock, 1983).

Our discussion of instruments that are available for the assessment of adolescent substance use involvement is by no means exhaustive or complete. There are many other instruments which are likely reliable, valid, and practical. The clinician or researcher should find the instrument or set of instruments which best fit program or project needs in terms of the variables assessed and their value in identifying both baseline problems in specific domains of functioning and change over time, perhaps in response to treatment interventions. Practical administration of instruments is also a primary concern. Valuable time should not be taken up in the assessment of variables which are not needed or will not be used in targeting treatment interventions within the treatment program.

SUMMARY

The assessment of substance abuse, its related behaviors, and psychosocial consequences and effects on adolescent functioning involves careful evaluation of multiple domains of the adolescent's life including behavior, family, school, and peer functioning. Evaluation of these areas determines whether a problem exists, identifies specific types of problems, and what type of intervention might produce the most change. The use of instrumentation to measure areas for assessment allows for more standard and quantifiable evaluation of baseline problems and potential evaluation of change on follow-up, that is, determination of treatment success or failure.

CHAPTER 7

Medical Evaluation

Substances of abuse are by their nature pharmacologic agents with acute, sub-acute, and chronic physiologic effects on not only the brain, but on a variety of other body organ systems as well. As a result of these physiologic effects or potential negative medical consequences of these effects, such as accidents, an adolescent using or abusing psychoactive substances often presents to a primary health care professional. Because adolescents do not commonly acknowledge their substance use, the psychoactive and physiologic effects and medical consequences of substance use may be the only overt manifestation of substance use. Knowledge of these effects and consequences allows those dealing with adolescents to potentially identify substance use by the adolescent and to provide appropriate education and information about the effects of substance use. Health care professionals who suspect or confirm the use of illicit substances can then refer the adolescent for further evaluation by clinicians with experience in the area of adolescent substance abuse.

With the physical effects and consequences of substance abuse in mind, a complete medical history and physical examination should be an essential part of any evaluation of an adolescent with behavioral or emotional problems. A comprehensive medical evaluation is especially important with suspected adolescent substance abusers.

POINTS OF ENTRY

Most adolescents who abuse substances are not health seekers; therefore, they rarely present for any type of health or medical care in an office setting. Even less common is an adolescent's presentation to ask for help with a substance abuse problem identified by the adolescent or others. A frequent point of entry of a substance-abusing adolescent into the health care system is for the emergency management of intoxication from substances, overdose, or the accidents resulting from these substance use-related conditions. Substance-abusing adolescents may be compelled to seek medical care for a variety of reasons, including vague somatic complaints, birth control, sexually transmitted diseases, chronic respiratory problems, dermatologic problems, and minor accidents.

Accidents

Accident-related behaviors are common in adolescents. In a study conducted in urban middle and high school settings, Milstein and Irwin (1987) found that 63.3 percent of the adolescents reported taking chances on bicycles or skateboards, 64.0 percent did not use seat belts while in a car, and 70.7 percent drove or rode in a car over the speed limit. Compounding these risk-taking behaviors is the use of psychoactive agents. The same study reported that 14.0 percent of the students used a bicycle or skateboard while under the influence, 48.3 percent had been passengers in a car with an impaired driver, and 6.8 percent drove a car or motorcycle while under the influence.

Accidents are the leading cause of death in the adolescent age group and are responsible for 79 percent of all deaths among adolescents aged 15 to 19 years (National Center for Health Statistics (NSHS), 1992). Motor vehicle accidents constitute the largest percentage of adolescent accident deaths (NCHS, 1992). Adolescents and/or other substances are frequently involved in motor vehicle deaths. Adolescents with positive blood alcohol levels and involved in fatal accidents appear to have lower alcohol levels than adult drivers involved in fatal accidents. Although less likely to drive after drinking than adults, adolescents who do drink are at higher risk than drinking adults to be involved in an accident, despite drinking less (Runyan & Gerken, 1989; Wagenaar, 1983). Magnifying the risk of death or injury to adolescents is their increased risk due to being less likely to use seat belts than other age groups (Williams, 1985). Recent legislation raising the legal drinking age to 21 years in all 50 states has resulted in a reduction of 10 percent to 15 percent in fatal motor vehicle accidents among youth (General Accounting Office, 1987).

Other types of accidents among adolescents, fatal or nonfatal, often involve alcohol or other drugs. Alcohol is estimated to be involved in as many as 40 percent of adolescent drownings (Howland & Hingson, 1988). Alcohol has been found to be involved in large percentages of deaths in accidents involving bicycles and all-terrain vehicles (Kraus, Fife, & Conroy, 1987; Newman, 1987).

There is a wide range of activities potentially affected by alcohol or other drugs. Unfortunately, adolescents who are more likely to use substances are also more likely to participate in risk-taking activities or behavior (Donovan & Jessor, 1985). Risk-taking orientation appears to be a strong predictor of driving while under the influence of alcohol.

Emergency Room Management

The psychoactive properties of alcohol and other drugs can affect perception, judgment, and coordination. Accidents and trauma can result, necessitating emergency evaluation and treatment. According to the Drug Abuse Warning Network (DAWN) reporting system of drug related emergency room visits, children and adolescents between 6 and 17 years had a drug-related emergency room rate of 58.8 per 100,000 for all drugs (NIDA, 1991). Problems resulting from intoxication from substances, overdose, or acute physical distress from either condition are certainly possible and not infrequent, thus also pointing to the need for emergency management.

While the adolescent may be surprisingly honest to health care workers given an acute and emergent medical problem or trauma, the health care professional is usually confronted with a situation or circumstances suggesting substance involvement, or with an adolescent who is uncooperative, unconscious, or otherwise having a compromised mental status. There are two common presentations of the substance-using adolescent to an emergency room setting: intoxication-injury and intoxication/overdose. Alcohol or other drug withdrawal states are much less common presentations for adolescents.

Initially, the role of the emergency room or other medical staff is to triage, stabilize, and acutely treat the presenting injury or illness. Given the significant percentages of adolescents using substances and the involvement of substances during other recreational activities, operation of motor vehicles, or use during work situations, any child or adolescent presenting to the emergency room with trauma should receive heightened suspicion of having used a psychoactive substance. Following the stabilization and acute treatment of the presenting problem, the medical staff utilize their heightened suspicion of substance use in a thorough mental status exam, toxicology screen, and acute treatment of the substance intoxication and/or overdose. The level of behavioral impairment is dependent on a host of factors in addition to the type of substance or substances used. The effects of all substances depend on age, weight, experience with the substance, and tolerance to the substance. For example, the presence of food while drinking alcoholic beverages will determine the rapidity in which the alcohol is absorbed and acts in the brain.

Mental Status Exam

In an emergency room setting, patients do not wear signs indicating their recent ingestion of substances. This unknown is further complicated by the altered mental status produced by the psychoactive substance(s) or the presenting injury. The adolescent may be unconscious, lethargic, or just uncooperative. However, prior to receiving the results of blood or urine toxicology (discussed later), several prominent behavioral and physical manifestations may leave solid hints as to the basic properties of the substance(s) involved.

A simplistic but practical way to divide the most common substances of abuse is between (a) psychomimetic or central nervous system (CNS) activating agents and (b) CNS depressants. Drugs of abuse frequently cause autonomic signs which are important cues to broad substance class. Cholinergic and anticholinergic syndromes are less commonly seen due to substance abuse by adolescents, but these syndromes should also be considered. In view of the prevalence of polysubstance use and abuse by youth, the use of multiple agents with divergent psychoactive and other pharmacologic effects may alter these common presentations.

Physical Exam

A thorough physical evaluation should include an evaluation for trauma and neurologic examination, especially to exclude brain injury or illness. Vital signs, especially heart rate and blood pressure, can indicate the presence of a drug. Medical staff should examine the skin for needle tracks or abscesses, especially in the arms, neck, supraclavicular areas, groin, and feet. Peri-nasal and peri-oral skin irritation can be produced by solvent inhalation. Red or injected conjunctiva (eyes) may be a sign of smoking marijuana. Pinpoint pupils may be a sign of opiate intoxication while dilated pupils can be evidence of opiate withdrawal or stimulant use. Mucosal irritation in the nose may likewise indicate cocaine use. Orifices, including oral cavity, rectum, and vagina should be examined for possibly hidden drugs. The acute onset of gastrointestinal distress (GI) should prompt radiographic exam to check for swallowed drug packets. Abnormal sensory and motor findings on a neurological exam may further suggest psychoactive substance use.

Diagnostic Studies

Especially in adolescents with unidentified intoxication or overdose states, the following basic studies should be obtained: electrolytes and electrocardiography (EKG). Electrolytes may determine the presence of metabolic acidosis and serum osmolarity changes produced by overdose of some substances. Electrocardiography will identify dysrhythmia, including conduction delays, produced by such substances as cocaine or antidepressants. Depending on the physical findings, chest x-rays or other films may be indicated.

Serum and urine toxicology can detect the presence of psychoactive substances. Medical personnel should obtain toxicologic screening on all patients, including adolescents, with unexplained mental status changes and/or injury prompting suspicion of ingestion of unknown agents which may affect acute management. Toxicological screening is limited by the time needed to obtain results, lack of correlation between drug concentration and observed effects, and the risk of false-positive and false-negative results (Schwartz, 1988). Nevertheless, "drug testing" is and can be useful in a variety of situations including emergency evaluation and later follow-up after substance abuse treatment.

There are several types of technologies for drug testing; the most appropriate method depends on the purpose of the test and other known and unknown variables (Gold & Dackis, 1986). *Thin-layer chromatography* (TLC) is a very commonly used method for use as a broad-spectrum screen for prescription drugs as well as drugs of abuse. TLC is the least sensitive drug-testing method, requiring a larger amount of the drug to be present for detection and yielding either a positive or negative without quantification of positive substances. Depending on the set level of sensitivity of the specific TLC in a particular lab, a negative TLC may be a false negative with positive results obtained by more sensitive testing methods.

The related methods of *gas chromatography* (GC) and *gas chromatography-mass spectrometry* (GC-MS) are more sensitive. GC-MS is also very specific, allowing quantitative as well as qualitative information. However, these methods are very expensive. Immunoassay methods, especially *enzyme-multiplied immunoassay technique* (EMIT), are becoming increasingly more common and perhaps the most common method utilized in clinical practice. Many RIA-based drug-testing kits are available to indicate the presence of specific drugs or combinations of drugs. Clinics and professionals can obtain these kits for low cost. Immunoassays are more sensitive than TLC for most drugs and therefore more likely to detect lower levels of use. Immunoassay methods are class specific with a positive response indicating that the drug being sought, and perhaps similar drugs, are present. Often, to obtain a valid result, positive results on immunoassays are followed by confirmatory testing using chromatographic techniques.

The type of fluid used for testing depends on the purpose and situation. In an acute, emergency setting, the testing of blood is needed as an index of recent use. If a particular substance or combination of substances is known to have been ingested, a method yielding quantitative results is preferred to assist correlating clinical findings with blood levels of the substance.

For routine screening, a sufficiently sensitive screening method such as RIA, yielding the presence or absence of a particular drug, is sufficient. Urine is the most common bodily fluid used for drug screening. To ensure a reliable result, specimen collection is important. Many substance abusers, adolescents obviously included, may wish to adulterate or substitute specimens in order to avoid a positive result. Urine specimens must be obtained under direct visual supervision with the responsible staff not leaving the specimen container, empty or full, out of sight at any time. Caution should be given in interrupting the results of positive drug screens. A single positive test does not necessarily mean that the adolescent is a substance abuser. Although drug screening may not be helpful in making a diagnosis, screening can be used to confirm the adolescent's self-report of use. This use of drug screening is especially valuable during ongoing follow-up after the start of treatment. For this use of drug-screening procedures, clinicians, parents, and other significant adults inform the adolescent to expect random drug screening to check compliance with treatment and expectations of abstinence. Before testing, the adolescent's parents or other authority figures should specify the consequences of a "dirty urine" (for example, grounding the adolescent from outside activities for a specified time period). Refusal to provide specimens should be considered a positive result.

History

If the adolescent is conscious and able to communicate, the medical staff should attempt to elicit as detailed a history as possible. This history should include the types of substances ingested, when they were ingested relative to the interview, and how much was ingested. The interviewer should be calm and supportive with the adolescent and stress the medical importance or necessity of the information to provide optimal medical treatment. This sense of medical necessity may lessen the resistance and possible denial of the adolescent. If time allows, the interviewer should take full advantage of this period of increased cooperation and obtain a complete substance use history. If the adolescent is resistant, not conscious, or if the mental status is compromised, the medical staff should seek similar information from other informants, including friends or family members. These interviews should be conducted in a room separate from the patient.

An important caution is *not* to assume that the ingestion or overdose was accidental and the result of the recreational use of substances. The medical staff should assess the circumstances for possible suicidal behavior, including specifically inquiring as to past suicidal behavior by the adolescent, current intent and/or plan, and assessing risk factors for adolescent suicide. These risk factors include the presence of major depression, substance abuse, and a history of suicide in the family (Brent et al., 1988).

Withdrawal

The past literature suggests that specific, overt signs of withdrawal from agents producing physiologic dependence syndromes are rare in adolescents (Vingilis & Smart, 1981). Nevertheless, medical personnel should consider the possibility of alcohol withdrawal, especially when an adolescent reports extreme levels of alcohol intake in terms of quantity, frequency, and duration of use, and a past history of even mild withdrawal symptoms. A history of opiate or barbiturate (or any history of the use of sedative/hypnotic agents or "downers") use should clue the clinician to monitor for these respective withdrawal syndromes. Especially in older adolescents from urban, lower socioeconomic backgrounds, characteristic signs and symptoms of opiate withdrawal should prompt appropriate management. I refer the reader elsewhere for more detailed discussions of the medical management of withdrawal syndromes (see Ciraulo & Shader, 1991). There are few salient differences in the management of withdrawal in adolescents as compared with adults. The clinician should be aware that the adolescent may be experiencing the withdrawal symptoms for the first time, resulting in more subjective distress. The younger addict may be more resistant than older addicts in revealing the nature or extent of use patterns.

HIV Risk and Infection

Substance use, poor judgment, and various risk-taking behaviors, including precocious sexual activity, by adolescents often go hand-in-hand. Due to these factors and the association of intravenous drug use with human immunodeficiency virus (HIV) infection, substance abusing and dependent adolescents are increasingly at risk for acquired immunodeficiency syndrome (AIDS) or HIV disease. Although adolescents constitute a small percentage of actual AIDS cases, the long latency from HIV infection to disease onset (i.e., mean of 10 years) and the high incidence of AIDS among young adults means that many affected individuals acquired HIV infection as teenagers (Centers for Disease Control, 1992). Thousands of adolescents have AIDS and more than 75,000 are estimated to be infected with HIV (Centers for Disease Control, 1992).

A decision to test for HIV infection should be based on the presence of specific risk factors such as intravenous (IV) drug use, specific, at-risk sexual behavior, sex with HIV-infected individuals or those at high risk for HIV infection. The existence of substance abuse in an adolescent does not necessarily mean that the adolescent is high risk for HIV.

Youth at Risk for HIV/AIDS

Although adolescents account for less than 1 percent of reported HIV/AIDS cases, many adolescents are infected as teenagers and may not display overt manifestations of HIV/AIDS disease until adulthood due to the long incubation period (Bacchetti & Moss, 1989). While nationally, HIV infection was the second leading cause of death in 1990 among men aged 25 to 44 years (National Center for Health Statistics, 1993), HIV has become the leading cause of death among young adults in many U.S. cities (Selik, Chu, & Buehler, 1993).

Almost 80 percent of adolescents were infected through sexual exposure or intravenous drug use. The subgroups of adolescents at highest risk for HIV infections are runaways, prostitutes, crack cocaine users, or IV drug users (St. Louis et al., 1991). Among ethnic/racial groups, African-Americans and Hispanics combined account for 75 percent of all pediatric AIDS cases (Selik, Castro, & Papparoanou, 1988). Among AIDS cases associated with intravenous drug abuse, African-Americans and Hispanics represent 51 percent and 30 percent respectively (Mascola et al., 1989). Disadvantaged, out-of-school youths are also at high risk for HIV infection in the United States (St. Louis et al., 1991). In areas of endemic HIV infection such as inner cities, risk-taking behaviors increase the risk of infection (D'Angelo, Gretson, Luban, & Gayle, 1991).

Sexually active adolescents have the highest rates of sexually transmitted diseases (Cates, 1990). Unprotected sexual intercourse is reported by approximately half of adolescents by adulthood (Centers for Disease Control, 1992). The heterosexual spread of HIV accounts for a larger proportion of HIV cases in youth than in adults (Vermund et al., 1989). Prostitution among female, adolescent substance abusers also increases HIV infection risk.

Young homosexual men often begin regular sexual interactions by mid-adolescence and are more likely to engage in high-risk behaviors, such as failure to use condoms and engaging in anal sex (Perkower, Dew, & Kingsley, 1991; Valdiserri et al., 1988).

Adolescent crack users show significant levels of behaviors that place them at risk for HIV infection, including a cluster of sexual risk behaviors (Fullilove et al., 1993). Substance-use related behaviors include engaging in sexual intercourse under the influence of drugs or alcohol and exchanging sexual favors for drugs or money (for drugs).

Factors increasing HIV infection risk among homeless adolescents include sexual risk behaviors being more common among homeless adolescents, increased levels of IV drug use, high rates of homosexual identity and behavior, and gravitation to areas where HIV is endemic and where HIV positive sex and IV drug use partners can be more easily found (Rotheram-Borus, Koopman, & Ehrhardt, 1991). It is estimated that 4 percent of homeless adolescents are infected with HIV (Rotheram-Borus et al., 1991). This is an infection rate more than twice that of other adolescent samples.

Given the increased risk of HIV infection among many groups of adolescent substance abusers, treatment or intervention programs need to consider HIV risk as an important part of the program (Kipke, Futterman, & Hein, 1990) evaluation procedures. Clinicians need to assess the risk of HIV via a complete, confidential evaluation of all high-risk behaviors including sexual behavior, medical history and, of course, drug use behaviors, especially IV drug use and needle sharing. This information may be used to identify and triage adolescents to appropriate services. For all adolescents meeting specific high-risk criterion (this includes most youth from special populations), HIV testing should be offered with prior informed consent and counseling. Those adolescent identified as HIV positive should be referred for appropriate specialized medical care and follow-up.

The treatment staff must keep the patient's HIV status confidential. Unfortunately, violation of this confidentially is common among staff and peers in treatment. The practice of universal infectious disease precautions throughout the program should eliminate the need for specialized treatment which might identify the adolescent's HIV status. Comprehensive staff training about HIV is obviously essential to reduce apprehension and to provide optimal service to youth having or at risk for HIV.

Despite HIV positive status and the poor ultimate prognosis for these individuals, substance abuse treatment should proceed. HIV-positive individuals may have years of quality life ahead and the potential of improved treatments for HIV could produce an even longer survival. The success of treatment also has implications for the general population in potentially reducing the transmission of HIV through decreases in IV drug use and associated high risk-drug use and sexual behaviors.

For all adolescents in prevention or treatment programs, education and information about HIV and risk is essential. Programs should provide basic, age-appropriate information about HIV infection, transmission, and prevention. Emphasis should be made on improving risk prevention and identifying potential high-risk behaviors in the adolescent's repetoire and lifestyle. While abstinence from sexual activity can be advised or encouraged, programs should offer explicit discussion of safe-sex practices including instruction and demonstration on the proper use of condoms as well as ways to avoid high-risk situations such as rape, substance use-induced poor judgment, and disinhibition. Improving knowledge and beliefs about HIV has been shown to decrease high-risk behaviors including drug use and unsafe sex practices (Jemmott, Jemmott, & Fong, 1992; Schinke, Gordon, & Weston, 1990).

Finally, clinicians and intervention programs must also target problems which underlie or promote HIV risk such as housing, financial needs, mental health, and community status (Rotheram-Borus et al., 1991). If adolescents are preoccupied by these and other issues, they are unlikely to be concerned about the potential risk of infection by a disease that they will develop and die from years in the future.

EFFECTS AND CONSEQUENCES OF
SPECIFIC SUBSTANCES OF ABUSE

Understanding the basic pharmacologic effects of specific substances of abuse, the routes of administration, and the acute and chronic health effects of these substances is necessary for basic and optimal medical management of the adolescent substance user or abuser. Psychoactive substances of abuse are used and abused in order for the user to experience their acute psychoactive effects. Depending on the pharmacologic properties of these substances, their use in combination with other substances, the quantity and frequency of use, and the age and baseline physical status of the user; the use of substances can produce a variety of acute, subacute, and chronic medical and physical consequences. As adolescents are more likely to be novice or inexperienced substance users, the appearance of more noxious substance-related effects may precipitate more extreme levels of distress, including anxiety and agitation.

The following discussion of specific psychoactive substances of abuse is a synthesis of information taken from several sources including Goodman and

Gilman (Balfour 1990; Gilman, Rall, Nies, & Taylor, 1990; Jacobs & Fehr, 1987). The reader is refereed to these references for further information about individual psychoactive substances of abuse, their pharmacologic properties, and the specific medical and psychoactive consequences of their use.

Alcohol

Ethyl alcohol or ethanol is the most widely used psychoactive substance in both adolescents and adults. Its use likely dates to the early portion of human existence. Since then it has become a central part of the social and religious life and culture of numerous civilizations, including most modern cultures. Ethanol or alcohol, as we generally call both the ingredient ethanol and beverage products containing ethanol, is a natural psychoactive substance which is produced from the fermentation of various grains and fruits by yeast. While the natural development of modest to moderate concentrations in the amounts of alcohol is possible in beverages such as beer and wine, we have been able to artificially increase the alcohol content or concentration through various distilling processes to create spirits or liquor and fortified wines. Generally, beer contains 3 percent to 6 percent alcohol; wine, 5 percent to 15 percent, and liquors such as whiskey, vodka, scotch, and so on, 40 percent to 50 percent. A serving of each beverage (that is, a bottle of beer, a glass of wine, a shot of liquor) has roughly equivalent amounts of alcohol. Alcohol is almost exclusively administered in beverage form. It is readily available in almost all parts of the United States and is legal for purchase or consumption by adults over the age of 21.

Alcohol is rapidly absorbed with effects noted in approximately 10 minutes. The psychoactive effects or level of intoxication generally corresponds to the blood alcohol level and is dependent on the amount and rate of alcohol consumed. Food, especially with high protein content, interferes with absorption. Without repeated doses—or drinks—the effects of a standard "drink" (about .6 oz. of absolute alcohol) last about an hour unless additional drinks are consumed.

Alcohol is classified as a central nervous system depressant. However, as the blood level rises, the user often experiences stimulation with depressant effects more evident as blood levels peak and decline. At modest blood levels below 100 mg/ml, there may be few, if any, psychoactive effects. As the blood alcohol level approaches and passes 100 mg/ml in an inexperienced user, the effects of alcohol include mild sedation, decreased anxiety, and increases in social disinhibition. As the blood alcohol level continues to rise above 100 mg/ml, impairment occurs in visual motor skills and coordination, integration of sensory stimulation, and information processing. Higher blood levels result in increasing levels of sedation and CNS depression with lethargy, stupor, and coma possible with blood alcohol levels above 300 to 400 mg/ml.

Acute physical consequences can include acute gastritis with nausea and vomiting, especially in the novice user. Impairment in cognitive and visual-motor functioning and judgment may result in accidents, injury, and death. Physical dependence or the presence of a withdrawal syndrome is rare in adolescents. However, mild withdrawal phenomena are possible, especially with heavier patterns of use or after heavy binges. Generally, cessation of use will result in the appearance of symptoms as soon as six hours after stopping alcohol use. Mild symptoms include shakiness and tremors, sweating, and restlessness. More severe patterns of withdrawal are characterized by autonomic hyperactivity (i.e., increased heart rate and blood pressure) and agitation. Rarely do adolescents experience seizures, hallucinations, or delirium tremens which may be noted in alcohol users with heavier and more prolonged use. Long-term abstinence symptoms may include increases in depressed mood, neurovegetative symptoms, and anxiety, although the existence of a specific chronic and long-term alcohol abstinence syndrome is controversial.

Due to its common use, alcohol is frequently used with other psychoactive substances. The effect may be to potentiate or to soften the psychoactive effects of the other substances. While alcohol may potentiate the depressant effect of opiates or sedative hypnotics and result in a more prolonged period of intoxication, the use of alcohol with marijuana and stimulants may produce anxiety. The effects of acute polysubstance use often depend on the type, amount, and timing of administration and can be variable between individual users. The more inexperienced user, such as the adolescent, is more likely to experience the adverse effects of polysubstance use.

Although acute intoxication of an adolescent is usually benign, the clinician should be aware of blood alcohol concentration (BAC) so that extremely high BAC levels can be monitored for potential respiratory depression.

Marijuana

Marijuana or cannabis sativa, the hemp plant, grows wild throughout much of the world and has been used for its tough fiber and psychoactive properties for centuries. The main active ingredient or cannabanoid is delta-9-tetrahydrocannabinol (THC) which is found concentrated in the leaves and flowering shoots of the marijuana plant. These plant parts can be ground and put into food or drink or dried and then smoked in a pipe or in cigarettes. Hashish, originally found in the Middle East, is the concentrated resin secretions of the cannabis plant. These secretions are dried and then formed into balls or cakes which are then usually smoked. A variety of methods have been used to concentrate the THC content. Smoking is the most common form of administration as the onset is more rapid and the effect more potent. Onset of effects occur within minutes, peak within 30 minutes, and may last for several hours. Metabolites of THC may be detected in the urine as early as an hour after inhalation and may be detected for periods up to one month due to its storage in fat tissue.

The psychoactive effects of marijuana are variable and depend on a number of factors, including the form of administration, concentration of active THC, the setting as well as the expectations and experience of the user. The most common effect is a mild euphoria and sense of well-being which serves to calm and relax the user. Many users report that time appears to slow and that they achieve insight and have greater sensitivity to sensory stimuli. Subtle alterations in visual and auditory perception, body image, and thought process may occur. Other effects may include fluctuating mood, rapid or fragmentary thoughts, and altered self-image. Acute panic or anxiety in reaction to disturbing thoughts or perceptions is a fairly common reaction, especially in an inexperienced user such as an adolescent. Marijuana can produce a reduction in short-term memory. High doses may result in significant perceptual distortion, loss of self-identity, and vivid hallucinations. Very high doses can result in a toxic psychosis or delirium with symptoms of agitation, confusion, and disorientation.

The physiological effects of marijuana are usually relatively mild, consisting of a mild increase in heart rate and blood pressure. Marijuana intoxication affects coordination, reaction time, and the ability to judge time, speed, and distance. This impairment may lead to accidents, especially in the operation of machinery or motor vehicles. Intoxication also interferes with cognitive functioning with decreased attention, short- and immediate-term memory. Repeated use causes irritation of the eyes and mucus membranes including the upper respiratory system. Long-term effects of chronic use include reduced sperm counts and testosterone levels, bronchial irritation and bronchoconstricicton. The existence of an amotivational syndrome due to chronic, heavy marijuana use is controversial.

Acute medical management of marijuana is rarely needed. If the adolescent is agitated or experiencing persistent psychotic symptoms, management should be directed toward decreasing the symptoms through controlling of limiting stimuli or providing medications such as benzodiazpines or haloperidol.

Hallucinogens

Hallucinogens include a broad variety of mostly unrelated substances that are able to distort the perception of objective reality. Prominent examples of hallucinatory substances are lysergic acid diethylamide or LSD, phencyclidine (PCP), mescaline as contained in peyote cactus, psilocybin/psilocin which are contained in psilocybe mushrooms, and a variety of synthetic variations of amphetamines including 4-methyl-2,5-dimethoxyamphetamine (DOM), 3,4-methylenedioxyamphetamine (MDA), 4-bromo-2,5-dimethoxyamphetamine (DOB), and 3,4-methylenedioxymethamphetamine (MDMA).

Oral administration of hallucinogens is the rule with nasal or IV use very rare, especially among adolescents. There are several examples of naturally occurring hallucinogens as part of plants. Mescaline is the active hallucinatory ingredient in the peyote cactus found in the southwestern United States. Peyote may be eaten or ground into a powder. Mescaline has also been synthetically produced. Psilocybin and psilocin, chemically related to LSD, are the active ingredients in psilocybe mushrooms. The Jimson weed, also known as loco weed or devil's weed, contains atropine and scopolamine. While this plant is very infrequently used, its anticholinergic effects can lead to severe medical consequences.

Synthetic compounds represent most hallucinogen use. LSD is commonly ingested either in solution with other liquids or absorbed onto a piece of blotter paper or onto a sugar cube. PCP administration is the most variable and includes oral ingestion, intranasal "snorting," IV-injection, and mixture with other agents such as tobacco or marijuana to be smoked. DOM, DOB, MDA, and MDMA like other synthetic clandestinely produced substances, are highly variable in their purity, potency, and effects. They may be produced and administered in tablet, capsule, or blotter-paper form.

Due to the variability in type and amount of drug, psychoactive and physiological effects may also vary. The hallucinatory state is usually characterized by alteration in perceptual orientation of time, distance, and direction; perceptual distortions such as the ability to "see" sounds or "hear" colors; and frank visual hallucinations. Perceptual experiences are intensified. Mood changes during hallucinogen use are highly variable from euphoric to depressive. Depersonalization, derealization, and delusions may follow. The distortion of reality may give rise to impaired judgment, bizarre behavior, and accidents. Anxiety and panic may result from the user experiencing these perceptions or distortions, resulting in a "bad trip." Hallucinogens are notoriously unpredictable in their effects and the user's reaction to those effects.

Phencyclidine (PCP) is a white crystalline powder in its pure form which easily dissolves in water, although it often contains contaminants. Its effects are extremely variable but usually somewhat different from other hallucinogens. The duration of action may last up to several days. PCP often produces a sense of detachment or derealization. Consistent with its early proposed use as an anesthetic agent, it can cause numbness in addition to slurred speech and incoordination. The observer can often notice an almost stereotypic blank stare, nystagmus or involuntary eye movements, and an exaggerated gait. As with other hallucinogens, visual and auditory hallucinations, image distortion, mood and anxiety symptoms can occur. Other patterns of PCP intoxication include psychosis with or without significant paranoia, gross confusion with disorientation, catatonia, and occasionally severe agitation, and violent and bizarre behavior. Physiological effects include mild hypertension and tachycardia. Increase muscle tone is often noted on physical examination. Overdose can be quite serious with seizures, coma, and respiratory arrest. Depression and/or irritability are often noted post-intoxication and there may be some risk of a persistent psychotic state.

Frequent and/or recurrent use of hallucinogens may produce tolerance. There is no evidence of physical dependance or a withdrawal syndrome. Acute medical concerns usually center on the possibility of accidents due to the impaired perception and judgment of the user. Acute anxiety or panic may require isolation from stimuli or sedation. The recurrence of hallucinatory phenomena or "flashbacks" may be experienced at a later time without warning. Flashbacks are more common with the frequent, repetitive user. Examples of flashback phenomena include intensification of perceived stimuli such as colors or shapes, the apparent motion of fixed objects, and a variety of geometric shapes or patterns often superimposed upon the field of vision.

Management should initially center on isolating the adolescent from sensory stimuli in a quiet, dark, and nonthreatening environment. Occasionally efforts to "talk down" the user through reassurance are useful, although physical restraint may be necessary. Chemical restraint should be avoided unless absolutely necessary to avoid injury. If the substance of use is known to be LSD or PCP, the use of haloperidol or a benzodiazepine (diazepam or lorazepam) is preferred.

Stimulants

The broader class of psychoactive stimulants includes a number of nonrelated substances. The two most commonly used stimulants are nicotine and caffeine. Nicotine and tobacco products will be discussed in a separate section. Although caffeine in the form of coffee and other caffeine-containing products (such as wake-up pills, nicotine-containing products, and a variety of over-the-counter stimulants) is readily available in many food products, beverages, and medicinal products, more potent stimulants are controlled substances and available by prescription only. Not infrequently, younger adolescents will experiment with over-the-counter stimulants.

Amphetamines constitute the protypical group of synthetic stimulants. Examples of stimulants include dexadrine, biphetamine, obetrol, and desoxyn. Amphetamines block the reuptake of norepinephrine and dopamine causes their release but, generally, have minimal effects on serotonergic systems. Other examples of stimulants include phenmetrazine (Preludin) and other anorexic agents or weight-reduction agents, and Methylphenidate (Ritalin) and Pemoline (Cylert) which are used to treat attention-deficit hyperactivity disorder and narcolepsy.

A significant number of adolescents report a lifetime experience with stimulants. Most use tends to be experimental or episodic. There appear to be several reasons for stimulant use among adolescents. A number of adolescents will use stimulants to stay awake to study or as an aid to weight reduction. Other youth use stimulants for their mood effects, more specifically a feeling of euphoria, exhilaration, increased wakefulness, and improved ability to concentrate. Other acute effects include an increased ability to concentrate, decreased appetite and, occasionally, irritability, anxiety, and apprehension.

While stimulants are usually taken orally with an onset in about 30 minutes and a duration of two to four hours, intravenous (IV) use produces an immediate onset and more intense psychoactive effects or "rush." Unfortunately, duration of effects is brief with IV use and a pattern of repeated injections often following. Cessation of use after such protracted use may produce a "crash" which consists of a period of intense dysphoria, irritability, or depression. Avoidance of the "crash" reinforces further stimulant use and produces a pattern which is very difficult to break. Episodes of use are then limited by availability of additional stimulant doses, exhaustion, or overdose characterized by delirium or psychosis. Stimulants may be used in combination with opiates, most commonly heroin, in a "speedball" which is administered intravenously. This combination allows for an immediate, intense "rush" followed by a more prolonged period of intoxication than would otherwise be available with IV stimulants alone.

Tolerance develops rapidly to the euphoric effects of stimulants. However, the large doses that are necessary to reproduce the original effect may produce a variety of adverse mental status changes. The toxic syndrome of stimulant use consists of variety of physical and mental changes. Early signs may include repetitive teeth grinding, touching and picking of the face or extremities, perseveration of speech and behavior, and a preoccupation or increased focus on one's own behavior and mental activity. Later, the individual may experience increased suspiciousness proceeding to overt paranoia with auditory and visual hallucinations. Extreme overdoses include hyperactivity, confusion, hypertension, tachypnea with palpitations, fever, and sweating. Without medical intervention, convulsions, cardiovascular collapse, and high fever may progress to death.

When chronic high-dose stimulant users are withdrawn from stimulant use, they often experience extreme dysphoria or depression, fatigue, somnolence (up to 20 hours per day), and apathy. Although the acute withdrawal syndrome may last up to several days, more persistent mood, anxiety, and minor perceptual changes may last up to several months.

The health effects of intravenous use of stimulants are the same as for oral agents and may also include a variety of infectious processes and embolic phenomena. Stimulants are also capable of producing cardiac arrhythmias, seizures, myocardial infarction, and sudden death.

Methamphetamine, a synthetic stimulant closely related to amphetamine, is an even more potent psychostimulant. A relative new form of methamphetamine is its crystalline hydroxide salt or "Ice." Ice is relatively pure and is usually administered by smoking due to the ability of the hydroxide salt to vaporize and be inhaled for a very rapid onset (Cho, 1990). Although similar to both cocaine and amphetamine in psychostimulant effects, the psychoactive effects of methamphetamine persist for hours.

A variety of stimulants are available as components of numerous over-the-counter agents. Most commonly, these substances, such as pseudoephedrine or phenylpropanolamine, are found in cold or cough remedies. These over-the-counter agents are readily available to children and adolescents. Some youth will use them in large quantities in search of a "buzz" or mood- or perceptually-altered state.

Cocaine

Cocaine is a stimulant of natural origin which is extracted from the leaves of the coca plant and is native to the Andean mountains of South America. Although the leaves of the coca plant have been chewed by natives since ancient times, pure cocaine was isolated only toward the end of the last century. Initially used as a local anesthetic, the identification of its psychoactive properties saw its use expanded to products such as wine, soft drinks, and numerous patent medicines. As the addictive potential of cocaine was appreciated at the beginning of this century, its use was limited to isolated use as a local anesthetic for ears, eyes, and nasal mucosa. During the past two decades, cocaine became popular as an initially expensive, high-status substance of abuse. However, the rapid spread of a cheap, available alternative form—crack—has brought cocaine use and addiction to lower socioeconomic groups with severe social, health, and economic consequences.

Cocaine for illicit use is distributed as a white crystalline powder. It is often mixed or diluted with a variety of usually inert substances such as mannitol or lactose; local anesthetics—although occasionally other psychoactive substance, most commonly other stimulants or PCP—are mixed with the cocaine. As cocaine is well absorbed from the mucus membranes, it is usually administered by nasal inhalation or "snorting." Intravenous administration is less common. Cocaine can be combined with heroin and injected intravenously in a form of "speedball." By conversion of cocaine hydrochloride, which decomposes when heated, to its freebase form, cocaine can be smoked and inhaled through the lungs. This method of use produces a more rapid and intense but brief experience.

Crack is a street term for cocaine which has been converted from cocaine hydrochloride to a freebase form by the use of ammonia or baking soda. In small, solid, rock-like form, crack can be made and sold in large quantities and at cheap prices as low as $5 to $10 per vial. Smoking crack results in a more rapid, intense but briefer euphoria than cocaine used intranasally. The rapid production of compulsive use of crack and its addiction results in preoccupation with its use and repeated purchases of crack doses progressing to more than several hundred dollars per week.

Crack smoking delivers cocaine through the lungs to the brain in a matter of seconds. However, the intense euphoria usually lasts as little as 5 to 10 minutes. Along with the euphoria comes emotional lability, anorexia, insomnia, hyperactivity, and hyperalertness. As the euphoric phase of crack use quickly subsides, it is replaced by dysphoria, paranoia, and even psychosis.

Cocaine produces an intense euphoria and feeling of well-being which is accompanied by increased motor activity, increased energy level, dilated pupils, loss of appetite, tachycardia, and hypertension. Duration is usually short-lived, lasting perhaps only minutes. A level of tolerance develops and cessation of chronic use may be followed by depression, hypersomnia, increased appetite, fatigue; craving for additional doses continues the "crash" which can appear as early as several hours after the last dose and last a week or more. High doses or repeated use can produce behavior similar to a manic state with rapid motor activity level, rapid, rambling speech, impaired judgment, and even paranoid and psychotic behavior. Irritability or acute, high levels of anxiety can also accompany use.

Due to its often intense and pleasurable psychoactive effects, cocaine use is highly reinforcing. The presence of intense dysphoria after cessation of use also reinforces continued use. This is particularly true of the freebase or "crack" form of cocaine in which the price of each individual dose is fairly low and the brief, intense high is suddenly replaced by dysphoria of the "crash." Crack use is often done in prolonged binges lasting up to several days or until money or the drug supply is gone or the user collapses from physical exhaustion.

Acute adverse behavioral effects include disinhibition, impaired judgment, grandiosity, impulsiveness, hypersexuality, perseverative behaviors, and extreme psychomotor activation. These changes may result in accidents and illegal behavior including assaults and inappropriate and dangerous sexual behavior. Medical complications of acute use include ulceration of nasal mucosa, pharyngeal irritation, and bronchitis when "snorting." Cardiac symptoms include irregular heartbeat, angina, and myocardial infarction; seizures, strokes, and respiratory arrest are secondary to effects on brain centers.

Crack or cocaine smoking can increase blood pressure and can potentially cause brain hemorrhages or seizures. The heart rate increases and may become irregular with possible cardiac arrest. Chronic effects are similar to those produced by other stimulants including amphetamines. Depressive syndromes and psychosis may occur with high doses and prolonged use, especially in a predisposed individual.

For the adolescent, the possibility of acute physical sequelae, especially cardiac problems, with little or no previous exposure, should cause much concern.

Problems secondary to the behavioral disinhibition and often extreme drug-seeking of cocaine use include HIV infection and other sexually transmitted diseases, neglect of education and other age-appropriate roles, and aggression, criminal, and other antisocial behavior.

Even prior to actual initiation into cocaine use, the child or adolescent may have significant exposure to cocaine and other drugs in the environment. The older child or young adolescent may be involved in drug sales as either a dealer or "runner," as drug distributors take advantage of their juvenile status.

Opiates

Opiates refer to opium and opium derivatives and their synthetic substitutes. Opiate use, including heroin, synthetic and other oral opiates, remains relatively infrequent by adolescents in the United States, especially outside central urban areas. Epidemiologic data demonstrates low lifetime prevalence and regular use patterns among adolescents.

Opiates can be taken by mouth, smoked, or injected. While many or most opiate abusers prefer intravenous (IV) injection or "mainlining" due to its immediate and stronger effects, adolescent abusers as a whole more commonly use oral opiates due to their availability and perceived lower danger. Variations in methods of use include subcutaneous injection or "skin popping."

Under medical supervision, opiate agents are usually administered for relief of intense pain, although additional uses include cough suppression and relief from diarrhea. Through the relief of suffering, or even in the case of users without pain, a brief period of euphoria may be produced, although the initial effects may often be perceived as unpleasant. Physiologic effects include drowsiness, pinpoint pupils, reduced cough reflex, reduced vision, and constipation. Larger doses may include sleep and possibly produce nausea, vomiting, and respiratory depression. Motor incoordination and slurred speech may be noted in only more severe states of intoxication. Acute behavioral effects include decreased physical activity and apathy.

The classic signs of acute opiate intoxication or overdose are miosis (pinpoint pupils), respiratory and central nervous system (CNS) depression. Associated symptoms may include hypothermia, hypotension, and bradycardia. For severe overdose resulting in coma, there is a risk for aspiration with pneumonia.

The onset of action is variable, depending on route of administration. With IV use, the opiate user may experience a sudden and intense perception of euphoria known as a "rush." The duration of action is likewise variable. The intensity of the euphoric "rush" use in IV is usually brief or even transient, followed by a dream-like state and subsequently diminishing sense of well-being, and finally resulting in overt withdrawal symptoms (discussed in a later section). The duration of the physiologic effects of most opiates is between 3 and 6 hours, although the effects of methadone (12 to 24 hours) and Levo-alpha-acetylmethadol or LAAM (48 to 72 hours) are considerably longer.

As the adolescent user is more likely to be inexperienced about opiate use, lack of knowledge about contaminants, and poor judgment regarding appropriate dosage for the desired effects may result in overdose.

Opiates produce physiologic dependence in that they produce tolerance to use with repeated use and a withdrawal syndrome upon cessation of use. All opiates produce a tolerance to use likely due to habituation (adaption) of opiod nerve receptors. Thus, increasing doses of a particular opiate agent are required to produce the same physiologic effects. Cross-tolerance exists between opiates, although not necessarily to the same extent. The level of tolerance also varies with the specific effect. Following withdrawal, tolerance decreases as the opiate nerve cells readapt to the absence of the drug.

As opiates are used, tolerance develops and the continued use of the agent is necessary in order to avoid the withdrawal syndrome. For short-acting opiates (e.g., heroin, most oral opiates), withdrawal symptoms begin 8 to 12 hours after the last use with peak intensity at about 48 hours and duration of 7 to 10 days. Withdrawal from opiates or from any addictive drug causes excitation of the same physiologic functions that were originally depressed by its use. The intensity of the withdrawal syndrome is directly related to the amount of opiate used.

For longer-acting opiates (like methadone), the withdrawal syndrome is more prolonged but less intense. Symptoms appear one to two days after last use, peak after three to four days, and may last several weeks with aches, pains, irritability, and disturbed sleep. Generally, opiate withdrawal is very uncomfortable but not life-threatening in an otherwise healthy individual.

Chronic opiate use has few documented direct toxic or adverse medical effects. Indirect medical dangers appear to be the most critical concerns. These concerns include the user's neglect of health, especially as opiates produce analgesic effects which can disguise the overt signs of developing medical problems. Intravenous administration can cause inflammation (phlebitis) or infections including abscesses with resulting scarring. Contaminants may produce a variety of physiologic effects and problems. Sharing needles may spread a number of infectious agents including HIV, hepatitis, and endocardia from bacterial agents especially staphylococus areas.

The treatment of withdrawal may include one or more of several options. Nonassisted withdrawal or "cold turkey," although not a critical danger, may discourage the user from cessation of use due to the extreme discomfort associated with the withdrawal syndrome. Assisted withdrawal can include the use of methadone or clonidine alone or in combination. For adolescents, I suggest avoiding opiate replacement whenever possible, especially if this is the adolescent's first withdrawal experience. The use of clonidine can attenuate much of the autonomic hyperactivity. Long-term opiate replacement or methadone maintenance should be reserved for cases which have failed drug-free (opiate) management.

Acute treatment of opiate withdrawal also necessitates attention to control of the airway, cardiovascular stability, and the use of IV naloxone (Narcan) to reverse opiate effects.

Sedative/Hypnotics

Sedative/hypnotic use by adolescents is no longer common. Drugs in this broad class include barbiturates, benzodiazepines, and a variety of agents belonging to neither group. These agents are all frequently prescribed by physicians for use as hypnotics, anxiolytics, and anitconvulsants. Barbiturates are used for sedation, sleep, and as anticonvulsants. They are classified as ultrashort, short-intermediate and long-acting with the duration of action determining such medical uses as anesthesia induction (ultra short-acting), sedatives or hypnotics (short- or intermediate- or long-acting), or anticonvulsant (long-acting). The intermediate-acting barbiturates include agents most sought after by abusers (e.g., pentobarbital, secobarbital, and amobarbital). Sedative/ Hypnotic agents are most frequently used by polydrug abusers, including such depressant substances as opiates and alcohol.

Benzodiazepines have appropriate medical uses in relieving anxiety and muscle spasms and as anticonvulsants and hypnotics. Their medical uses are determined by their duration of action. A number of other sedative/hypnotic agents, including glutethimide (Doriden), methaqualone (Quaalude, Sopor, Somnafac), and Meprobamate (Miltown, Equanil) have been more extensively used—and abused—in the past and have no particular therapeutic advantages over other sedative/hypnotic agents.

Almost all sedative/hypnotic agents are taken in oral form with widely varying duration of effects and onset of effects. Low doses of these agents produces a mild sedation. With higher doses, the user may experience a sense of well-being or even euphoria. Intoxication is characterized by symptoms quite similar to alcohol intoxication. These effects include slurred speech, ataxia and impaired motor coordination, impaired judgment, and even disorientation. Higher does may also produce apathy, lethargy, or depression. Overdose is similar to extreme alcohol intoxication with cold, clammy skin, shallow respiration, and coma and respiratory depression as the most critical consequence.

There is a rapid development of tolerance to most sedative hypnotics. Although benzodiazepines have a wide margin of safety, other sedative/hypnotics can more easily produce an overdose. It is not uncommon for an abuser to use up to 10 to 20 times a normal therapeutic dose for these agents.

Acute medical consequences of sedative/hypnotic use include overdose, accidents secondary to motor incoordination, and impaired judgement. The sudden cessation or reduction of high-dose sedative/hypnotic use may result in a withdrawal syndrome. The onset of this syndrome depends on the duration of action of the agent and may not be apparent for up to several days with some agents. Initial symptoms may include agitation and anxiety, insomnia, decreased appetite, hypersensitivity to sensory stimuli, gastrointestinal distress, sweating, and increased heart rate. During the peak of the withdrawal syndrome, grand mal type of seizures can occur and may progress to frank delirium in some cases. Due to the possibility of extreme withdrawal symptoms, sedative/hypnotic withdrawal and detoxification necessitates close medical supervision. It is important to note that some sedative/hypnotic agents, particularly benzodiazepines, may produce physical dependence after prolonged periods of use at therapeutic doses.

Anabolic Steroids

Attention has turned only recently, during the late 1980s, to the use of anabolic/androgenic steroids by youth for athletic enhancement. Anabolic steroids are synthetic analogues of the male sex hormone testosterone. While minimizing the masculinizing or androgenic effects, these steroids maintain the growth-promoting of anabolic actions. Anabolic steroids are used legitimately to treat a variety of diseases and conditions. In adults, anabolic steroids may be used in the treatment of certain anemia, hereditary angioedema, and breast cancer (Council on Scientific Affairs, 1988). In children and adolescents, the indications for accepted usage include: (a) initiation of delayed puberty, (b) treatment of micropenis, and (c) hypogonadism (Moore, 1988). Steroids approved for clinical use include stanozolol (Winstrol), methandrostenolone (Dianabol), and nandrolone phenpropionate (Durabolin). There are numerous black market preparations which have no approved therapeutic use in humans.

For the past four decades, scientists and athletes have suggested that sex hormones and eventually anabolic steroids could enhance physical performance, body mass, muscle strength, and aggressiveness (Council on Scientific Affairs, 1988; Yesalis, 1992). Whether there is an advantage in the use of these steroids above diet and training techniques is uncertain, with conflicting evidence (American College of Sports Medicine, 1987; Wilson, 1988). Whatever benefits anabolic steroids provide, their use is associated with a variety of harmful effects, including liver abnormalities, changes in cardiovascular risk factor (e.g., changes in lipoproteins and hypertension), endocrine effects, and psychological effects including severe mood changes and aggressive behavior (Hallagan, Hallagan, & Snyder, 1989).

Physical risks to adolescents potentially include the same adverse risks for adults, as well as acne and premature skeletal maturation, spermatogenesis, and an increased risk of injury if sexual maturity has not been reached (Buckley et al., 1988). No characteristic pattern of mental status or physical abnormalities is usually observed.

Steroid abuse is common among athletes in strength sports such as weightlifting, body building, and field events. Steroids are usually taken in "cycles" of use from 6 to 12 weeks duration in preparation for a competition, followed by a drug-free period which may last up to a year. Doses are much larger than medically therapeutic. Drugs are often "stacked" when several steroids are taken simultaneously for a desired synergistic effect. Other steroid use patterns include "plateauing" to avoid tolerance and "pyramiding" when doses are incrementally increased then decreased during a cycle (Yesalis, 1992).

Athletes likely constitute the adolescent population most at risk for anabolic steroid abuse. However, given a pattern of steroid use among noncompetitors, adolescents with a low self-image and a persistent desire to enhance their appearance may also be vulnerable (Buckley et al., 1988).

Anabolic steroids likely have addictive potential. In one study, one-fourth of 226 male high school students admitting to anabolic steroid use reported that they would not stop steroid use despite a definite knowledge of extreme debilitating physical effects such as cancer, sterility, or increased risk of heart attack (Yesalis et al., 1990). Among heavy users, over 40 percent indicated that they would not stop despite the potential risks. The existing literature suggests that some adolescents who abuse anabolic steroids will display signs and symptoms of psychoactive substance dependence including continued use despite adverse consequences, tolerance, and even withdrawal (Bower, 1992a, 1992b).

Despite the similarity of steroid abuse and dependence to the abuse and dependence of other substances in adolescents, anabolic steroid use is perhaps more often seen in isolation from the use of other agents. Medical evaluation should include somatic complaints chronologically related to use, common withdrawal symptoms, mood and neurovegetative symptoms, and aggressiveness.

The physical exam is often remarkable for an overdeveloped body habitus. Among the more prominent findings may be high blood pressure, rapid weight gain, jaundice, gynecomastia, and testicular atrophy in males; hirsutism, deep voice, and breast atrophy in females (Kibble & Ross, 1987). Lab studies should include urine drug screen, liver functions tests (bilirubin, SGOT, SGPT, LDN, CPK), lipid and cholesterol profile, and endocrine and cardiac function tests when specifically indicated.

Tobacco

Although commonly overlooked as a drug of abuse, tobacco, and its primary psychoactive constituent nicotine, is one of the most frequently used substances by adolescents. Over 18 percent of senior high school students report daily use of cigarettes and over 10 percent report use of one-half pack or more of cigarettes per day (University of Michigan, 1992).

Cigarettes are by far the most common vehicle for tobacco and nicotine use. Due to cigarettes' status as a legal substance for adults and their ready accessibility to adolescents, cigarettes, along with alcohol, are considered a gateway drug. The prevalence of alcohol, marijuana, and even cocaine use is significantly higher in adolescents who have tried cigarettes and even higher in daily smokers than in adolescents who have never tried cigarettes (U.S. Department of Health and Human Services [DHHS], 1988). By their senior year in high school, over 60 percent of students report having tried smoking cigarettes at least once (University of Michigan, 1992).

All tobacco products contain substantial amounts of nicotine and other alkaloids. Tobaccos from low-yield and high-yield cigarettes contain similar amounts of nicotine (DHHS, 1988). Smokers can manipulate their nicotine dose by the number of cigarettes, frequency, and depth of inhalation (Young, Robinson, & Wickert, 1981). Nicotine readily crosses the blood-brain barrier, is rapidly distributed throughout the brain, and activates several central nervous system (CNS) neurotransmitter pathways including release of acetylcholine, norepinephrine, dopamine, serotonin, vasopressin, growth hormone, and ACTH (Benowitz, 1988). The most prominent CNS effect is arousal. Acute and chronic tolerance to CNS and other nicotine effects develops. Although a novice smoker—usually a preteen or an adolescent—may initially experience dizziness, nausea, and even vomiting, repeated smoking produces rapid tolerance to subjective distress and cardiovascular effects (Benowitz, 1988). The pharmacologic actions of nicotine include central nervous system stimulation, skeletal muscle relaxation, and endocrine and cardiovascular effects (DHHS, 1988). Smoking activates the sympathetic nervous system, resulting in an increase in heart rate, blood pressure, and coronary blood flow (Cryer, Haymond, Santiago, & Shah, 1976).

Smoking produces CNS and behavioral arousal. Many studies show improvement in attention, learning, reaction time, and problem-solving (Benowitz, 1988; Wesnes & Warburton, 1983). Smokers report relaxation, particularly in stressful situations, and reduced anger, tension, and depression (Warburton, 1987). Regular and heavy adolescent smokers score higher on perceived stress compared with nonsmokers (Mitic, McGuire, & Neumann, 1985). A study of students in grades 2 through 10 reported that a measure of affective distress was related to rapid transitions from experimental to regular smoking (Hirshman, Leventhal, & Glynn, 1984). Other studies have correlated students with high stress with smoking (Silverstein, Kelly, Swan, & Kozlowski, 1982; Wills, 1986).

Up to 80 percent of smoking individuals experience a nicotine withdrawal syndrome when cigarette smoking is suddenly stopped. This syndrome includes irritability, insomnia, restlessness, increased somatic complaints, difficulty concentrating, hunger, depression, and craving (Fagerstrom, 1978; Hughes & Hatsukami, 1986; Shiffman, 1979).

The presence of a frequently compulsive pattern of cigarette use, a withdrawal syndrome upon abstinence, frequent use despite knowledge of a risk of or actual severe physical consequences, forms the core of a nicotine dependence syndrome which is currently recognized by the *Diagnostic and Statistical Manual of Mental Disorders, 4th Edition* of the American Psychiatric Association (APA, 1994) and the *International Classification of Disease* (ICD-10) of the World Health Organization (World Health Organization, in preparation). The nicotine dependence syndrome is similar to other drug dependencies in the user's response to environmental stimuli or cues which can influence the initiation, maintenance, and relapse; frequent relapse despite desire and intent to quit and the role of nicotine in reinforcing tobacco-seeking and tobacco-using behavior.

SUMMARY

Psychoactive substances of abuse have both acute and chronic psychoactive and physical effects which may have important consequences for the health of the adolescent who uses or abuses these substances. Although adolescents use psychoactive substances for their seeming pleasurable effects on brain function (including changes in mood, cognitive, and sensory processes), each of these abusable substances have not only less desirable and noxious effects on brain processes, but also significant physiological effects on other bodily functions. Many of these substances have the potential to create life-threatening conditions. Medical professionals should have a high level of suspicion when an adolescent presents for emergency care or with an unusual condition, not easily explained. Many of the substances commonly used by adolescents have general patterns of use to alert medical professionals and prompt reasonable suspicion. Medical personnel must be aware of the acute and chronic stigmata of psychoactive substance use. Management should take into account the adolescent's acute mental status as well as the observed and expected effects of the substances that have been used. Similarly, clinicians who care for substance-using and -abusing adolescents in other nonmedical settings should be aware of the common medical problems caused by psychoactive substance use.

CHAPTER 8

Treatment Settings and Special Treatment Populations

The identification of any level of substance abuse requires intervention or treatment to minimize the level of current and potential dysfunction, morbidity, and mortality. Presently, in the mid-1990s, we are at a transition point in the development and implementation of treatments for adolescent substance abuse and dependence. Two basic factors account for this transition and, perhaps, a bit of uncertainty as to what kind of treatment(s) we will be able to utilize in the future.

The first factor is an ongoing effort to achieve cost-containment for health care, in general, and specifically to control the costs of substance abuse treatment. Many policy makers and many in the general public view treatment for substance use or addictive disorders as too often a futile measure and even as a waste of time. Despite studies demonstrating the efficacy of treatment for addictive behaviors, the seeming intransigence of serious drug problems in society has produced a skepticism that treatment does little more than line the pockets of those running treatment facilities.

Managed care standards by both public and private payers for health care are forcing a restructuring of the addictions treatment industry. Limitations on who is acceptable for detoxification treatment or rehabilitation treatment (rehab) and for how long they may receive what level of treatment are now the rule rather than the exception. As a result, treatment programs have vacancy rates of up to 50 percent and an estimated 200 inpatient programs (both adult and adolescent) have closed during the past several years (Spicer, 1994).

The second basic factor is the recognition that despite our knowledge that treatment of some kind can work, many of those with substance abuse or dependence do not benefit from a standard, traditional treatment. Different individuals likely need different types, amounts, and combinations of treatment(s). This is especially the case for adolescents.

THE UNIQUE TREATMENT NEEDS
OF ADOLESCENTS

As previously discussed in Chapter 4, considering the adolescent within a developmental context presents several unique characteristics of adolescents (versus adults) which must be considered when developing or selecting appropriate treatment interventions or modalities. Within a developmental context, adolescents are undertaking substantial changes in their physical maturity as they pass puberty; changes in their social viewpoint with the development of friendships, sexual interests, relationships and intimacy; and changes in cognitive abilities or the ability to see the world and oneself in a more abstract and less self-centered fashion. Because they have not fully matured in terms of their social, cognitive, and emotional functioning, they are more vulnerable to make poor choices and to be adversely influenced by peers and other outside factors. Adolescence is a critical time for the shaping of vocational interests through secondary education. Finally, adolescents are usually a dependent member of a family system; they have less choice as to decisions affecting their lives. Together and separately, each of these developmental changes contrasts the needs of adolescents against the needs of adults. Ultimately, these developmental characteristics and the unique needs arising from them demand specific approaches to the treatment of adolescent substance abuse. While these treatment approaches have many similarities to those traditionally directed toward adults, approaches for youth should be developed and delivered specifically for youth.

Despite an obvious recognition of the unique status and needs of adolescents, treatment designed specifically for adolescent substance abusers has been present for only the past two decades. The first dedicated program for adolescent substance abusers was the inpatient program, opened in 1974 at St. Mary's Hospital in Minneapolis, Minnesota (Wheeler & Malmquist, 1987). Designed on the 12-Step model of Alcoholics Anonymous (AA) and Narcotics Anonymous (NA), this program served as a model for a generation of adolescent treatment programs. For most of the past 20 years, the establishment of programs for substance-abusing adolescents has been a growth industry.

In 1987, according to the National Drug and Alcoholism Treatment Unit Survey (NDATUS), 313 alcohol treatment units offered specialized programs for youth and another 2,155 units offered combined alcohol and drug programs. Adolescents consisted of approximately 10 percent of the total population in all treatment units. In 1987, 59,790 youth were in drug and alcohol treatment with 86 percent in outpatient treatment and the remainder in inpatient programs. A total of 21,009 adolescents were admitted to alcohol treatment programs with approximately 87 percent as outpatients.

As with alcohol and drug treatment in older populations, treatment for adolescents is currently undergoing rapid change and transition. In 1990, 52,457 youth under 18 years of age were admitted to alcohol treatment units or programs with at least some state funding (National Institute on Drug Abuse, National Institute on Alcohol Abuse and Alcoholism, 1992). Such units represent a majority, but usually not all, treatment programs in most states. Another 72,923 youth were admitted to drug treatment units in 1990. Presumably many of these adolescents also had significant problems with alcohol. This represents a substantial increase from the admissions in 1985 when 26,967 and 24,070 adolescents were admitted to alcohol and drug treatment units, respectively (National Institute on Drug Abuse, National Institute on Alcohol Abuse and Alcoholism, 1986).

However, managed care for addiction services and increased scrutiny of the need for treatment in various settings has virtually collapsed the industry. Presently, a previous emphasis on inpatient and residential treatment for adolescent substance abuse is being replaced by outpatient and briefer treatments. Many traditional 28- or 35-day programs are decreasing their length of stays and are establishing expanded outpatient services, such as partial hospitalization or intensive outpatient services. Many programs that are unable to achieve this transition are closing or downsizing.

The Goals of Treatment, Treatment Setting, and the Selection of Modalities

The manifest goal of treatment for adolescents with substance abuse problems is achieving and maintaining abstinence from substance use. A closer examination of the risk factors for adolescent substance abuse and the varied deficits of adolescent substance abusers in the areas of psychopathology, social skills, family functioning, academic, and school functioning, and the ability to find and participate in prosocial activities points to addressing these deficits as a part of a more comprehensive treatment approach. The perceived poor response of many adolescent substance abusers to past treatment efforts may, in fact, be due to a one-dimensional approach to treatment. In the past, most substance abuse treatment programs were based on an often rigid interpretation of the disease model of addiction. Accordingly, substance abuse was always the primary problem and likely perceived as the cause of any additional problems plaguing the adolescent. By achieving abstinence, the other problems would or could be solved, although little direct, specific, or immediate attention might be given to these problems.

Increasingly, goals for substance abuse treatment are becoming more comprehensive, including the broad goal of a total change in the adolescent's lifestyle (DeLeon, 1988). A change in lifestyle presumes total abstinence from psychoactive substance use, developing prosocial attitudes, values and behavior, and development of more adaptive skills for improved interpersonal relationships and academic and vocational functioning.

Should We Treat Smoking and Tobacco Use?

In most localities, the purchase of cigarettes and other tobacco products by minors is illegal. Tobacco in the form of cigarettes is a gateway drug whose use usually precedes the use of other substances and their later potential abuse. While the negative health consequences of smoking and tobacco use are well known, the absence of an acute intoxication syndrome and significant behavioral effects has produced an atmosphere of complacency about targeting tobacco use in the same way as other substance use. Besides prevention programs that specifically target cigarette smoking, treatment program interventions are rarely directed toward tobacco use. Nicotine, the active agent in tobacco, is addictive. Because its use has potentially ominous consequences in terms of the risk for later substance use and abuse and adverse health effects, treatment must deal directly with the use of tobacco.

Treatment programs should enforce a strict on-site, no-smoking policy for adolescents, their families, and program staff. Psychoeducational efforts should include information about the acute and chronic health effects of tobacco. Programs should emphasize tobacco as a psychoactive substance to be avoided.

Evidence of Treatment Efficacy

The research into the effectiveness of treatment for adolescents with alcohol abuse/or dependence is remarkable for its paucity and lack of evidence to support the superiority of any general or specific approach. Several other treatment studies point to the benefits of treatment in general while failing to identify the superiority of one approach over others (Catalano, Hawkins, Wells, Miller, & Brewer, 1990–1991). Many attempts at establishing treatment effectiveness have been severely hampered by a variety of methodological problems including poor preassessment measures, the lack of clear, valid definitions or measures of treatment success or relapse (i.e., What constitutes successful treatment outcome?), poor or inadequate measures of outcome variables, and poor follow-up procedures including very low rates of follow-up.

The relative high rates of treatment outcome success from some studies may be due to a significant follow-up contact bias. Difficult-to-contact groups who are likely omitted in studies with approximately 50 percent response rates show consistently poorer outcomes when compared with the easy-to-contact groups (Stinchfield, Niforopolos, & Feder, 1994). Thus, the outcome results reported by many studies may not be generalizable across the entire treated population. However, one should not necessarily count the noncontacted or difficult-to-contact samples as treatment failures.

As part of the Drug Abuse Reporting Program (DARP) study in which youth were followed up four to six years after admission to 52 different treatment programs across the United States, Sells and Simpson (1979) reported that adolescents using alcohol were generally unaffected by treatment, although a reduction in heavy alcohol use was reported for drug-free outpatient programs. In a treatment outcome study for the Pennsylvania substance abuse system, individuals with better psychosocial functioning did better during outpatient treatment and had lower rates of relapse on follow-up than those requiring inpatient or residential treatment (Rush, 1985). Finally, in the Treatment Outcome Prospective Study (TOPS), significant improvements in drug-related problems, depression, and education were noted (Hubbard, Cavanaugh, Craddock, & Rachel, 1985). Drug-free outpatient clients reported reductions in heavy alcohol use, although these reductions were less than those in residential treatment settings. Although both the DARP and TOPS studies provide comparisons between outpatient and residential treatment, their results are inconclusive and contradictory (Catalano et al., 1990–1991). All programs had some success in reducing problems associated with substance use and in reducing substance use other than alcohol or marijuana use.

In a review of the adolescent treatment research, Catalano and associates (1990–1991) reviewed a number of studies using experimental, quasi-experimental and one-group, pre-post designs. They identified factors associated with relapse or lack of relapse back to alcohol use. Studies report that younger age of onset, more serious alcohol use, the abuse of multiple drugs deviant behavior, and criminal involvement are associated with noncompletion of treatment. Among treatment factors, time in treatment is related to reduced alcohol and other drug use in residential programs. Staff characteristics (including staff attitudes and level of training), the availability of special services, and family participation are also associated with improved outcomes. Post-treatment predictors of relapse include thoughts, feelings and cravings about alcohol, less involvement in school or work and less satisfactory leisure-time activities.

In summary, Catalano and colleagues point to four conclusions: (1) some treatment is better than no treatment, (2) few comparisons of treatment modalities have demonstrated the clear superiority of one approach over another, (3) secular trends in public attitudes toward substance use and specific substances may affect the efficacy of treatment, and (4) more controlled studies of substance abuse treatment outcome are needed.

Based on existing studies, a number of basic recommendations can be made as to the general content of adolescent treatment programs. Treatment for adolescents should have achieving and maintaining abstinence from alcohol and all illicit substances as the primary goal for treatment. Treatment should also seek to improve the overall psychosocial functioning of the adolescent. Although improved functioning is obviously a worthwhile goal in itself, improvements in specific areas of functioning may directly or indirectly improve the adolescent's prospects for maintaining abstinence and preventing relapse.

There are treatment program characteristics associated with improved abstinence rates and lower relapse rates (Fleisch, 1991; Friedman & Beschner, 1985). These characteristics provide guidelines for the treatment of adolescents with substance use problems and include the following:

1. Treatment programs should be intensive and of sufficient duration to achieve changes in attitude and behavior.

2. After-care or follow-up treatment after a more intensive level of treatment is essential. Adequate transition and continuity between treatment components involves reinforcing changes that are achieved earlier in treatment.

3. Treatment approaches should be as comprehensive as possible and potentially target psychosocial dysfunction within multiple areas or domains of the adolescent's life. These areas include coexisting psychiatric disorders, vocational or educational needs, recreational or leisure-time activities, birth control services, and education/information about alcohol and other substance abuse and medical issues, particularly HIV/AIDS education.

4. Treatment programs should be sensitive to and address the cultural issues and the socioeconomic realities of the adolescent, his family, and environment. Examples of relevant interventions include having treatment program staff representative of the racial and/or ethnic groups of the adolescents, assisting families to obtain additional social services or financial resources such as welfare assistance. The adolescent, the family, and staff should perceive the program as practical to real-life circumstances.

5. Treatment programs should encourage family involvement and work with families to improve interpersonal communication between family members, to improve the ability of parents to consistently provide structure and limit-setting for their children, and to address addiction patterns in the parents through both referral of the parents for treatment and acknowledgement of the parental role in the adolescent's problems.

6. Treatment programs should attempt to obtain and use a wide range of social services such as juvenile justice, child welfare, and recreational programs to assist the adolescent and his or her family in planning and preparing for an alcohol and drug-free lifestyle. Programs should require or strongly encourage adolescent attendance and participation in self-support groups such as Alcoholics Anonymous (AA) and/or Narcotics Anonymous (NA) to develop a drug-free peer group and models for abstinence.

TREATMENT SETTINGS

Crisis Intervention and Evaluation

The adolescent presenting to hospital emergency room or other medical facilities with acute injury or medical conditions that suggest a substance use etiology or involvement require at least a screening evaluation for possible drug involvement. There are also other settings, such as school, where the acute presentation indicating a substance use problem may dictate some immediate form of intervention.

Researchers dealing with adult substance abusers are studying the effects of brief, focused interventions (Daley & Marlatt, 1992). The development of similar interventions for youth holds the potential for a brief, but cost-effective form of intervention. For example, there are many programs for adolescents arrested for underage drinking and/or driving while intoxicated. Brief programs lasting up to eight sessions serve the purpose of a more complete evaluation of the adolescent's patterns of substance use as well as providing an intensive program of psychoeducation (about the dangers of substance use) to discourage further substance use.

Inpatient Treatment

Inpatient or short-term treatment is seen as the preferred setting for most adolescents with substance use disorders for several reasons: (1) control of the environment by preventing the adolescent from running away, from exposure to substance-promoting influences such as music, radio, or television, from contacting deviant peers, or from bringing in contraband such as alcohol or other drugs; (2) separation from often problematic family circumstances; and (3) increasing the intensity of treatment by having each daily activity assume a therapeutic role in which the adolescent must participate.

Indications for inpatient or acute forms of treatment include adolescents who present with ideation or behavior indicating an actual or potential danger to self or others (e.g., suicidal ideation or behavior, more extreme forms of aggressive behavior), adolescents requiring acute medical attention (e.g., withdrawal or significant medical complications of substance use), and adolescents with significant coexisting psychopathology, especially psychotic symptoms. A history of treatment failure should also be strongly considered, within the context of other severity factors, as an indication for inpatient treatment.

Traditionally, short-term programs were based on a set time period, ranging from 28 days to as much as 60 days. Reimbursement limits and managed care have shifted the basis of length of stays to patient needs. Not only are programs required to justify admission to programs based on medical, psychiatric, or substance abuse severity, but also continued stay based on response to treatment and the continued documentation of severity factors. Such a variability in the length of stays between patients makes it difficult to develop and maintain set programming. As perhaps intended, treatment has become increasingly individualized and flexible in many settings.

While many short-term treatment programs are truly inpatient programs in hospital settings, there are also free-standing programs which often offer a range of treatment options from short- to long-term care. Many such programs are best subsumed under the category of residential treatment. Hospital-based programs have several salient advantages, including the availability of medical and psychiatric backup. Although almost all short-term programs have access to medical detoxification services, these are rarely needed for adolescents (Harrison & Hoffmann, 1989).

The milieu of inpatient treatment is an important component of treatment. Almost all programs have some kind of behavioral management system that optimally rewards appropriate, treatment-promoting behavior and provides explicit, consistent consequences for negative behavior(s). Behavior management systems range from a simple set of rules with a limited set of contingencies for compliance and noncompliance to more complex token economies with adjunct methods, such as a levels system and behavioral contracting (Bukstein & Van Hasselt, 1993). Such a system of consistent expectations, limits, and consequences for behavior often stands in stark contrast with the poor supervision and inconsistent limits which contributed to the adolescent's substance abuse and deviant behavior. Milieu behavior management systems also prepare the adolescent for the hopefully improved parent management systems to be implemented upon their return home.

Inpatient programs are usually staffed by multidisciplinary teams consisting of chemical dependency or substance abuse therapists/counselors, physicians including psychiatrists, nurses, social workers, teachers, and occasionally representatives from the clergy.

Outpatient Treatment

Outpatient treatment settings and modalities for adolescent substance abusers range from very intensive day-long and partial hospitalization to regular or occasional follow-up by an individual therapist. While the former setting may be every bit as intensive as some inpatient or residential treatment programs, the essential difference is that the adolescent resides either at home or in a less restrictive residential placement such as foster care or a group home. In outpatient settings, a significant amount of control may be sacrificed. However, the primary advantage (and in some ways disadvantage) of outpatient settings is that the adolescent participates in treatment while remaining in the community with, presumably, exposure to the circumstances, stressors, and problems that may have contributed to the development and maintenance of substance abuse problems. Given the concern about generalization of treatment progress from a protected, controlled inpatient setting to the exposed community or home environment, one might expect appropriate outpatient treatment to be preferable.

Residential Care and Therapeutic Communities

The difficulty in achieving success in short-term substance abuse treatment for adolescents has prompted the development of intermediate and long-term treatment options. Residential care or intermediate care settings range from one to nine months while long-term treatment can last as long as two years. They are less structured and usually less staff-intensive than inpatient programs. In longer term settings, there is a more diverse collection of treatment approaches than is found in shorter-term settings (Wheeler & Malmquist, 1987). Treatment modalities may include group and individual counseling, drug education, and educational and recreational activities. Although some programs offer family services, the distance from the adolescent's home may prevent optimal family/parent involvement. Some programs have attempted to address this issue by inviting and encouraging family attendance during family weeks or weekends. During these special programming periods, the family participates in an intensive array of groups providing support, psychoeducation, and counseling.

Longer-term programs appear to be increasingly admitting adolescents with a host of behavioral and psychiatric problems which indicate a greater level of severity of dysfunction. A decade-old study found that adolescents in residential programs had multiple problems including lower educational backgrounds, more criminal or juvenile justice contact, and more severe substance abuse histories in terms of duration and levels of substance use (Beschner & Friedman, 1985). Most longer-term programs required previous treatment in a short-term or rehab setting.

Many long-term programs operate as therapeutic communities (TC). The typical TC is based in the 12-Step, AA/NA philosophy. The TC is truly a community where the adolescent assumes an important role in the maintenance of the community. While developing responsibility and a sense of purpose, the adolescent receives support and further exposure to AA/NA. The TC is often a more structured, less permissive form of long-term treatment. As in many forms of substance abuse treatment, long-term settings, especially TCs, rely on counselors who are themselves in more advanced stages of recovery from substance abuse/dependence. Many long-term programs, including TCs, serve urban youth and depend upon public funding and support. Such programs are often the setting for the treatment of adolescents addicted to opiates or to crack cocaine (Plaut & Kelley, 1989).

As previously noted, there is a wide variability in the structure and philosophy of longer term programs. Straight, Inc combines a structured day program with housing by volunteer parents (Friedman, Schwartz, & Utada, 1989). These volunteer parents may also have or have had their own adolescent involved in the Straight program. Half-way houses, while more extensively used for adults in recovery, offer close supervision and an intermediate step from a structured, protected treatment setting back to home and the community. Often actual treatment programming is minimal in half-way houses. Outpatient facilities and other local agencies provide additional treatment services and support. Group homes have similarities to both TC and half-way houses. While widely variable in the structure and support provided directly, group homes may provide therapeutic groups and access to AA/NA meetings and adjunct mental health services.

Other Treatment Settings

School-based programs dealing with substance use are usually concerned with prevention (see Chapter 10). However, student assistance programs (SAP) often provide after-care counseling and/or groups for high-risk youth. Several school-based programs offer support groups and more intensive intervention experiences than prevention programs (Fleisch, 1991).

Treatment Matching and Selection of Treatment Setting

Ideally, a given treatment setting would provide the individual adolescent with the right modalities at the appropriate intensity in the best environment, and would produce the optimal outcome in terms of improving treatment targets. The idea of *treatment-patient matching* has received much attention for the treatment of adult substance abusers. McLellan, Woody, Luborsky, O'Brien, and Druley (1983) reported that psychiatric severity may be an important guide to treatment-patient matching. Adult substance abusers with low psychiatric severity did well whether they were placed in inpatient or outpatient settings. Those with high psychiatric severity tended to do poorly regardless of setting, while those with a moderate level of severity did best in inpatient settings. A number of additional adult treatment matching studies are in progress (McLellan & Alterman, 1991).

In the only published report of a patient-treatment matching study for adolescents, Friedman, Granick, Kreishner, and Terras (1993) reported that compared to short-term inpatient treatment, long-term outpatient treatment had significantly greater effect in reducing substance use/abuse for patients who had relatively more severe social, family, and employment problems. This study also found a trend toward better outcome for adolescents with more severe psychiatric problems. While this study may have limited application across all potential treatment settings and for all groups of adolescents, it suggests that programs designed to provide treatment for the long-term may be preferred to brief, intensive, and restrictive programs.

The concept of treatment-patient matching suggests that different groups of adolescents may have different treatment needs and that the philosophy of "one size fits all" may not be appropriate, efficacious, or cost-effective. Without treatment research to guide us in the selection of appropriate settings for individual adolescents, clinicians will need to rely on the experience and guidance of others. The American Society for Addiction Medicine (ASAM) has developed placement criteria based on explicit decision-making rules (Mee-Lee & Hoffmann, 1992). While not strictly based on research involving substance-abusing adolescents, the criteria do provide a reasonable departure point for considering treatment-patient matching. The ASAM criteria represents the further development of the Cleveland Admission, Discharge and Transfer Criteria (Hoffmann, Halikas, & Mee-Lee, 1987). The ASAM criteria have components for admission, continued stay, and discharge. For admission, a clinician rates the adolescent along six dimensions: intoxication/withdrawal, biomedical complications, emotional/behavioral problems, treatment acceptance/resistance, relapse potential, and recovery environment. Depending upon the severity criteria met within each dimension, there are four possible levels of care : (1) outpatient treatment, (2) intensive outpatient/partial hospitalization, (3) medically-monitored intensive inpatient treatment, and (4) medically-managed intensive inpatient treatment. By considering the levels of care specified by the severity criteria in a dimension, the clinician can determine an admission profile which will be the basis for placement decisions and the level of intensity of treatment required for the adolescent. Similarly, the continued stay and discharge components are based on the same dimensions and levels of care, but different severity criteria which are relevant to continued stay and discharge status. The summary continued stay profile can be the basis for justifying continued stay in a particular treatment setting. Likewise, meeting discharge criteria for a level of care indicates that the adolescent is ready for discharge to a less intensive level of care.

Despite the potential usefulness of such placement criteria, especially in this era of managed health care, there are no published empirical studies that validate the criteria and the decision rules. In addition, treatment programs at various levels of care or intensity are not consistent in the types and modalities of treatment provided and the skill of staff to provide treatment. In other words, there is often considerable variability of quality between treatment programs. Given the absence of a research literature documenting the efficacy of specific treatment modalities for adolescents with substance abuse problems, it becomes very difficult to match patients to specific treatments or levels of care.

SPECIAL TREATMENT POPULATIONS

Dually Diagnosed Adolescents

Dual diagnosis treatment refers to concurrent treatment of adolescents with both substance abuse problems and coexisting psychiatric or mental health problems such as depression, anxiety, attention deficit hyperactivity disorder. Dual diagnosis is perhaps somewhat of a misnomer given the likely existence of multiple problems (two or more) in addition to substance abuse in adolescents presenting for treatment. Terms such as "multidiagnosed" or "multiproblem" may be more appropriate. Given the significance of coexisting psychiatric problems in substance-abusing youth, attention to this prominent special population is not surprising (Bukstein, Brent, & Kaminer, 1989). Coexisting psychiatric and behavioral problems often have a critical role in the risk for, onset, maintenance, severity, and relapse to substance abuse.

It is difficult to describe the extent of dual diagnosis programs for adolescents. Pressures from managed care are prompting the conversion of previously traditional programs to dual-diagnosis programs. The label dual diagnosis is not specific or really descriptive, as many programs may use this label when they merely accept youth with multiple diagnoses for treatment. The actual transition of programs to ones that truly deal with multidiagnosed adolescents is much less certain. Some programs go on with business as usual while others have made greater or lesser modifications to their existing programs to accommodate the special needs of multidiagnosed youth. This is certainly an improvement as many programs would previously not accept such special needs youth for admission, would discharge them due to poor adherence to their existing program, or would transfer them to psychiatric units or programs. Unfortunately, psychiatric programs might routinely ignore the adolescent's substance abuse every bit as much as their psychiatric problems were ignored in the substance abuse treatment program.

Regardless of how treatment programs choose to label themselves, the following criteria should be used to determine whether a specific program truly serves youth with multiple diagnoses.

1. The program should provide careful assessment of both substance abuse problems and psychiatric and behavioral problems through a comprehensive diagnostic assessment.
2. The program should develop and deliver treatment modalities that directly and specifically address psychiatric and behavioral problems. This includes behavioral approaches and medications when appropriate.
3. The program should involve a qualified child and adolescent psychiatrist at all levels of treatment including, assessment, treatment planning and aftercare.

Beyond these basic criteria and recommendations, there continues to be much controversy as to the role of psychiatric modalities within any substance abuse treatment program. In truth, most substance abuse treatment modalities are generic to the extent that they potentially target both substance abuse problems and psychiatric/behavioral problems. Milieu management, skills and problem-solving training, and family therapy are not specific to either a mental health or a substance abuse treatment approach. The real controversy arises in the level that a substance abuse treatment program wishes to evaluate and consider psychopathology such as depression, anxiety, attentional problems, and aggressive behavior as separate issues that may influence or be influenced by substance use or abuse, but require attention nonetheless. Are programs willing to tackle depression or anxiety with cognitive therapy or medication rather than merely dismissing these "symptoms" as the consequence of substance abuse? Specific comments on the potential use of different behavioral modalities, family interventions, and medication for adolescents with multidiagnoses are mentioned in Chapter 9.

The cardinal feature of a practical approach to the treatment of multidiagnosed adolescents is flexibility. Although almost all of the adolescents, regardless of their diagnoses, can benefit from any combination of a variety of treatment modalities, the delivery of these modalities may need to be individualized to the particular characteristics of the individual adolescents. For example, approaches for an aggressive adolescent with ADHD will likely differ from the approach for a socially avoidant, anxious teenager. For many cases of multidiagnosed youth, the use of highly confrontative techniques is not recommended. All programs should emphasize structure and consistent limit-setting. Power struggles may reinforce the cognitive distortions and attributional biases often present in adolescent substance abusers. Treatment programs and staff should model adaptive adult behavior and responses to adolescent limit-testing.

Racial and Ethnic Groups

While the previous chapters in this volume have described the endemic nature of substance use among adolescents and patterns of pathologic use among adolescents, we have also come to an appreciation that substance use among adolescents is not a unitary phenomenon. Such factors as comorbid psychopathology, history of parental substance abuse, and other environmental factors can greatly influence the presentation, development, response to typical treatment and, ultimately, the prognosis of an individual adolescent's psychoactive substance abuse disorder. Specific populations of adolescents have differing types and levels of risk factors for the development of substance use and abuse. Because these differences can affect the screening assessment and treatment of adolescent substance use or abuse, the clinician should become familiar with the special population characteristics.

In dealing with or providing any type of intervention for any specific racial, ethnic, or cultural group, the clinician must understand the cultural realities and context for that specific group. Both the process and the content of interventions and treatment must be culturally relevant and must target the specific needs and cultural experiences of the specific racial or ethnic group of adolescents. This "fact" of intervention is hardly surprising when one considers the "peer" nature of many approaches to substance abuse treatment. For African-American adolescents, for example, the peer group is not only other adolescents, but more specifically other African-American adolescents.

African-American Adolescents

Treatment planning for African-American youth must consider African-American culture including its history, values, and attitudes. Engagement, rapport-building strategies, and counseling techniques must take into account such culturally determined variables as eye contact, touching, time perspective, language, and social distance (National Institute on Alcohol Abuse and Alcoholism, 1986). Among the counseling techniques that consider culturally determined behavioral styles are directive, confrontational, and action-oriented techniques.

There are several guidelines to approaching a culturally sensitive treatment for African-American youth in substance abuse treatment (Thompson & Simmons-Cooper, 1989). Facilitating the development of a positive self-identity and cultural identity for African-American youth appears to be an essential element in any intervention. African-American youth must learn to accept themselves before they can develop a motivation to achieve and to develop positive and responsible behavior. Values clarification from an African-American cultural perspective involves exploration of the youth's behavior and whether that behavior supports his or her values. African-American adolescents must distinguish between the coping behaviors of living in their environment and those behaviors arising directly from substance use or abuse. As the adolescents learn which types of behavior represent dysfunctional coping, they should be encouraged to develop the ability to formulate options for their behaviors. Finally, the adolescents should begin to understand the role of emotions and their own response to feelings as a determinant of their behavior.

Group treatment approaches, such as AA, are useful for African-American populations of youth in that groups reflect the communal nature of the African heritage and culture. There are several cultural characteristics and values of African-Americans which make treatment modifications necessary (Sue & Sue, 1990). African-American language is often nonstandard English and communication is often based on nonverbal behavior. African-American culture tends to be more action-oriented, has a different time perspective, and responds preferentially to concrete, tangible, and structured approaches to counseling and treatment. Intermediate and short-term goals are especially important. Added emphasis is given to the extended family and a sense of being part of a larger group. While cultural sensitivity is essential for all treatment staff, the necessity of a critical mass in the number of African-American staff members cannot be understated. African-American youth, just as any other group of adolescents, need role models for appropriate behavior. Given the frequent absence of these role models in their immediate communities, having role models involved in treatment or intervention is critical. A variety of African-centered treatment approaches have been described. Rowe and Grills (1993) propose that effective drug and alcohol treatment directed toward African-Americans must adopt culturally-centered precepts and emphasize the empowerment of African-Americans to develop spiritual, personal, familial, communal, and institutional awareness.

Aftercare issues are particularly important given the fact that adolescents are likely to return to an environment where drug access is easy, and the lack of material, emotional, and social support will increase the risk of a rapid relapse back into substance use. To combat these factors, the adolescents need to have increased knowledge and skills to problem-solve and negotiate the realities of their lives in a more functional manner. As much as possible, the acute treatment environment and aftercare services must create and support a safe, healthy environment. Obviously, family interventions will be necessary. Social agencies, such as child welfare and community centers, may need to be summoned and become involved when necessary. Community interventions by governmental and nongovernmental groups, agencies and individuals will be necessary to develop and maintain an environment where not only a permanent remission of substance abuse is possible, but also the prevention of future abuse by other African American youth is less likely.

In the 1990s, the frequent occurrence of major environmental, family, and social problems in addition to the obvious substance use behavior(s), deviant behaviors, and psychiatric comorbidity demand more intensive intervention approaches in addition to traditional substance abuse treatment approaches. Intensive case management and family preservation models are intensive approaches which deal with a broad range of personal and environmental problems within the adolescent's social context (Henggeler, 1991).

Hispanic Adolescents

Although many of the same issues in the process of cultural sensitivity that are applied to African-Americans are applicable to Hispanics, the specific content is obviously different. The bilingual nature of U.S. Hispanic culture makes language and communication even more important. Conflicts between Hispanic youth and their elders, or society in general, often present prominent themes of ethnic identity, biculturality, sex roles, skin color, and a sense of self in relationship with the family (Sue & Sue, 1990). Given the strong family ties of Hispanics, intergenerational conflict in the context of inevitable acculturation appears to be the primary issue seen among Hispanic youth. In general, Spanish-speaking groups differ from whites in several cultural variables (Sue & Sue, 1990). In addition to language, Hispanics are more likely to be group-centered with a strong allegiance and ties to an extended family and, like African-Americans, place an emphasis on being action-oriented. Hispanics are more likely to respond to concrete, structured approaches with intermediate and short-term goals.

The cultural differences of Hispanics translate to several major concerns in the intervention of adolescents with substance abuse. Assessment and treatment should not only be culturally sensitive, but also culturally specific with an emphasis placed on the role of family, adolescent identity, language preference, social network, and the process of acculturation in their specific Hispanic community. Because family pride, support, and solidarity are important characteristics of Hispanic culture, including the family in treatment is necessary, to engage other family members as part of a supportive network. Utilizing such nontraditional elements as folk-healers and spiritists (*Espiritistas*) along with other more traditional substance abuse treatment methods can be quite useful.

Native American Adolescents

Although Native American youth comprise a very small minority of U.S. adolescents, the extremely high rate of substance abuse in the Native American population demands a discussion of relevant issues regarding this group. Native American youth are geographically isolated. Many live in poverty and are subject to high rates of disease and suicide (LaFromboise, 1988). The high rates of substance use among Native American adolescents have been previously discussed. It is not surprising that Native Americans lead the United States in the rates of alcohol-related cirrhosis, diabetes fetal abnormalities, and homicide and accident fatalities (Moncher, Holden, & Trimble, 1990). Native American youth may tend toward experimentation with psychoactive substances at an earlier age than other ethnic groups (Oetting, Edwards, Goldstein, & Garcia, 1980). Acculturation theory proposes that youth from minority cultural backgrounds experience more stress if they have not developed bicultural skills (LaFromboise, 1988; Schinke, Moncher, Palleja, Zayas, & Shilling, 1988). Bicultural skills are those skills which allow productive, comfortable interaction between the majority culture and the minority cultures. A deficiency of these skills can lead to stress with substance use as a coping response.

Native Americans and whites are quite similar to African-Americans and Hispanics in terms of language, action orientation, valuing the extended family, emphasizing short-term goals, and a preference for a concrete, structured approach (Sue & Sue, 1990). Native Americans may often use folk or supernatural explanations of environmental phenomena or circumstances. Many Native American youth are more isolated from the prevailing 1990s culture than other racial/ethnic groups. It is also essential to remember that Native Americans are not a homogenous group as there are over 500 federally recognized tribes and over 300 federal reservations (Manson & Trimble, 1982) found in a variety of different geographic locations. During evaluation and treatment, including staff from the same tribe is often essential to elicit personal information and specific attitudes and values of the individual and his or her tribe. Modification of traditional self-help groups such as AA is necessary as public disclosure and discussion of personal problems as well as a tradition of noninterference in the affairs of others are likely to impede the success of more traditional AA or NA approaches (GNAW, 1986). Native Americans can often be motivated through encouragement to assist their families, tribes, and communities. Special aftercare concerns include education, employment, and training which are necessary for the Native American to assume a productive lifestyle.

Specific intervention issues and treatment approaches for Native American youth are similar to those for the other racial and ethnic groups discussed. Assessment and treatment must be culturally-sensitive and specific and must deal with the economic and social realities of Native Americans. Dealing with the identity issues and the acquisition of appropriate bicultural skills of Native American adolescents is essential. Given the geographic isolation of many Native American groups, running a homogenous, locally specific program without multiple-cultural concerns is usually possible.

Asian Adolescents

Asian-American youth have low rates of substance use and abuse. Whether the effects of acculturation will bring future substance-use related problems to succeeding generations of Asian youth remains to be seen. Asian-Americans comprise several dozen separate national and ethnic identities, each with its own prevailing attitudes, beliefs, and traditions. Several salient issues arise in the treatment of Asian-Americans. Language barriers, the stigmatization of any deviant behavior in Asian cultures, and the role of the family in taking responsibility for its members create formidable barriers for treatment staff to overcome. As in other ethnic and racial groups, one should strive to include staff from the same group and include the patient in self-support groups with same-culture members.

In summary, approaches to the screening, assessment, treatment, and aftercare of substance-abusing adolescents from different racial and ethnic backgrounds need to consider several basic criteria in order to provide effective services. These criteria include:

1. The development of *cultural sensitivity* in terms of knowledge of the racial/ethnic population characteristics, values, behaviors.

2. The availability of *minority staff* from the specific racial/ethnic group to serve as role models.

3. Maintaining *sufficient numbers of similar minority youth* within the treatment population served.

4. Development of *modified intervention approaches* to serve the needs of the racial/ethnic population served.

5. Increased emphasis on *comprehensive services* to address the significant environmental and social needs of many racial/ethnic youth and their families.

Pregnant Adolescents

Foremost in the treatment of the pregnant adolescent is the realization that treatment considerations must be extended to two individuals—the adolescent and her child in utero. During the course of treatment from recognition of pregnancy and concurrent substance use to well beyond delivery, the adolescent's pregnancy never ceases to be a primary issue for both the adolescent and treating clinicians.

Initially, the clinician should not only assess the extent of substance use as a problem, but also obtain appropriate consultation as to confirm the pregnancy, the duration of the pregnancy, and the presence of any further high-risk characteristics for pregnancy, labor, and delivery. If the adolescent is inclined, strong considerations should be given to aborting the pregnancy. However, the program staff should also consider the potential negative reaction by family and other staff members to a decision for abortion. In terms of motivating the adolescent for treatment and/or stopping or severely curtailing use, the knowledge of pregnancy can be a significant motivator. Research has shown significant decreases in the use of most substances after a pregnancy becomes known (Cornelius, Day et al., 1993). However, transient improvements in motivation or in substance use should not deter the clinician from considering the short-term effects of recent substance use on the pregnant adolescent and her fetus.

Suspicion or knowledge about withdrawal in the potential mother in the presence of physiologically addictive substances such as opiates, sedative-hypnotics, or significant patterns of alcohol use requires careful management.

Apart from the obvious concerns about specific treatment for substance use, the provision of prenatal care is essential, especially given the high-risk status of the patient as an adolescent as well as a substance abuser. The stresses of adolescent motherhood are considerable; therefore, it is essential not to delay treatment efforts until after the pregnancy. The content of much of the substance abuse treatment of pregnant adolescents is similar to that directed at adolescents in general. Treatment staff should exercise caution in attempting to prevent the adolescent's pregnancy (or abortion) from becoming a distraction to either other patients or treatment staff. Pregnancy and post-partum status often elicit sympathy and other enabling behaviors on the part of others. This allows the adolescent to escape a more careful scrutiny of her problems related to substance use. As in the case of other racial/ethnic groups or special patient populations, specialized treatment programs, sensitivity, and specialized training for staff members are essential for treatment success. Nevertheless, the adolescent's pregnant status is an inescapable fact. Any treatment setting dealing with pregnant adolescents must have appropriate obstetric coverage and access to facilities treating high-risk pregnancies and deliveries.

The most successful intervention efforts with pregnant adolescents are comprehensive and address broader social and environmental support issues (Hardy & Zabin, 1991). Obtaining and maintaining family involvement and support is important in ameliorating the long-term effects of adolescent motherhood. Family planning, including education about contraceptive methods and selection, when appropriate, of the most practical and effective birth control method is a critical component of programming and follow-up. Treatment should also include access to education and resources and/or job-training opportunities.

Many of the same treatment and management issues for the pregnant, substance-abusing adolescents apply after pregnancy as well. Better outcomes for adolescent mothers are noted in comprehensive programs which meet both medical and social needs (Hardy & Zabin, 1991).

Aftercare presents many potential problems. High-risk adolescents often become substance-abusing, pregnant adolescents. After acute treatment and after delivery, the adolescent and her child often continue to live in a high-risk environment. Not surprisingly, the stress of adolescent motherhood holds a high potential for relapse. Child abuse and neglect are frequently consequences when a parent abuses substances (Kaplan, Pelcovitz, Salzinger, et al., 1983). In this way, another generation is placed at risk for a variety of negative psychosocial consequences, including eventual substance use and abuse.

Homeless/Runaway Youth

The severity of the social and psychological problems and heterogeneity of the population of homeless/runaway youth requires comprehensive interventions which integrate clinical treatment with intensive, extensive social supports. Regardless of their point of entry into the system—for example, seeking medical care, substance use treatment, shelter, housing, or general public assistance—the clinicians and social agency staff need to be aware of the multitude of additional problems that this population of youth often carry. Treatment cannot be one-dimensional. Homeless/runaway youth are usually suspicious of "the system." They often perceive that the system has failed them. Motivation for engagement into treatment is often tenuous. From the clinician's perspective, homeless substance abusers are among the most undesirable and difficult candidates for treatment, given their multiple problems (Wright & Weber, 1987).

To deal with the many problems in treating homeless/runaway youth, outreach, including supportive housing arrangements and individualized treatment programs or plans, are necessary. These efforts are directed to the functional level of the adolescents and consider any coexisting problems or psychiatric disorders (Institute of Medicine, 1988). Intervention must provide for their multiple needs by establishing and maintaining appropriate services for mental health, housing, education and vocational training, and public assistance or welfare. This effort requires the best efforts of specific treatment programs, but also the cooperation of multiple social service programs.

In terms of specific approaches to substance abuse treatment in the homeless/runaway adolescent population, there are several obvious limitations. The most prominent limitation is the absence of an appropriate support network, especially a family. The lack of a supportive and functional family is the single largest factor associated with homeless youth (General Accounting Office, 1989). When a family is absent or reconciliation is too problematic, alternative support systems must to be created. When family reconstitution is possible, available resources are directed to reducing family conflict and reducing family stress by addressing familial addiction problems, housing, and employment (Shane, 1989).

Among the homeless population, the frequency of gay or sexually-abused youth with significant other psychopathology such as depression often requires specific treatment interventions directed toward these issues. Medical care, including HIV-related interventions and education, are also critical components of a comprehensive system of care for homeless/runaway youth.

Homosexual Youth

Although a sizeable percentage of male adolescents have had at least one homosexual experience (Sorenson, 1973), only a very small subset of adolescents clearly identify themselves as homosexual (Remafedi, Resnick, Blum, & Harris, 1992). Data from studies of adult homosexuals suggests an incidence of substance abuse in the gay population of about 30 percent (Cabaj, 1992). Many of the same factors which explain an increased incidence of substance abuse in gay adults may be applicable to gay adolescents. The stress of violating societal and cultural prohibitions against homosexuality and the common ambivalence about dealing with one's sexual identity may lead to substance use as a way of dealing with unacceptable feelings. Alcohol or other drugs are often needed to socialize and to ultimately overcome their internal fear, denial, anxiety, or even revulsion about gay sexual activity (Cabaj, 1992). This may be particularly true of earlier homosexual experiences during adolescence. In adopting a gay identity, the homosexual adolescent assumes a "deviant" identity in the eyes of society; therefore, the concurrent existence of other deviant behaviors such as substance abuse should not be surprising.

Assessment and treatment concerns for gay youth are similar to those for other special populations of adolescents. In most adolescent treatment settings, unless the clinician is very experienced and perceptive, or unless the adolescent is honest, it is unusual and difficult to identify homosexual youth at initial assessment. If an adolescent's homosexuality becomes known, the adolescent usually reveals this during the course of treatment, often at very sensitive stages when the adolescent begins to let down defenses and reduce his or her denial. Unless the clinician and treatment setting are experienced and prepared to deal honestly with homosexual youth, the adolescent's revelation may be quite distracting and even disruptive to peers and treatment staff. Adolescent peers in treatment who may already have a significant level of anxiety dealing with more common, but sensitive treatment issues, may be overwhelmed by a peer's disclosure of a gay orientation. Whether this uncovers the peer's own ambivalence about his or her sexual identity or it taps into cultural homophobia, the risk for program disruption is real. In most treatment settings, an experienced therapist can direct attention back to the pertinent topic at hand, that is, substance abuse and related behaviors. However, one must account for the staff's and one's own views on homosexual behavior. If the existence of homosexual youth in a particular treatment setting violates the treating staff's personal views to the extent that treatment quality is affected, the adolescent should be discretely referred to another program which is more accepting of gay youth and experienced in their treatment. Although one is likely to encounter male homosexual adolescents more frequently, the existence of lesbian or female homosexual youth is possible. Little is currently known about substance abuse and treatment in this population of adolescents.

If homosexual issues become prominent, members of the treatment staff should assist the adolescent in exploring conflicts around identity and should be reasonably supportive and realistic about sexual identity decisions without imposing their own values and judgements.

Youth in the Juvenile Justice System

Antisocial behavior is among the most robust of risk factors for the development of substance use in adolescents. A number of studies have demonstrated a relationship between adolescent substance use and the involvement in crime and delinquent behavior (Elliot, Huizinga, & Menard, 1989; Kandel, Simcha-Fagen, & Davies, 1986). Drug offenses comprised 7 percent of all delinquency cases in 1989 and 10 percent of all cases in youth 16 years or older (Office of Juvenile Justice and Delinquency Prevention, 1992). Delinquent youth have multiple problems including histories of physical and sexual abuse, psychological distress, family problems, and poor academic functioning (Dembo, Williams, & Schmeidler, 1993). Antisocial behavior is also quite persistent over time and highly resistant to treatment interventions (Kazdin, 1987). Given the cost to society of both delinquent behavior and substance abuse, intervention becomes necessary.

As critical as multiproblem, comprehensive treatment is for youth with multiple psychiatric diagnoses and substance abuse, the same holds true for delinquent youth. Similarly, comprehensive intervention approaches are necessary for delinquent youth. Early intervention and diversionary programs have provided psychoeducation for youth and their families, resulting in changes on knowledge, attitudes and feelings about substance use (Klitzner, Fisher, Stewart, & Gilbert, 1991). Hawkins, Catalano, and Wells (1986) provided a 10-week cognitive-behavioral skills training program for institutionalized delinquents. This program was followed by six months of case management to promote adaptation to the prevailing environment.

The importance of aftercare services cannot be underestimated as this is often the weakest part of the service delivery system (Dembo, Williams, & Schmeidler, 1993). The high risk of recurrence of delinquent behavior and/or relapses to substance use suggests that long-term assistance or intervention is often necessary. The greatest promise for the ultimate success of treatment and adaptive functioning for the delinquent adolescent probably lies in repeated interventions over a long period of time. These interventions should be reinforced by improved educational, social, and vocational skills (NIDA, 1992; Pickens, Leukefeld, & Schuster, 1991).

Henggler (1991) provided multisystemic therapy (MST), based on a family-systems conceptualization of behavior and behavior change, to serious juvenile offenders and their multiproblem families. Consistent with a family-preservation model of service delivery, MST was usually provided on-site, that is, in the adolescent's home and up to several hours per week as necessary. Henggler has included substance abuse interventions as part of this intensive program (Henggler, 1993). The success of this program in reducing recidivism and aggression and in increasing family cohesion provides a promising model for future intensive intervention for seriously antisocial youth with substance abuse (Henggler, Melton, & Smith, 1992).

Approaches for the Assessment and Treatment of Special Populations

The risk for deviant behavior is not spread uniformly through the general population of adolescents. Similarly, substance abuse, like other deviant behavior, is not found in equal proportions among all groups of adolescents as defined by racial or ethnic status, sexual orientation, or adequacy of living arrangements. In fact, the level of risk is often defined in terms of such characteristics as race, environment, sexual activity (which can and does often lead to pregnancy in females).

Interventions, whether they are preventative or for treatment, must be relevant to the individual adolescent, his or her family, and the social/economic environment. Assessment should fully identify important characteristics such as race, pregnancy, or homeless status, which influence the adolescent's behavior and serve to either encourage or discourage substance use or abuse. In the spirit of "treatment matching," interventions should be individualized to address these characteristics.

For the clinician, training and experience should be directed toward the development of broad sensitivity to individual adolescent differences. These include differences in race, culture, and sexual orientation. The clinician should also understand that special populations of adolescent substance abusers often require special expertise, training, and facilities. Because some adolescents are frequently members of several special populations—for example, pregnant African-American females or homeless gay adolescents—more intensive treatment services are often necessary. This can go far beyond acute treatment for substance abuse into areas such as housing, vocational training, and intensive case management.

Perhaps most important, treatment is most relevant to the adolescent when it involves those to whom he or she relates best—peers. Treatment settings should develop appropriate programming for groups of similar adolescents. Adolescents should not feel isolated from peers with similar characteristics. This need speaks to the development of specialized treatment for specific adolescent populations, but also in the specific communities where the adolescents live and where sensitive and relevant treatment can be optimally delivered.

CHAPTER 9

Treatment Modalities

For many years, the specific content of treatment for adolescent substance abusers has taken a back seat to an emphasis on the process of treatment. As long as the treatment focused on eliminating denial about the problem and engaged the youngster in the 12-step philosophy and self-support groups to achieve and maintain abstinence, little attention was paid to the specific content of treatment; that is, what is provided as treatment and how these elements work to achieve and maintain the goals of treatment. Whereas the previous chapter focused on the general aspects of treatment, including treatment setting and dealing with specific populations, this chapter will attempt to describe the major components or content of several major treatment modalities for adolescent substance abuse (Table 9.1). I will discuss the theoretical, empirical, and research basis for each modality; provide an outline of the basic content of each modality, emphasize critical areas in the provision of each modality including common problems; and finally, show how each modality might fit into a model for the comprehensive treatment of adolescent substance abuse.

TABLE 9.1.   Treatment Modalities for Adolescent Substance Abusers

12-Step Programs
    Step-work and other group therapy
    Self-support groups (Alcoholics Anonymous, Narcotics Anonymous)
    Step-work books and written assignments

Familiy Treatment
    Specific theory-based therapy (e.g. Functional Familiy Therapy)
    Multi-family therapy
    Parent/family support groups
    Behavioral therapies
        Parent management training
        Contracting, negotiation skills

Cognitive-Behavioral Methods
    Social skills training
    Anger control training
    Cognitive therapy
    Relapse prevention

Psychopharmacology

TRADITIONAL METHODS: AA, NA, AND
THE 12-STEP MODEL

The first and still the most widely used approach to the treatment of adolescent substance abuse is an approach based on the philosophy and principles of Alcoholics Anonymous (AA) and Narcotics Anonymous (NA) (Wheeler & Malmquist, 1987). Treatment programs based on the AA/NA model have been alternatively called Minnesota model programs (after the geographical location of the three founding centers of this model) or self-help programs (Cook, 1988a, 1988b). The principles of AA and NA are summarized in the "12-steps" which provide a plan for recovery from addiction to alcohol, other drugs, or presumably any one of a number of other "addictions" such as gambling, overeating, or sexual behavior.

The AA/NA philosophy is rooted in the belief that change is possible, but only if the addicted individual recognizes his or her problem with addiction and admits that he or she cannot control this addiction but must learn to live with it in an adaptive manner. Spiritual awareness and growth are seen as critical to this process and to later steps which promote taking more individual responsibility for one's past behavior and what needs to be changed in order to achieve a healthier, more adaptive lifestyle and better interpersonal relationships. In the past, AA/NA, 12-step philosophy has held that the resources for change lie within the individual and require only the 12-step process and support from others in recovery to discover and use these resources. Acceptance of the disease model of addiction and commitment to an ongoing personal recovery program are necessary to achieve total abstinence for alcohol and other drugs.

Program components of AA/NA-based programs include group therapy, lectures, work assignments including 12-step work, a therapeutic milieu, attendance at AA/NA meetings, family therapy, or counseling, and recreational activities. Although most programs have multidisciplinary staff including physicians, psychologists, social workers, nurses, and sometimes clergy, most of the treatment is usually provided by counselors many of whom are recovering addicts. Although AA/NA-based programs have been inpatient, residential, or "rehab" programs designed to deliver a basic level of treatment over 28 to 42 days, managed health care pressures have made residential stays much more variable, depending on individual needs. Many long-term (60 days up to two years) programs such as "half-way houses" and therapeutic communities are also based on AA/NA principles.

Group Therapy

Group therapy is the primary mode of treatment delivery within most AA/NA, 12-step programs, although the types and number of group experiences vary among specific programs. Nonstructured, process-oriented groups have a primary goal of breaking through the denial of group members. Other goals include expressing and clarifying feelings, especially painful affective states, developing relationships, and confronting negative characteristics or behaviors of adolescents that appear to limit or impede the recovery process. A confrontational approach often characterizes the atmosphere of many treatment programs. While occasionally useful in motivating some adolescents, this approach is less useful for others. It is not difficult for a confrontative approach to deteriorate into bullying and mental abuse. Some adolescents might take advantage of confrontation to punish other peers, irrespective of any therapeutic value of this process. Many substance-abusing adolescents do not have the appropriate level of social and communication skills to use confrontation in a motivating, therapeutic manner. Given the frequent presence of negative attributional biases in adolescents with substance abuse, confrontation is liable to create more denial, resistance, and roadblocks to accepting and using treatment.

Within the AA/NA 12-step-based programs, group therapies are expanding their focus to cognitive-behavioral methods such as social skills training which often includes alcohol and other drug refusal skills, problem solving, and relapse prevention.

Lectures and Psychoeducation

In AA, NA, and other 12-step-based programs, the staff, including counselors, nurses, psychologists, psychiatrists, clergy, and social workers will often present information on the psychcosocial and medical consequences of substance use and abuse, the 12 steps and 12 traditions of AA/NA, the nature of substance abuse/dependency, personal testimonies about addiction, and ways of dealing with common problems of adolescence. Didactic lectures are often supplemented by video and audio tapes as well as reading assignments, mostly from the big books of AA/NA.

Family Counseling

Usually within large, multifamily groups, AA/NA and 12-step-based programs present psychoeducational topics similar to those presented to the adolescents. Additional topics include explaining the process of "enabling" and basic parent management techniques. Multifamily groups also serve an important support function. Families share stories, problems, and advice on adolescent management and problem-solving. Parents learn, as do their children, that they are not alone and others have similar problems. Family programming promotes further parent involvement in such support groups as parents of teenage alcohol and drug abusers (POTADA).

Both the term "enabling" and the closely related "codependency" are subject to much misunderstanding within both the treatment and lay community. Both terms reinforce the notion of substance abuse/dependency as a family "illness" that has great effects on all members of a family system—not merely on the affected adolescent. *Codependency* basically refers to the negative effects of the adolescent's addictive or substance use related behaviors on the family or a particular family member and their behavior. A significant other, in this case a parent or sibling, develops a set of dysfunctional behaviors in response to the adolescent's substance abuse. In a real sense, these dysfunctional behaviors are a "disease" called codependency. Among the dysfunctional behaviors of codependency is enabling. Enabling refers to behavior or a set of behaviors that positively reinforce the adolescent's substance use behavior. *Enabling* behaviors by family members and others in the adolescent's life include allowing the adolescent to escape from suffering from the full consequences of his substance use behavior. For example, writing excuses to school when the adolescent is truant due to substance use or getting charges dropped when substance use leads to violation(s) of the law are among the more common enabling behaviors by parents or other family members. Parental codependence may be a common response to adolescent problem behaviors in general, rather than a reaction specific to substance abuse (Hawks, Bahr, & Wang, 1994).

Family-oriented modalities within AA/NA-based programs attempt to reinforce the idea of the adolescent and not the parent taking ultimate responsibility for the adolescent's behavior. Similarly, the adolescent's problem should not be used as an excuse for the parent's behavior which might include avoidance of marital conflict or job-related problems.

Written Assignments and Stepwork

Although the 12 steps of AA/NA are discussed frequently in a number of settings, the need for reflection and individual work suggests that "step work" is a valuable component of treatment. A life history or story, while not necessarily a part of step work, is often a critical lead-in or preparation for an honest, critical examination of the adolescent's life and problems.

Usually, the adolescent is expected to finish the first 3 to 5 steps during inpatient or residential treatment. While recovery through the AA/NA 12-step philosophy is described as a life-long process, completion of the first 5 steps is considered sufficient as a satisfactory commitment to abstinence and to continuing the 12-step process after discharge (Jaffe, 1990). During the past several years, individual professionals and treatment programs have developed stepwork books designed specifically for adolescents. Jaffe's *The Step Workbook for Adolescent Chemical Dependency Treatment* (1990) is one of the best examples of a simple, but complete guide for adolescents to work the first 5 steps of AA/NA. As in Jaffe's workbook, it is important to explain and work through the 12 steps in a developmentally appropriate fashion. Generally, individual stepwork is checked and discussed with a counselor on an individual basis and later may be presented to peers in a step study group. Given the reduced time presently allowed during residential stays, the availability of a guide to treatment as well as the importance of outside checks and discussion by both peers and counselors becomes increasingly important.

Most of all, the 12 steps provide a structure for treatment and recovery. Both the explicit and implicit messages and lessons of each of the 12 steps serve as a useful guide for the adolescent to admit to, confront, and to ultimately solve substance use and other life problems.

Step 1

The acknowledgement of an inability to control substance use is both a confrontation of denial and a development of motivation to participate in treatment. The writing and discussion of a life history or an alcohol and drug use history are often incorporated into step one. This may allow the adolescent to examine his or her problems and their connection with substance use.

Steps 2 and 3

Steps 2 and 3 are also motivational in nature. The spiritual aspect of these steps is occasionally controversial and often difficult for some adolescents to accept or understand. However, when reduced to their simplest form, these steps ask for an acknowledgment of the need for help with one's problem(s) from someone other than themselves. The alienation and hopelessness often present in many adolescents often demand that the adolescent look outside himself or his immediate world for guidance, structure, and meaning. Even when the spiritual orientation of the 12 steps leads to a development or reaffirmation of religious beliefs or behavior, this is certainly preferable to the negative lifestyle and behavior of the adolescent substance abuser.

Step 4

The development of a moral inventory involves a description of past behavior(s), including embarrassing and difficult experiences and painful effects. Essentially, the adolescent asks, "What have I done," "Who am I," and "What are my issues and problems." In identifying issues and problems, step four lays the groundwork for subsequently dealing with each of these problems and advancing to a more adaptive lifestyle.

Step 5

Although step 5 explicitly asks for a verbal disclosure of the inventory from step four, the implicit message is that the adolescent begins to deal and work on his or her issues and problems with a helping person.

Steps 6 through 12

The remainder of the 12 steps describe a guide to proceeding with and maintaining recovery. The message of these steps is that by using these steps as a guide to life and recovery, relapse is much less likely.

In completing stepwork, it is important to allow the adolescent's work to proceed on a developmentally appropriate level. For many adolescents, their answers will be very concrete and will have to be discussed specifically rather than easily generalized to every other adolescent. Many adolescents have limited reading and writing skills; therefore, much of stepwork may have to take place through oral discussion.

AA/NA Meetings

Exposure to and eventually participation in AA/NA meetings can take several forms. Many programs have institutional meetings on a treatment unit. During these meetings, adolescents may hear a "lead" or testimonial from a recovered addict that is followed up with a brief discussion. This exposure prepares the adolescents for regular AA/NA meetings both on-site (within the treatment facility) and out in the community. While in residential treatment, adolescents are accompanied by staff to community meetings. The adolescent's participation and talking at meetings is encouraged so that he or she might recognize the value of the meetings to the recovery process. While on pass, attendance at local meetings is usually required. This serves to acquaint the adolescent with local or "home" meetings and their attendees.

For both adolescents and treatment programs, the identification of AA/NA meetings that are peer-oriented or attended by adequate numbers of adolescents is often critical to the success of recovery and the maintenance of abstinence. Adolescents must feel that meetings are relevant to their concerns. The availability of youthful role models for recovery and the presence of abstinent peers for friendship and support is really the basis for the self-support movement for adolescents.

Aftercare

The follow-up aspects of traditional treatment approaches have undergone the most change over the course of the past several decades. In the past, aftercare might consist of merely sending the adolescent out to the community to attend AA/NA meetings, perhaps with a 90/90 (90 meetings in 90 days) or similar frequency requirement and with a strict parent contract requiring strict limits on outside activities and a prohibition of contact with substance-using peers. Progressively, over the last decade or so, formal aftercare groups, individual counseling and/or family counseling modalities have been established to continue more formal treatment after discharge from inpatient or residential treatment.

With limited inpatient or residential stays, aftercare either in partial/day hospital or outpatient setting has become the site for much of adolescent substance abuse treatment. In addition to offering many of the same treatment modalities as inpatient or residential settings, outpatient settings for aftercare often have to concentrate on threats to the adolescent's relapsing back into substance abuse. Even for highly motivated youth, the highly protected and structured inpatient setting produces change which cannot be maintained or generalized to functioning at home and in the community. More than AA/NA meeting attendance is needed; therefore, aftercare involves more intensive treatment using behavioral, family modalities, and even medication should psychiatric status warrant.

Strengths and Weakness of Traditional Approaches

Research investigating AA/NA, 12-step program methods and outcome is sparse for adult treatment and even more rare for adolescent programs. Alford, Koehler, and Leonard (1991) examined the substance use and social functioning of 157 male and female adolescents at 6, 12, and 24 months after leaving an AA/NA-based program. Both treatment completers and dropouts demonstrated less substance use after than before treatment. Although significantly higher percentages of both male and female treatment completers reported abstinence at six months when compared with dropouts, abstinence rates declined sharply by one and two years following treatment. Abstinence was associated with more successful, adaptive psychosocial functioning. A minority but sizable percentage (17 percent) of treatment completers were found to be frequent substance users, but also exhibited successful functioning at two years posttreatment. Frequent attendees of AA/NA meetings were more often abstinent than less frequent or nonattendees. Thus, abstinent treatment completers, especially those attending AA/NA meetings after discharge, had better functioning than dropouts, nonabstinent teens, or those not attending AA/NA meetings. Abstinent youth, whether treatment completers, had better functioning than nonabstinent youth.

AA/NA, 12-step-based treatment for substance-abusing youth is evolving. In previous years, many 12-step programs tended to be rigid with very little toleration given to missteps or any behavior deemed indicative of denial. Dropouts, expulsions from treatment, and other treatment failures were blamed on patient denial or the adolescent's not having yet "reached bottom." Substance use was the focus, the only focus, and attention toward psychological problems, family and peer problems discussed only in terms of their relationship to substance use. The AA/NA philosophy was interpreted from a disease model with substance abuse/dependency as the primary disorder and other problems—depression, anxiety, and other types of psychopathology—as secondary and not deserving of attention until the adolescent demonstrated abstinence and control of the primary disorder. Other treatment orientations or modalities—cognitive-behavioral, medications—were eschewed as having little value for substance abusers or addicts. Interpretation of the 12-step philosophy indicated that adolescents need only to accept their status as addicts, follow the 12 steps, and attend meetings to get better. Little attention was paid to skills deficits and learning better, more adaptive ways of handling problems. Finally, many proposed that the 12-step method was not only the best way to recovery but the only way—for all adolescents. One size fits all.

These attitudes are changing. There are few "pure" 12-step programs remaining, especially among mainstream treatment programs. Cognitive-behavioral techniques for groups, individuals, and families have gradually but steadily assumed a more prominent role in many programs. Medications for a variety of psychiatric problems are not only being tolerated, but also being aggressively used by an increased psychiatric presence in many 12-step treatment programs.

The addition of other treatment approaches to the core 12-step approach appears to strengthen the positive elements of the 12-step approach for adolescents. The 12-step approach supplies a useful structure for treatment. In addition to providing a rationale for dealing with denial of both substance abuse/dependency and other problems and increasing motivation for treatment, the 12-step approach offers a method of accepting help, that is, treatment, and cataloging the adolescent's treatment needs. The availability of support and role models through meetings is an important element in prevention of relapse and developing a lifestyle without psychoactive substances.

FAMILY TREATMENTS

It is an inescapable fact that almost all adolescents are dependent members of a family system. Many risk factors for the etiology and maintenance of substance abuse are related to the family. As per the discussion in Chapter 4, such family-related factors as parental substance use or abuse, poor parent-child relationships, low perceived parental support, low emotional bonding, and poor parent management of the adolescent's behavior have each been identified in raising the risk for substance abuse among adolescents. Targeting the family for treatment intervention seems obvious, although the specific approach to be used in family treatment of adolescent substance abuse has varied. The various family treatment approaches used for adolescent substance abusers include structural family systems approaches, multifamily therapy, and behavioral approaches.

Structural Family Systems Approaches

Many early case reports of family treatment have involved the use of structural family systems approaches (Minuchin, 1974). In this approach, the adolescent is viewed as the symptom bearer and the family is viewed as the patient (Kaufman & Kaufman, 1992). The goal of structural interventions is to restructure the family so as to produce change and improved functioning in all family members (Kaufman & Kaufman, 1992). In one of the only examples of a controlled outcome study using family structural methods with the families of adolescent substance abusers, Szapocznik and associates (1983, 1986) compared conjoint family therapy with one-person therapy. While both conditions produced improved family functioning, the one-person therapy also reduced the identified patient symptomatology.

Structural family therapy (SFT) is a family systems approach based on the work of Minuchin (1974) and Haley (1976). SFT views the family unit as a social system with established patterns of "transacting business" among its members and its environment. These repetitive patterns of interactions define the family's structure. Dysfunction results from the maladaptive manner in which a family organizes itself to cope with stressors both within the family and outside of it. In SFT, the therapist assesses family interactions and attempts to implement strategies to restructure maladaptive patterns in order to achieve change. Through the use of such SFT techniques as joining (forming an alliance between the therapist and each family member), restructuring (therapist directs alternative interfactional patterns, challenges the family "status quo"), reversals, detriangulation, and reframing, SFT alters dysfunctional patterns within the family in order to achieve change.

Functional Family Therapy

Functional family therapy (FFT) is another family-based approach that was originally developed for treating juvenile delinquency. Given the relationship between delinquency and adolescent substance abuse, FFT may be applicable to adolescent substance abusers and their families. Studies have demonstrated the effectiveness of FFT in reducing recidivism (Alexander & Parsons, 1973) and a reduction in the referral of siblings (Klein, Alexander, & Parsons, 1976). FFT includes principles that apply across most families, as well as goals and techniques that are individualized for each family and its unique environment (Alexander, Waldon, Newberry, & Liddle, 1990). FFT consists of five basic phases. Within each phase, goals are developed which require specific therapist skills and techniques. Initially, the therapist creates positive expectations for change by each family member. In subsequently identifying the affective, behavioral, and cognitive expectations of each family member, the therapist can then identify what family processes must be changed to meet those expectations. For families with an adolescent substance abuser, the therapist creates a context for change and changes the meaning of the adolescent to other family members and to decease their negative attitudes toward this adolescent.

Multi-Family Therapy

Multi-family (MFT) approaches involve interventions with multiple families and their affected adolescents. These interventions can involve as many as 50 people in 10 to 15 families. Multi-family approaches are commonly used in 12-step programs and serve a psychoeducational function and a support function among the participating families. Although somewhat more difficult to organize than individual family sessions, MFT can be much more cost-effective by minimizing staff effort to reach a maximum number of families. MFT appears to work better within the context of a residential treatment program and other treatment modalities.

Behavioral Family Methods

Among the behavioral methods used in the family therapy of adolescent substance abusers are contingency contracting, parent management training, and problem-solving training. Teicher, Sinay, and Stumphauzer (1976) used trained paraprofessionals to treat alcohol-abusing adolescents in their homes. The paraprofessionals used behavioral contracting to find areas of agreement regarding privileges and home responsibilities, as well as to target such problems as alcohol or other drug use, school attendance, and gang activity (Messer, Kush, & Van Hasselt, in press). Contingency contracting can be used to target problem behaviors and areas such as home responsibilities, family relationships, and school attendance.

Bry, Conboy, and Bisgay (1986) adapted Robin's (1981) problem-solving training approach with three substance-abusing adolescents and their families. Problem-solving training consisted of identifying the desired changes, assessing maintaining variables, generating solutions, and reinforcing positive changes.

Contingency management involves teaching the family to identify problem behaviors and controlling variables, changing the consequences through the provision of consistent rules, reducing negative commands and demands, and systematically reinforcing desired behaviors while eliminating reinforcement for negative, undesirable behaviors (Bry, 1988). A specific form of contingency contracting is the *behavioral contract*. Families learn to develop specific behavioral contracts or written documents which specify the behavior(s) to be changed and the reinforcing consequences that are agreed upon by all family members (Nichols, 1984). Behavioral contracts appear to be effective for adolescent problems since they provide for clear and consistent positive consequences that are established through negotiation and compromise. Communication skills focuses on the reduction and elimination of negative and coercive family interactions and increasing positive interactions. Problem-solving skills training consists of instruction (including modeling) and rehearsal (role-playing) of behaviors which are required to resolve conflicts and to solve problems.

General Family Approaches

Each of the family approaches previously described offers a useful guide for intervention with the families of adolescent substance abusers. There is even research to suggest that integrating the most effective elements of structural, strategic, functional, and behavioral family therapies can be effective. Lewis and colleagues designed the *Purdue Brief Family Therapy model* to combine these models of family therapy in a 12-session treatment *of the families* of adolescent substance abusers (Lewis, Plercy, Sprenkle, & Trepper, 1990). The goals of the Purdue model were:

1. To decrease the family's resistance to treatment.
2. To redefine substance use as a family problem.
3. To reestablish parental influence.
4. To interrupt dysfunctional sequences of family behavior.
5. To assess the interpersonal function of the drug abuse.
6. To implement change strategies consistent with the family's interpersonal functioning.
7. To provide assertion training skills for the adolescent and any high-risk siblings.

More than one half of the adolescents receiving this brief therapy model made clinically reliable decreases in their substance use as compared to just over one third of adolescents whose families received a parent skills training program using a psychoeducational approach.

Regardless of what method or approach is used, the family must be involved. Regardless of what specific family interactions are targeted for change, there are several common goals that should be addressed with families. The first principle of family treatment is breaking through any parental denial about the existence of a substance-abuse problem and persuading them to initiate efforts to achieve at least a temporary abstinence and level of control over the adolescent. The next step is helping the parents to establish or reestablish structure with consistent limit-setting and careful monitoring of the adolescent's activities and behavior. This step is perhaps the most difficult, as other factors often block the way. These factors include parental substance abuse/dependency and other psychopathology, weak parental coalitions, and the adolescent's substance abuse serving as a functional, albeit maladaptive, purpose within the family. Finally, the therapists seek to develop a healthy family system through the improvement of interfamilial communication and other family coping mechanisms.

The chances for success of family interventions often presume a minimum level of family involvement and motivations. In families where parental addiction, physical, and/or sexual abuse are issues, the absence of parental support will likely diminish the effectiveness of family approaches. In some programs serving urban youth, including runaways and essentially emancipated adolescents, family issues might be presented as an issue to understand to promote recovery rather than for resolution with family unification as a reasonable goal.

COGNITIVE-BEHAVIORAL METHODS

In view of the variety of environmental and learning factors associated with the development and maintenance of adolescent substance use and abuse, behavior therapists and other professionals have developed a variety of behavioral and cognitive-behavioral methods to target both substance use behaviors and a host of associated behavioral and emotional problems. Among the behavioral and cognitive behavioral methods most commonly used are social skills training including problem-solving skills and anger-control training, cognitive therapy, relapse prevention, and aversion therapy. The use of these interventions alone or together, especially in concert with more traditional methods such as 12-step work, offers the core of a potential integrated approach to the treatment of adolescent substance abusers. Other treatment modalities also have inherent behavioral elements. Family therapy often incorporates operant techniques, such as contingency contracting. Self-support groups, such as AA and NA, appear to have cognitive elements as members learn to think in alternative ways in response to substance use cues.

Social Skills Training

Numerous studies have pointed to an association between poor interpersonal skills in childhood and later problems in adolescence (Furnham, 1986). The rationale for the use of social skills interventions is based on evidence that individuals use psychoactive substances to decrease social anxiety and to increase assertiveness and perceptions of self-efficacy in interpersonal contexts (Van Hasselt, Hersen, & Milliones, 1978). Mostly designed for adult substance abusers, a variety of social skills interventions have been developed (Chaney, 1989; Van Hasselt, Hersen, & Milliones, 1978). Social skills are a prominent component of many recent prevention efforts with children and young adolescents (Kumpfer, 1989).

Although increasingly incorporated in the treatment programming in a variety of adolescent treatment settings, social skills interventions have been the focus of evaluation by researchers on several occasions. In a program called "Project Skills," Hawkins, Catalano, and Wells (1986) used a combination of behavioral skills training, involvement in prosocial activities, and social network development to treat adolescents in therapeutic communities. The skills sessions used such behavioral techniques as instructions, role-playing, modeling, feedback, and group discussion and evaluation to improve social introductions and assertion, alcohol and drug refusal, giving and receiving praise and criticism, problem-solving, and stress management. Results from the project demonstrated improved performance in situations which involved the previously listed skills. Haggerty, Wells, Jenson, Catalano, and Hawkins (1989) developed a similar approach in "Project ADAPT" for institutionalized delinquents with significant substance use problems. This project identified seven skills areas for intervention:

1. Consequential thinking to identify the antecedents and consequences of substance use behavior.
2. Self-control in resisting impulses to use substances and peer pressure and to develop drug refusal skills.
3. Avoiding trouble by identifying and avoiding high-risk situations for substance use and associated problem behaviors.
4. Social networking by identifying prosocial activities and new, nonsubstance-using friends.
5. Coping with authority by using negotiation and compliance skills.
6. Problem-solving by generating effective and prosocial solutions in difficult situations.
7. Relapse-coping by developing strategies for dealing with subsequent substance use behavior.

An inventory of social skills can be quite enormous (Table 9.2). To review each of these areas in an adequate fashion by using techniques such as role-playing, modeling, and feedback would be beyond the scope of all but the most long-term of treatment programs. A reasonable solution is to provide a framework for *social problem-solving skills* (SPSS) (Bukstein & Van Hasselt, 1993). Problem-solving involves the teaching of a four-step problem-solving sequence that can potentially be applied across difficult or high-risk situations: (1) Stop and identify the problem, (2) identify your goal(s), (3) generate possible solutions and determine the consequences of each solution, and (4) choose the most effective solution, evaluate its actual effectiveness, and self-reinforce for appropriate, adaptive behavior.

TABLE 9.2.   Social Skills for Adolescent Substance Abusers

Drug and Alcohol Refusal Skills

Relapse Prevention

Communication Skills
  Nonverbal communication
  Assertiveness training
  Negotiation/conflict resolution skills

Problem Solving Skills

Anger Control Training

Relaxation Training

Leisure-Time Management

Specific instruction can be applied in several performance areas that predict adequate social functioning. These areas include: conversation skills, friendship-making skills, dating skills, positive assertion (giving and receiving praise and compliments), and negative assertion (refusing unreasonable requests, including alcohol and drug refusal and standing up appropriately for one's rights). SPSS also includes instruction in social perception or the ability to identify the feelings and emotional states of others.

Anger control is a problem experienced by many adolescent substance abusers who describe poor impulse control, angry outbursts, and aggressive behavior and outbursts. An adaptation of Ecton and Feindler's (1990) anger control strategy incorporates a variety of cognitive-behavioral methods such as identification of anger triggers, relaxation techniques, the "broken record" technique, emphatic assertion, escalating assertion, and fogging by confusing the provoker with agreement.

Outlines of the basic skills to be covered are important with a specific skill or set of skills to be discussed during a particular session. The use of examples from the adolescent's experience is critical in order to engage the adolescent and convince him or her of the practical relevance of working on these skills. Staff should provide adolescents with "homework" or assignments to collect problem situations that might be later discussed individually or in group. Staff, parents, and other adults should appropriately and positively reinforce any success in using learned skills.

Behavioral contracting consists of the staff and adolescent mutually identifying specific problems and areas of deficit. Multiple treatment goals are developed weekly with positive reinforcers provided upon attainment of specified goals in planned incremental changes. Specific criteria are set for time and frequency limitations which constitute the behavior explicitly stated on the contract. The behavior must be observable and, preferably, measurable. Upon attainment or maintenance of goals, contracts are usually renegotiated to require further progress toward a final, long-term goal. Behavioral contracting serves as a prompt for the patient to focus on specific treatment goals and to improve patient motivation by involving the adolescent in the development of goals and rewards (Bukstein & Van Hasselt, 1993). Contingency contracting also prepares the adolescents for contracting with his or her parents upon return home.

Cognitive Therapy

Cognitive therapy is the label given to a variety of therapeutic approaches that seek to modify the patient's or adolescent's thinking, especially the premises, assumptions, and attitudes underlying his or her cognition (Meichenbaum, 1977). For adolescent substance abusers, the high prevalence of depression, the existence of distorted attributions about the ability of alcohol and/or other drugs to affect the adolescent's life in a positive manner are each potential targets for cognitive approaches. Preliminary evidence indicates that a significant portion of adolescent substance abusers report cognitive distortions and negative internalized self-statements (Van Hasselt, Kempton, Null, & Bukstein, 1993). Although cognitive therapy is being used increasingly in the treatment of adults with substance abuse problems (Beck, Wright, Newman, & Liese, 1993), there is currently little research to demonstrate the efficacy of cognitive methods for adolescent substance abusers. Cognitive approaches appear to show promise for adolescents with depression (Lewinson, Clarke, Hops, & Andrews, 1990).

A cognitive approach is characterized by being collaborative, active, and highly structured and focused (Beck et al., 1993). Beck and colleagues propose a set of addictive beliefs that fuel substance use behavior. Among these beliefs are the fear of intolerable withdrawal effects and the individual's sense of helplessness in controlling the craving for further substance use.

Relapse prevention can also be seen from a cognitive perspective. Cognitive therapy can provide practical techniques for predicting and controlling relapse, identification of and coping with high-risk situations for relapse, keeping a lapse from becoming a relapse, using advantages-disadvantages analysis, and using social support networks (Beck et al., 1993).

Relapse Prevention

Relapse or a return to substance use or a previous pattern of substance abuse is a critical concern for any treatment program using lifetime or even indefinite abstinence as a goal for treatment success. Unfortunately, a return to some level of substance use is more likely the rule rather than the exception for adolescents at some point after treatment (see Chapter 8). Relapse need not be intentional, but the result is the same with a real risk of a return to previous levels of substance abuse and psychosocial dysfunction.

The adult research literature identifies several salient characteristics of relapse. Relapse situations often involve interpersonal conflict, social pressure to use, exposure to substance-related environments, or experiencing negative emotional states including social anxiety (Marlatt & Gordon, 1980). For adolescents, research suggests that two or more relapses within the first three months after treatment are a major risk for returning to a pathological pattern of substance use (Brown, Vik, & Creamer, 1989). Brown and associates (1989) reported that a majority (approximately two-thirds) of post-treatment relapses involved direct social pressure to drink; over half of the relapse situation occurred within a social context. In the same study, one third of the adolescents experiencing a relapse reported attempts to cope with a negative affective state (depression and/or anger and frustration) at the time of relapse. While a single relapse does not necessarily portend treatment failure, repeated, severe relapses within the first three months of post-treatment are more ominous in predicting a return to abusive patterns of use.

In response to this information about relapse in both adolescents and adults, professionals have developed extensive, cognitive-behavioral-based interventions to prepare substance abusers for post-treatment experience and exposure to situations that are high-risk for a return to substance use and abuse. The goal of relapse prevention is to increase the adolescent's awareness of relapse risk, high-risk situations for relapse, and the development and implementation of strategies for dealing with these situations and the relapse should it occur. Although relapse prevention should be individualized so that each adolescent can identify his or her own high-risk situation and negative effects as well as specific responses to these situations, relapse prevention is often presented in group form similar to other skills interventions. Modeling, role-playing, feedback, and other behavioral group techniques are very important. As previously noted, relapse prevention can be considered another "problem" to be included in a more comprehensive problem-solving skills curriculum. Identification of "triggers" or high-risk situations is useful within a generic set of problem-solving steps that can be easily remembered and hopefully utilized by the adolescent in any one of a number of problem situations.

Aversion Interventions

The goal of *aversion interventions* is to reduce or eliminate the craving or desire for alcohol or other drugs. Usually noxious stimuli such as nausea or electrical shock is paired with urges or impulses to use psychoactive substances via a classical conditioning paradigm. Such methods have a very limited usefulness in adolescents due to the stressful nature of the noxious experiences, the need for medical supervision, and the high dropout rates (Rimmele, Miller, & Dougher, 1989). Covert sensitization involves cognitive pairing uncomfortable feelings (e.g., nausea or vomiting) and situations with exposure to illicit substances. Participants are asked to imagine these situations or scenarios and to experience relief from the uncomfortable feelings when the imagined exposure is ended. Covert sensitization appears to be safe, inexpensive, and involving minimal time; it has the potential for self-administration. These procedures usually require high levels of motivation and presumably the existence of a conditioned response to substances; therefore, covert sensitization procedures may be applicable to a limited number of adolescents.

Disulfiram (Antabuse) use for adolescents with alcohol abuse or dependency is not advised because of its potential for medical problems and high rate of poor compliance among youth.

Aversive methods likely have limited usefulness in the adolescent treatment population. However, the most effective aversive method may be the consistent use of negative consequences from those who possess some level of control over areas of the adolescent's life, such as a probation officer or a parent.

Other Behavioral Methods

Contingency-management procedures may offer a potentially successful strategy in the treatment of adolescent substance abusers. Higgins and associates (1993) describe an approach used for cocaine-abusing adults where negative urine specimens are rewarded retail items, activities, lottery tickets, and vouchers. In addition, a community reinforcement approach was provided by significant others in agreed-upon activities when urine tested negative. These behavioral approaches were combined with education in recognizing the antecedents and consequences of cocaine use, employment counseling and assistance, and recreational activity counseling. This combined approach produced higher rates of program completion and abstinence than a comparison group treated with individual and group sessions providing supportive and confrontative therapy and didactic material based on the disease model and self-help orientation.

While many may argue that abstinence and freedom from the consequences of substance abuse should be sufficient motivation for treatment success, adolescents—by virtue of their concrete way of viewing their lives and the world around them—may require some level of real, material incentives and/or social reinforcement for their efforts rather than the absence of punishment.

PSYCHOPHARMACOLOGY

Within most treatment programs for substance-abusing adolescents, medication has only recently become a viable treatment option. Despite the change in attitudes of many treatment professionals and the arrival of more pragmatic, eclectic treatment professionals, there remain individuals who strongly believe that medications should be used in addicted individuals only in cases of medical emergency, that is life or death. Among these individuals, the use of psychoactive medications to therapeutically change mood or to control anxiety is antithetical to the AA/NA, 12-step philosophy. "Drugs" are why the patient, in this case the adolescent, is in treatment in the first place. Fortunately, our overall understanding of psychopathology, including comorbid conditions has developed considerably over the past decade. Alcoholics and other substance abusers can be depressed or anxious and these conditions can affect their response to other treatments and their risk for relapse. There is no compelling evidence that other forms of psychopathology cannot be treated concurrently with substance abuse/dependence in adolescents.

Knowing that we *can* treat comorbid psychopathology is not necessarily knowing *how* to treat it successfully. Guidelines for the treatment of coexisting psychopathology are only now being developed for adults (American Psychiatric Association, Work Group on Substance Related Disorders, in preparation). Given the uncertainty of treatment approaches for children and adolescents in general, treatments for adolescent substance abusers remains uncharted territory with few, if any, quality research studies to back up specific treatment recommendations. *Psychopharmacology,* or the use of medications to treat emotional and/or behavioral disorders, can be an important treatment component for adolescents. Based on the existing adult literature and experience using medications with substance-abusing youth, I will review some basic guidelines for the use of psychopharmacologic agents.

Pharmacotherapy can be effective in the treatment of adults with a variety of substance abuse disorders. For cocaine treatment, dopamine activities such as bromocriptine and amantadine have been used to decrease craving and dysphoria during cocaine withdrawal (Giannini, Baumgartel, & DiMarzio, 1987; Tennant & Sagerian, 1987). A number of studies have indicated the value of tricyclic antidepressants, particularly desipramine, in attenuating the craving and dysphoria associated with cocaine withdrawal (Giannini, Malone, Giannine, Price, & Loiselle, 1986; Tennant & Tarver, 1984). However, these agents may have limited efficacy for use in cocaine abuse in specific adult populations (Meyer, 1992). For alcohol dependence, disulfiam (Antabuse) may be helpful in maintaining abstinence in adults through the threat of a noxious reaction when alcohol is consumed. The efficacy of lithium carbonate in helping to reduce drinking is uncertain due to conflicting evidence (Fawcett, Clark, & Aagesen, 1987; Goodwin, 1982). For opiate addiction, a variety of agents can be used for withdrawal (methodone, cloinidine), maintenance (methadone, LAAM), and opiate antagonists and activities that block opiate receptor sites and prevent the reinforcing psychoactive effects of opiates (naltexone) (Greenstein, Fudala, & O'Brien, 1992).

Although past evidence is equivocal regarding the efficacy of tricyclic antidepressants for depression associated with alcoholism (Liskow & Goodwin,

1987), recent preliminary data indicates that selective serotonin activities may significantly reduce problem drinking in nondepressed social drinkers (Naranjo, Kadlec, San Leieza, Woodley-Remus, & Sellars, 1990) and in nondepressed alcoholics (Lawrin, Naranjo, & Sellars, 1986), although these changes in alcohol intake did not appear to be related to changes in depressive symptoms. In another preliminary report of the treatment of suicidal depressed alcoholics, Cornelius and associates (1993, 1994) reported both improvement in mood and alcohol consumption in both open and double-blind placebo trials.

Unfortunately, similar data does not exist in demonstrating the efficacy of antidepressants for depressed adolescent substance abusers. In fact, pharmacologic studies of adolescents have usually attempted to avoid comorbidity, especially that of substance abuse, for fear of contaminating pure depression and the search for proof of psychopharmacologic effectiveness (Rudorfer, 1993). The reality of high levels of comorbidity in adolescents demands the trial of therapeutic agents on both an open clinical basis and in controlled research trials of comorbid populations. There is no compelling reason why agents used for pure disorders may not be tried with adolescents having comorbid disorders.

A comprehensive review of the psychopharmacologic treatment of adolescent psychiatric disorders is beyond the scope of this chapter and book (see Green, 1991; Rosenberg, Holttrum, & Gershon, 1994; Werry & Aman, 1993).

There are three broad potential target areas for pharmacotherapy among adolescent substance abusers: (1) treatment of withdrawal effects, (2) specific treatment of the substance use behavior itself, and (3) treatment of coexisting psychiatric disorder(s). General principles of the treatment of withdrawal syndromes is covered in Chapter 6. While infrequent, the treatment of withdrawal symptoms in adolescents should proceed as the treatment of these symptoms does in adults. Unless the clinician obtains a history of withdrawal symptoms or quantities and/or frequencies of specific substance use sufficient to produce a withdrawal syndrome, careful monitoring for the emergence of symptoms followed by treatment of observed or reported symptoms is the suggested course.

Specific treatment of substance abuse behavior includes drug substitution (for example, methadone maintenance), antagonist therapy (e.g., naltrexone), aversion agents (e.g., disulfiram), or agents theoretically directed toward brain neurotransmitter systems which may underlie neuroadaptation to the particular substance, craving, or other substance use-reinforcement mechanisms (e.g., carbamazepine or serotonergic agents such a fluoxetine or sertraline). Results of pharmacologic trials of adult cocaine addicts with such agents as desipramine, amantadine, and buproprion are mixed, at best (Meyer, 1992). There are case studies of adolescents treated effectively with desipramine for cocaine dependence (Kaminer, 1992). While there are opiate-dependent adolescents, especially in urban, inner-city areas, the use of maintenance strategies such as methadone is often discouraged or prohibited by law.

Given the absence of a proven efficacious agent, the pharmacologic treatment of substance-abusing adolescents without significant coexisting psychopathology should be considered and reserved for only the most treatment-resistant cases.

Pharmacologic treatment of substance-abusing adolescents with coexisting psychiatric disorders may be the most commonly encountered clinical situation. Perhaps the biggest potential error in considering medications in the treatment of adolescent substance abusers with comorbid psychopathology is an overemphasis in attempting to determine the primary disorder. For example, if substance abuse is primary, then abstinence is the cure. This may not be the case, at least for depressive disorders. In one available study (Bukstein, Glancy, & Kaminer, 1992), the primary-secondary distinction did not predict remission of depressive symptoms upon short-term abstinence. Although initial, short-term attempts to treat depressive symptoms with abstinence should be made. Persistence of the symptoms beyond several weeks should alert the clinician that antidepressants or other medications may be needed. Other factors which may prompt more aggressive medication treatment include: (1) psychiatric symptoms definitely predating the substance use or abuse, (2) a significant family history of the psychiatric disorder, (3) past treatment failures and relapses, and (4) past successful treatment of the psychiatric disorder with medication.

The major objection to the use of psychoactive agents to treat substance abusers has been the fear of abuse of that agent or seeming to promote a drug-use philosophy which may prompt future substance use or abuse by adolescents. While understandable, there is no empirical evidence to support these fears. Many, if not most adolescents, can take medications without abusing them or becoming dependant on them. Compliance with a medication regimen over a sufficient period of time is a much greater problem than abuse according to our experience. Psychotherapeutic agents may be abused or sold by addicted or sociopathic parents. Some agents present a greater risk for abuse than others.

The use of stimulants (that is, methylphenidate, dextroamphetamine, pemoline) in the high percentage of adolescent substance-abusers who are diagnosed with attention-deficit hyperactivity disorder is a difficult and often vexing decision. Stimulants are among the most efficacious psychotherapeutic agents for children and adolescents, yet they are potential agents of abuse by both adolescents and their families (Goyer, Davis, & Rapoport, 1979; Fulton & Yates, 1988). The presence of ADHD with symptoms and behaviors of impulsivity and poor problem-solving can assist the development and maintenance of a substance abuse problem. Stimulants are often quite effective in reducing a variety of problematic, deviant behaviors that are often related to adolescent substance abuse. For another class of potential agents of abuse, benzodiazepines, the clinician almost always has an alternative agent (usually antidepressants) or behavior therapy to target significant anxiety symptoms or disorder. Pemoline, unlike methylphenidate and dextroamphetamine, is a stimulant that is classified as a schedule IV drug by the Drug Enforcement Administration (DEA). With less abuse potential, pemoline can be considered for adolescents with coexisting ADHD and substance abuse. Alternatives to stimulants for ADHD include desipramine and buproprion.

With careful supervision by parents or other responsible adults (including school personnel), stimulants may be given to substance-abusing adolescents without being abused. To prevent stimulant abuse or decrease its risk, the clinician should evaluate both adolescent and family members for histories of stimulant or other substance abuse or antisocial behavior.

Community Modalities

It is usually difficult to participate in a deviant activity such as substance use while one participates in prosocial activities. It is important not only to identify such activities within a community for adolescents in recovery, but also to make these activities accessible to them and to maximize the chances that an adolescent will succeed in and benefit from these activities. Prosocial activities may be the vehicle for the adolescent to develop social skills and to meet nonsubstance-using peers. The participation of nonsubstance-abusing peers is often essential to the success of these programs or activities.

Many adolescents will need vocational training in order to develop skills to support themselves in later life. Such training needs to be practical and tied to employment opportunities.

In addition to prosocial activities, the adolescent often will require support that he or she does not receive from the family. Sources of such support can

TABLE 9.3. Target Symptoms/Disorders and Medications for Adolescent Substance Abusers

Target Symptoms/Disorders	Medication Options
Depression/Dysthymia/Poor Mood Regulation	Tricyclic antidepressants Serotonin re-uptake inhibitors Bupropion
Bipolar Disorder/Cyclothymia	Lithium Carbamazepine Valproic acid
Attention Deficit Hyperactivity Disorder	Pemoline Methylphenidate Dextroamphetamine Tricyclic antidepressants Clonidine
Severe Aggressive Behavior	Serotonin re-uptake inhibitors Lithium

include counselors, clergy, teachers, and other school staff. Mentoring by positive community role models offers an alternative method of exposing the adolescent to positive activities, role models for behavior, and support (Freeman, 1993).

Alternative Modalities

Some treatment programs have adopted wilderness or other outdoor experiences as part of their programming. Most of these experiences are adaptations of Outward Bound courses which utilize a variety of outdoor or wilderness experiences. The most common outdoor experiences used by adolescent treatment programs are "ropes courses." The term *ropes course* is a generic term to describe a variety of physical activities which can be used to satisfy a wide range of educational and therapeutic activities (Fischesser, 1991). Simpler courses typically involve group problem-solving and target-establishing cooperation, communication, listening, and planning. More advanced experiences also target group support, but place more emphasis on personal challenges, risk-taking, and development of a sense of accomplishment. These experiences range from a brief experience (several hours) in some programs to wilderness trips of several months. Many of these experiences are intended to be well-integrated into the overall programs of the treatment programs.

How well such programs have fared in this era of managed health care scrutiny is uncertain. There is no significant evidence that such programs achieve their goals, especially beyond the short-term. While these experiences often provide an exciting alternative "high" and may be seductive in attracting adolescents and their families, they are unlikely to be readily available in the adolescent's general environment. There is also some question as to whether the improved trust, communication, and problem-solving can be generalized to the adolescent's home environment and produce lasting change.

While there is no reason why a modest amount of these experiences should not be incorporated into the treatment modality mix of some treatment programs, the decision to involve individual adolescents should be based on the adolescent's specific needs and characteristics. For example, some adolescents with significant levels of coexisting psychopathology may not be good candidates.

Wilderness activities, along with any other alternative treatment experiences, should emphasize the development of prosocial interests, skills, and activities which can be maintained when the adolescents returns home.

COMBINING TREATMENT APPROACHES:
A COMPREHENSIVE MODEL

Despite originating from varied theoretical orientations, traditional treatment methods, family treatment, cognitive-behavioral methods, and medication are not inherently incompatible. In fact, my experience using a comprehensive approach allows me to suggest that these modalities are potentially complementary. Traditional approaches appear to work best to confront denial, motivate for treatment, and provide a framework or guide to recovery through the 12 steps. The provision of support, role models for recovery, and new peers presumably similarly motivated to remain abstinent are important aspects of the traditional model essential for successful maintenance and prevention of relapse. Family treatment offers the opportunity to improve communication between family members and increase structure, limits, and supervision within the household; it allows the constituent family members to better function in their appropriate family roles. Cognitive-behavioral methods give the adolescent and his or her family the skills necessary to improve psychosocial functioning and communication. Medication, when appropriate, targets the extreme affective states (mood and/or anxiety), impulsivity and poor attention which may predate substance abuse or may be persistent following the achievement of abstinence. Each of these seemingly diverse approaches or modalities targets important aspects which contribute to the onset, maintenance, and threat of relapse of substance abuse in adolescents.

In view of the multiple risk factors for the development of substance abuse problems in adolescents, the frequent presence of comorbid psychopathology, and the multiple deficits in social skills and family functioning, the use of multiple modalities is often required in the treatment of adolescent substance abusers.

THE FUTURE OF TREATMENT FOR ADOLESCENT SUBSTANCE ABUSE

As the little research available appears to demonstrate, treatment, at least in general, works. What we do not know for certain are the differential effects of various modalities, either alone or together. Nor do we know the effects of certain types of treatment on certain subgroups of adolescents who vary on racial or ethnic status or some special characteristic such as hopelessness, pregnancy, or HIV-positive. That we continue to pursue treatment for all adolescents manifesting problems with substance abuse seems obvious. However, we should proceed with caution, asking questions about what we are doing for youth, how we are doing it, and what effects our actions have—positive and negative—for the adolescents that we treat.

CHAPTER 10

Prevention

While acknowledging the importance of treatment for substance-abusing adolescents, the most effective intervention is preventing the initial development of substance use or abuse in adolescents. Prevention has received much attention and funding during the past two decades. However, we continue to search for truly effective prevention interventions for adolescent substance abuse, although both past and current efforts appear to have marginal, if any, success in preventing substance abuse. This chapter will explore important issues in the conceptualization, development, implementation, and evaluation of programs for the prevention of substance abuse in adolescents. By examining the success—or lack of success—of past programs, we can identify ingredients for future prevention programs that may hold more promise for success.

What Are We Preventing?

One factor inhibiting the development of effective prevention efforts is the lack of a consensus of a conceptual goal of prevention efforts. Exactly what are we attempting to prevent (see Table 10.1)? Prevention of the onset of substance abuse by adolescents appears to be the most obvious goal. However, others have proposed a range of prevention targets or goals including prevention of the onset of any substance use by children or adolescents, the onset of use or progression to the abuse of specific substances, the early onset of substance use, and the prevention of the consequences of substance use. On a broader view, many consider the most salient prevention goal to be the prevention or attenuation of the risk factors for adolescent substance abuse. While ultimately more costly and

TABLE 10.1. **Targets for Prevention**

Prevent onset of substance use
Prevent onset of substance abuse
Prevent *early* onset of substance use
Prevent *consequences* of substance use
Prevent or reduce *risk factors* for substance use/abuse
Increase *protective factor* which reduces risk of substance use/abuse

requiring more intensive interventions across a wide variety of social, environmental, psychological, and behavioral domains, prevention efforts aimed at
risk factors are more likely to be more effective and influence the development of a wider range of dysfunctional behaviors and psychosocial problems.

Prevention in a Historical, Cultural Context

As mentioned in the first chapter of this book, perhaps the first "prevention"
efforts consisted of often rigid cultural and societal sanctions. In colonial days,
while drinking was taken for granted as a normal part of colonial and frontier
life, overt drunkenness was usually not tolerated and the offender was subject
to both legal proscription and public censure. Local custom and pressure influenced alcohol use by youth. Formal efforts at prevention would not be seen
until the moral education efforts of the Women's Christian Temperance Union
(WCTU) and other religious organizations. Moral education primarily consisted of appeals to religious beliefs, quotation of scripture, and threats of eternal damnation. Moral education in churches, schools and other social outlets
would remain the dominant attempt at prevention into the twentieth century
and up to the adoption of prohibition. Following the repeal of prohibition, prevention efforts, while losing some of the religious zeal, continued to focus on
appeals to fear. If real physical or social consequences of substance use could
not be found, they could easily be fabricated. Films such as "Reefer Madness"
pictured even the infrequent substance user as treading down the road to ruin.

Fear arousal would continue to be the primary mode of prevention as part of
efforts at drug education, starting in the 1960s (Battjes & Bell, 1985). In the
1970s, there was a significant change in emphasis from fear to a review of the
facts, that is, the established health consequences of substance use or abuse.
Few of these efforts, which were largely modeled on traditional heath educational models, proved to be very effective in preventing substance use or abuse
in the targeted adolescent populations.

Fortunately, research into the antecedents of adolescent substance abuse
began to provide guidance for policymakers, clinicians, and educators in their
attempts to develop effective prevention strategies. The identification of peer
factors as well as beliefs, attitudes, and values prompted a focus on these factors as targets for prevention interventions. Adolescents who used or abused
substances or those at risk for the development of substance abuse were seen as
deficient in certain social or adaptive skills and/or as having deviant attitudes
and beliefs which left them at increased risk for substance abuse. Prevention
interventions increasingly focused on values clarification, affective education,
social and coping skills. In the 1970s and into the 1980s, the role of family,
community, and social factors in promoting substance abuse became increasingly apparent as additional prevention efforts focused on these environmental

factors. Finally, during the past decade, the possible role of genetic and biologic factors such as tempermental traits (for example, impulsivity, high motor activity level, negative affect, and novelty-seeking) has suggested prevention efforts address these factors (Tarter, 1992).

Regardless of the specific focus of prevention interventions, current interventions are almost always based on addressing risk factors for the development and/or progression of substance use or abuse among children and adolescents (see Table 10.3).

FOCUS ON THE RISK FACTORS FOR
ADOLESCENT SUBSTANCE ABUSE

In devising and developing potential prevention interventions, researchers and clinicians look to research identifying risk factors, categories of risk factors, and their incorporation into theories that will explain the natural history for the development of substance abuse. Examples of types of prevention interventions are listed in Table 10.2. Presumably, prevention interventions will be devised to interrupt this progression to substance abuse by eliminating or decreasing risk factors or by strengthening or developing protective factors. Risk and protective factors in the context of theory form the basis for models for prevention and ultimately for interventions (see Table 10.3).

TABLE 10.2.   Types of Prevention Efforts

- Legal proscription
- Public/societal disapproval
- Moral education
- Targeting risk factors
- Fear tactics
- Education
- Improve attitudes/knowledge
- Improve values/decision-making
- Improve social competency skills
- Family-focused
    Family therapy
    Behavior management training
- Community-focused interventions
    Education/information
    Media messages
    Recreation/alternative activities
    Reduce access (e.g., laws, outlets)
- Early psychiatric/mental health intervention

TABLE 10.3.   Matching Risk Factors with Prevention Interventions

Risk Factors	Type of Intervention
Peer-related factors	Skills-based intervention
Individual factors	Skills-based intervention
Poor social skills	
Aggression/conduct disorder	Early MH referral
Poor academic progress	Academic assistance (tutoring, placement)
Family factors	Family therapy
	Parent management training
	Social support services/agency involvement
Biological factors	Early MH intervention treatment
	Behavioral oral treatment
	Medication treatment
	Family-oriented treatment
Community factors	
Access to substances	Changes in policies/laws
Community attitudes/ values	Improve socioeconomic conditions
Lack of recreational/	
alternative activities	
Lack of jobs	

Social Learning Theory and Models for Prevention

The large number of environmental risk factors or antecedents for substance use have suggested that substance use behavior is learned within an environmental context. Children, adolescents, and even adults learn a variety of behaviors through a process of modeling by parents and peers, and through reinforcement if specific behaviors are adopted or rejected. A child's or adolescent's susceptibility to various social influences is medicated by knowledge, beliefs, and attitudes, as well as by individual characteristics such self-esteem and tempermental traits.

Problem behavior theory (Jessor & Jessor, 1977) is a primarily developmental theory based on social learning theory concepts (Bandura, 1969) which states that the social environment (social supports, access, behavioral models) along with individual factors (attitudes, beliefs) places the adolescent at greater or lesser risk for problem alcohol use in the context of a variety of other problem behaviors. Adolescents will be motivated to engage in problem or deviant behaviors in as much as they perceive these behaviors as helping them to achieve desired goals such as coping, being accepted into a particular peer group, or achieving a desired self-image. The practical focus for prevention efforts based on *social learning theory* (SLT) or problem behavior theory is to reduce not only alcohol abuse but also other problem behaviors through delaying onset, minimizing use, and prevention of abusive patterns of use. This would be accomplished by first convincing adolescents that the risks outweigh the risk of substance use. Subsequently, alternative methods of achieving desired goals would be taught. *Domain theory* (Huba & Bentler, 1982) supports the role of self-perceived behavioral pressure from the adolescent's support system in determining the initiation of substance use. Prevention efforts based on the domain theory would focus on behavioral pressure and modifying the youth's support system including changing peer values, developing more prosocial role models, and providing more positive reinforcement for nonuse of substances.

There are many examples of prevention efforts based on social learning models. In fact, most prevention interventions fit SLT. SLT-based interventions include educational approaches, family-based interventions and many community-based projects.

Educational Approaches

Educational approaches include three major models for changing behavior (Moskowitz, 1989): (1) knowledge/attitude models, (2) values/decision-making models, and (3) social competency or skills models.

The *knowledge/attitude model* claims that an increase in knowledge will produce both a change in attitude and a subsequent change in behavior as well. For example, knowledge about the risks and negative consequences of substance use will produce negative attitudes toward substance use and reduced substance use. Knowledge-based approaches are rarely based on scare tactics, but attempt to provide information about the pharmacologic effects of various substances of abuse, the health and social consequences of substance use, school and community attitudes and norms, including legal sanctions for possession and use, and often general health education. In addition to videos, films, and written materials, outside speakers representing medical, sports, entertainment, and law enforcement fields provide testimonials to the danger of substance use. While many prevention projects have demonstrated significant improvements in adolescents' knowledge about substances, this has not translated into real behavior change.

Values/decision-making models promote the ability of adolescents to develop greater insight into themselves and to develop a self-concept and values on which they can base decisions about their behavior. Unfortunately, modern society presents so many mixed messages about values and behavior through peers, the media, and parents that a logically consistent message is difficult to sustain (Moskowitz, 1989).

Social competency or skills models suggest that youth at risk for substance abuse lack many psychosocial skills to behave appropriately and to refuse social pressure to use substances. In addition to including substance refusal or resistance skills, social competency-based approaches include the teaching of many generic skills involving improving interpersonal communication and problem-solving. A sample of the typical content of skills-based prevention interventions is listed in Table 10.4.

In one of the earliest examples of a social competency approach, Evans (1976) proposed countering social pressures or influences to smoke cigarettes by inoculating students with exposure to progressively more intense prosmoking influences and providing them with counterarguments to resist these influences or pressures. Despite minimal effects, this work has served as a model for the development of more sophisticated prevention interventions. Approaches dealing with peer pressures or social influences were expanded to include peer leaders and the use of role-modeling and social reinforcement techniques.

Almost all of the earlier examples of social influence and social competency approaches have targeted prevention of cigarette smoking. Evaluating the effectiveness of such programs finds modest but real reductions in the proportion of participants beginning to smoke or advancing to regular cigarette use (Botvin & Botvin, 1992). Upon follow-up, some effect continues, although generally decaying over time. The focus on cigarette smoking has allowed little evaluation in terms of program effects on the use of other substances, although one study reported reduced use of alcohol and marijuana (McAlister, Perry, & Killian, 1980). Unfortunately, researchers have used general populations of students, failing to focus on high-risk populations.

Researchers and prevention programmers have broadened the earlier focus on changing attitudes, beliefs, and behaviors specific to substance use to include the development of more generic skills to deal with a variety of interpersonal and intrapersonal factors. Botvin and associates (1990) developed *life skills training* (LST) to facilitate the development of generic life and coping which could also be specifically used to resist substance use. Specific goals include increasing self-esteem, resisting peer pressure, coping with anxiety, communication skills, and social skills. LST consists of three components: (1) a substance-specific component, (2) a personal skills component, and (3) a social skills component.

TABLE 10.4.   Content of Skills-Based Prevention Interventions

Education: Understanding effects/consequences of substances and substance use/abuse

Resisting peer pressure

Changing attitudes, values, and norms about substance abuse

Identifying and dealing with adult influences

Problem-solving strategy
    Techniques to promote self-control
    Relieving stress, anxiety, and pressure
    Developing assertiveness skills

Developing self-esteem (including goal-setting)

Communication skills

LST involves instruction, modeling, rehearsal, feedback, reinforcement and extended practice through homework. Botvin has reported significant reductions in the incitation of regular smoking for adolescents participating in two years of prevention programming when compared with nonparticipant controls. LST produced significant effects for alcohol and marijuana use. Work by Botvin and associates suggests that more intensive programming (several session per week) may be more effective than less intensive formats and that booster sessions may enhance and maintain program effects.

Wills and Schiffman (1985) developed a *decision skills curriculum* to target decision-making and cognitive coping to assist the adolescent in dealing with environmental stress which predisposes to substance abuse. Included in the eight modules of decision skills are values clarification, decision-making skills, dealing with social influences, assertiveness training, stress management, and health consequences.

Pentz's (1985) *social assertiveness skills training* is also based on a social competency model. The curriculum addresses social competency and self-efficacy via improving assertiveness, that is, the ability to appropriately disagree, agree, and refuse as well as to initiate conversations. Skills dealing with a variety of social situations are taught through modeling, rehearsal, and feedback. After learning concepts and practicing the identification of pressure situations, the students observe appropriate models and then practice these skills in a variety of situations. Achievement of skills is evaluated by behavioral assessment techniques, such as video taping role-play situations. The training consists of 10 approximately hour-long sessions. The curriculum provides a student manual and workbook, a parent workbook, student/parent workbooks, and suggested community outreach projects.

Pentz (1985) reports that evaluation of this prevention intervention demonstrates increased social competency and improved academic performance, and reduced substance use.

Cognitive behavioral skills training (Schinke & Gilcrist, 1984, 1885) deals with the development of decision-making and problem-solving skills for adolescents. This format teaches self-instruction techniques to assist youth achieve and maintain adequate self-control through high-risk situations. Participants also learn coping and relaxation techniques to deal with stress and anxiety. Similar to other skills approaches, modeling, feedback, reinforcement, and homework assignments are used to teach the curriculum.

Gilcrist and Schinke have reported the effectiveness of this approach in improving problem-solving, decision-making, and assertiveness skills as well as changing attitudes (Schinke & Gilcrist, 1985).

While each of these models suggests that skills acquisition is the key to prevention, some efforts concentrate specifically on skills to deal with substance use behaviors while others propose generic skills to deal with a range of problem situations and behaviors.

Despite the apparent effectiveness of such skills-oriented programs in at least delaying the onset of tobacco use in the participants, there remain many concerns about the overall effectiveness of these programs. Prevention researchers have questioned the real versus the statistical effectiveness of prevention interventions, especially in preventing substance use or abuse other than tobacco. Do these programs prevent significant numbers of youth from using alcohol or other drugs? High attrition rates, lack of a focus on high-risk youth, and lack of consideration of the prevention of substance abuse versus use tend to further raise questions about the ultimate effectiveness of these interventions in prevention.

For the most part, most educational approaches to the prevention of adolescent substance use or abuse have been school-based. For those programs that are voluntary, there is a concern about the potential for high rates of nonparticipation, especially by high-risk students, and attrition. Many programs have high costs and may intrude into the regular academic schedule.

Family-Focused Preventions

Family-focused prevention interventions are based on substantial research pointing to the role of parents and families in the development of adolescent substance abuse (Kumpfer, 1989). Although such family-focused interventions specifically for substance abuse prevention are scarce, there is considerable support for family or parent skills training for related problems, such as conduct disorder or delinquency (Dinkmeyer & McKay, 1976; Patterson, Chamberlain, & Reid, 1982). Family therapy for youth at risk for delinquent behavior appears to be an effective prevention strategy (Klein, Alexander, & Parsons, 1977). Family involvement in school-based programs or other prevention programs can reduce risk factors and affect parent management practices (Bry, 1985).

The *strengthening families program* (Demarsh & Kumpfer, 1985, 1986) combines parent training, children's social skills training, and a family skills training program for children of adult drug abusers in treatment. Within the family skills component, there were three phases: (1) a play therapy phase in which parents are taught to enjoy the child, (2) a family communications training, and (3) an effective discipline training phase. Each component appeared to reduce risk factors that were related to its goals.

Community-Focused Interventions

Community-focused prevention includes a variety of usually broad-based efforts that are targeted at the social environment of communities. Community organizations and media campaigns are the best examples.

Specific organizations formed to combat and prevent substance use among adolescents and others involve parents (e.g., Mothers Against Drunk Driving

(MADD), the National Federation of Parents), students (e.g., Students Against Drunk Driving (SADD)), teachers (PTA), and others. These community prevention groups act primarily as a method of education and information dissemination to increase community awareness of substance abuse, for parent and community support, and to support specific changes in laws, law enforcement, and public policy. The efficacy of community groups is very difficult to establish (Moskowitz & Jones, 1985). These groups may be limited in their effectiveness due to their high turnover and the absence of skills and knowledge to achieve real change.

Community organizations with more general goals (for example, the Chemical People) often develop prevention projects alone or in concert with other community groups or sponsor projects in the schools or the community. Frequently, coalitions of community groups form with an explicit goal of preventing and/or reducing substance use or abuse in youth.

The media, including television, radio, and magazines is a potent influence on the attitudes, beliefs and, ultimately, the behavior of youth. Although cigarette advertisements have been absent from television for decades, magazines are filled with glamorous images of smokers and drinkers. The use of cartoon camels in a cigarette ad has prompted much controversy when it was discovered that most children could readily identify both the character and the product (Fischer, Schwartz, Richards, Goldstein, & Rojas, 1991). Until recently, television programming often offered a similar characterization of substances users—smokers and/or drinkers—as models to emulate. Beer commercials use sports figures and other celebrities as spokespeople for their products. How much these media images influence adolescent substance use is uncertain. Atkin, Hocking, and Block (1984) found that patterns of beer and liquor consumption by adolescents were related to exposure to advertising and that adolescents with greater exposure to alcohol ads were at higher risk for heavy drinking and drinking while driving.

The abundance of pro-substance use messages are countered by public service advertising which is less frequent and often appears at times that the targets are less likely to view or hear them; in other words, these ads fail to reach their audience. Media efforts have often relied on a relatively narrow range of persuasion strategies. The messages provide information which ranges from the scare tactics of comparing a frying egg to your brain on drugs to factual information on the harmfulness of drugs on health. Unfortunately, the viewer is rarely left with ways of avoiding or saying "no" to drug use. Evaluation of media prevention efforts is rare and almost always inadequate. A consensus is that most of these media efforts have failed to change behavior (Flay & Sobel, 1983).

A coalition of media, advertising, and other corporate sponsors established the Partnership for a Drug-Free America in 1987 to decrease the social acceptance of drug use among youth and to provide information about drugs (specifically cocaine, crack, and marijuana) and drug use. The Partnership donated time and money to produce anti-drug messages. These messages did achieve a wide viewership and produced more positive views on nondrug-using individuals and more negative views of drug users, although these changes were smallest among adolescents (Black, 1988).

Despite the absence of evidence for the effectiveness of media prevention efforts, media prevention offers a number of potential advantages, including low cost per intended target, the ability to increase exposure through repetition of the message, and access to high-risk groups such as low-income and minority families who often view a particular medium such as television with greater frequency than other groups (Schilling & McAlister, 1990). Similar to other prevention efforts, media prevention models should use existing research and consider how to design messages to change attitudes and behaviors to change the perception of acceptability of substance use and support nonuse. Media efforts should target high-risk groups with messages that are designed specifically to reach those groups. The messages should be delivered by credible communicators. Media campaigns are likely to be most effective in reinforcing prevailing attitudes and societal norms and when combined with other prevention strategies (Flay & Sobel, 1983).

Prevention approaches targeting the prevailing school climate is a community-based approach that potentially offers an important adjunct to educational-based prevention efforts. In addition to emphasizing "drug-free" status and a no-tolerance attitude, multicomponent programs can improve school atmosphere by increasing cohesion and support among students, teachers, and administration.

Recreational activities and other alternative programs are becoming a very active area among community prevention approaches. The rationale is that by encouraging participation in prosocial activities and making these activities available to youth, then their attraction to and participation in more deviant activities such as substance abuse will diminish. These alternative activities can also be combined with other prevention approaches, such as skills development, to become more comprehensive interventions. The few available outcome results from such projects are mixed with participation in some activities producing decreased substance use while others show increased use (Swisher & Hu, 1983).

Many potential community interventions are only indirectly related to substance use or abuse. Community or neighborhood characteristics such as low socioeconomic status, high population density, low population mobility, physical deterioration, and high crime are associated with greater substance use in adolescence (Brook et al., 1990). Addressing larger social and economic problems, while costly and often politically difficult, may have the most significant potential effect on many of the most salient risk factors for substance use among youth.

Public Policy and Legal Efforts

Numerous regulatory efforts have had a modest but real effect on adolescent substance use (Moskowitz, 1989). The increase of the minimum legal drinking age to 21 in every state has reduced alcohol-related motor vehicle accidents, injuries, and fatalities among youth (Joksch, 1988; Saffer & Grossman, 1987). Other regulatory measures include increasing price and excise taxes, reducing the number of outlets selling alcoholic beverages for consumption, eliminating sales from poorly supervised outlets such as service stations, and restricting sales at public events. The efficacy of these latter measures for alcohol prevention is uncertain, although increases in the price of alcohol (achieved through increases in taxes) may negatively affect both the frequency and level of alcohol consumption (Moskowitz, 1989).

Laws for other substances which are illicit for the entire population also have an uncertain effect on adolescent use patterns. Increases in the enforcement of drinking-driving laws have produced short-term reductions in the incidence of drunk-driving, especially when accompanied by media exposure to these efforts (Moskowitz, 1989). Unfortunately, many efforts at increasing interdiction or increasing the arrests of the dealers has produced little effect in the price or availability of illicit substances (Polich, Ellickson, Reuter, & Kahan, 1984). The effect of the illicit nature of substance abuse in promoting use by appealing to the rebellious side of adolescent development is debatable. The Draconian laws against the sales of many illicit substances may have raised the exposure level of younger adolescents to many illicit substances as their juvenile status allowed a safer alternative to adults in acting as pushers, messengers, and other foot soldiers in the drug wars.

Despite legal prohibitions against substance use, alcohol and other drugs are still used and abused. Different communities have different influences which determine what is normative behavior, especially normative or acceptable alcohol and other drug abuse behavior. Adolescents who reside in communities that condone levels of substance use behavior are more likely to use substances (Grossman, 1985). When informal control institutions such as church and family break down, formal control systems with laws, regulation, and statutory consequences are needed to control substance use (Kumpfer, 1989). Unfortunately, the formal control system has failed to show lasting changes in substance use (Polich et al., 1984).

Targeting Biological Risk Factors

An emerging literature suggests that there are biological risk factors or vulnerabilities which may take the form of certain tempermental traits that place specific youth at risk for eventual substance abuse (Tarter, 1992). At this time, it is difficult to imagine a specific prevention intervention targeted to such biological risk factors as differences in evoked potentials, electroencephalograph (EEG), body sway, or differences in subjective responses to alcohol challenges. These risk markers offer more value as more specific identifiers of youth at risk for later substance abuse rather than as targets for intervention themselves. One such trait, high behavioral activity level, may also predispose to more discrete behavioral or psychiatric problems such as attention-deficit hyperactivity disorder and conduct disorder, which together are a risk factor for early onset substance use and abuse in adolescents. Data from the Epidemiologic Catchment Area Study shows a two- to two-and-a-half times increased risk for subsequent substance abuse for adolescents having depression or anxiety disorders.

While the secondary prevention of problems in youth involves the early treatment of behavioral and emotional problems, early, aggressive psychosocial treatment of psychiatric problems may result in diminished risk for substance abuse. Psychiatric treatment also involves somatic treatments such as medication (for example, stimulant treatment for ADHD or antidepressants for mood disorders). Despite the reluctance of many to use any psychoative medication—illicit or therapeutic—medication treatment of early psychiatric problems holds promise for decreasing the risk for subsequent substance abuse.

Comprehensive Prevention Programs

Programs targeting a single risk factor or set of related risk factors for substance abuse may be insufficient to produce significant and persistent changes in adolescent substance use and related behaviors (Battjes & Jones, 1985). Given the multitude of risk factors for adolescent substance use and abuse, research strongly suggests the targeting of multiple risk factors or influences to use substances as part of a comprehensive approach to prevention. The *Midwestern prevention program* in Kansas City involved eight communities which were randomly assigned to one of two types of programs (Johnson et al., 1990). The first, a more comprehensive program, involved school programming (social resistance skills training and normative influences modification), parent involvement, mass media, and training of community organizations. This comprehensive program was compared with a control program utilizing only the mass media and community organization components. The school-based program, delivered at either grades 6 or 7, showed a reduced rate of increase of marijuana and tobacco use three years later when compared with adolescents from the control program. Equivalent reductions were found for youth with both low and high levels of risk. Unfortunately, there did not appear to be significant effects on alcohol use.

A recognition of the importance of a community focus in the prevention of substance use and abuse among high-risk adolescents has resulted in prevention initiates from government agencies and the creation of the Office of

Substance Abuse Prevention (OSAP) through the Omnibus Anti-Drug Abuse Act of 1986. OSAP funded numerous community demonstration grants into the early 1990s. Unfortunately, many of these grants appeared to be awarded on the sole basis of their community orientation and emphasis with little attention to evaluating outcome; that is, did these programs work? Despite the likely development of many worthwhile prevention programs, we may never know if they were effective. With the reorganization of the Alcohol, Drug Abuse, and Mental Health Administration and the evolution of OSAP into its successor agency, the Center for Substance Abuse Prevention (CSAP); requests for applications for future grants will require an outcome evaluation component. The Midwestern prevention project represents an exception to the surprising paucity of evaluation and outcome data from recent prevention projects in the community.

The Current Status of Prevention

Does prevention work? From a review of past prevention efforts, one can only offer qualified assessment of the entire field. There are significant successes in each area of prevention. However, when considered next to the extent of adolescent substance use and abuse and its ultimate cost to society, these successes appear rather limited. Prevention can delay the onset of substance use, and in some cases, decrease the extent of substance use. Yet, in almost all cases, this effect is usually temporary and time-limited. Prevention efforts can change factors contributing to the high-risk status of youth. Changing these factors does not appear to necessarily produce changes in substance use or abuse.

Why? There appear to be several common problems to most prevention interventions. Some approaches are based on theories that are suspect. The specific goals of the program may not be clearly stated or may be too complex. The poor involvement or targeting of high-risk youth is common to many prevention efforts, especially past educational- and school-based approaches. Quality control of the specific intervention is often variable or poor. The design and implementation of many programs results in programs that are not intensive enough for the target population of youth. In addition to carefully matching the type and process of intervention to the target population, prevention programs must consider the developmental and cultural appropriateness of the intervention. Finally, in order to learn what works and for whom, prevention programs should develop and complete both process *and* outcome evaluation. Outcome evaluation should include the measurement of all meaningful outcome variables and substance use patterns as well as adaptive functioning in such major life domains as psychological, behavioral, family, academic, and social functioning. As discussed in the review of the prevention literature, prevention efforts should target broader areas of risk factors. Changing the short-term incidence of substance use or abuse may not be sufficient to alter the longer-term risk or extent of substance abuse among high-risk youth.

What works? Generally, the more successful programs are comprehensive programs which are skills-oriented, of sufficient intensity and duration, peer-led, and have follow-up or booster sessions. A more inclusive list of recommendations for future prevention programs or trials is provided in Table 10.5.

In stressing the community aspects of prevention, it is important to recognize the broader cultural-societal context of adolescent substance use/abuse. Regardless of the explicit messages of prevention programs, we must consider the implicit messages that may promote substance use or abuse within society as a whole or within specific subcultures. Alienation and poverty are among the most prominent factors that may help to perpetuate deviant behavior, including substance abuse, within many communities. These are the larger "risk factors" for substance abuse among youth that combine with an assortment of other risk factors to produce an often malignant problem that even the most comprehensive of prevention programs cannot hope to influence.

Unified Theories and Models for Prevention

What do we really know from more than a decade and a half of prevention projects and studies? The results suggest that several characteristics of prevention programs may predict their effectiveness. These characteristics include: quality and length of intervention, participation of parents/family, multicomponent interventions, and support of the program by administrators from relevant agencies (Johnson & Solis, 1983). The Midwestern prevention project offers a useful model of a comprehensive prevention program. The diversity of communities demands that prevention efforts take into account the characteristics and needs of communities that differ in socioeconomic, ethnic, and racial status. As adolescents at high risk for substance abuse are also at high risk for other problem behaviors such as delinquency, early sexual activity and pregnancy, and other risk-taking behaviors, programs should also be broad enough to incorporate interventions to target all or most of these high-risk behaviors.

TABLE 10.5.   Recommendations for Prevention Interventions

Interventions should be developmentally appropriate.

Interventions should be targeted and tailored to serve specific, high-risk populations.

Interventions should be comprehensive in targeting multiple risk factors across several life domains.

Interventions should proceed concurrently with changes in social policies and community variables.

Interventions should be longitudinal, providing reinforcement of previous interventions.

FUTURE ISSUES AND PROSPECTS

Prevention of adolescent substance abuse can work. However, similar to treatment efforts, prevention, as currently delivered, may not work very well. We have enough knowledge about past successes and failures to design potentially more effective prevention efforts. To truly make these newer prevention efforts more effective, we must be willing to make them count through an increased emphasis on comprehensiveness, targeting high-risk youth, appropriate evaluation of outcome, and additional efforts by society to improve the socioeconomic conditions in the communities where youth live. The latter issue is likely the most important and is certainly the most costly and socially controversial. Not to recognize the importance and impact of socioeconomic conditions on the escalation of substance experimentation to hard-core use, abuse, dependency, and severe negative consequences is to put a bandaid on cancer. Prevention does not involve doing a little, but doing a lot to produce the greatest effect possible on the many risk factors for adolescent substance use or abuse.

CHAPTER 11

Future Directions

The reason for presenting a book on adolescent substance abuse is to empha-size the unique nature of adolescents and their problems, including substance abuse. As adolescents are not adults and not the same as adults, their problems are also different. While adolescent substance abuse is similar in some respects to substance abuse in adults, this book has described its differences. One can-not expect to understand adolescent substance use or abuse merely by apply-ing adult standards of assessment and treatment. We know adolescent substance abuse is different, but we hardly know anything else about it.

Currently, almost all youth have some experience with alcohol. A substan-tial minority of adolescents use alcohol frequently and many develop problems related to use. Although patterns of use—in terms of types of substances used and prevalence of use—are constantly changing, many adolescents experiment with one or more substances (other than alcohol or tobacco). Whether prob-lems develop, most difficulties do not persist and most adolescents go on to adulthood without persistent substance abuse problems and without treatment. We need to account for such developmental patterns, including time-limited patterns of problem substance use, in our conceptualization of what substance abuse is.

We also need to consider the role of other problems, such as other types of deviant behavior and coexisting emotional or psychiatric problems, in the de-velopment and persistence of substance abuse in youth. It is becoming in-creasingly obvious that while substance abuse is a critical problem for an adolescent, it is seldom the only problem. A one-dimensional focus will rarely remedy the multiple ills that plague problem youth.

The presence of multiple problems usually requires multiple interventions, each targeting one or a variety of targets which represent areas of dysfunction in the adolescent's life. Similarly, prevention efforts need to have multiple tar-gets and interventions. We also need to be more focused in the targets and in-terventions that we select. Identifying risk factors for the development of adolescent substance abuse should proceed identifying affected, specific pop-ulations, and the development of specific, appropriate interventions for these high-risk youth.

Several critical areas are essential for study and action in the future.

1. *Define what adolescent substance abuse is.* Further empirical study is necessary to establish a valid diagnostic system for substance abuse among youth. Future research might include establishment of identifiable subgroups of adolescents differing from other subgroups in a variety of patterns of substance abuse, family factors, coexisting psychopathology, natural history, and treatment response. Research should also focus on relevant differences between individual substances of abuse and whether a broad definition of abuse fits for all substances in adolescents.

2. *What are specific risk factors for specific populations of youth?* Adolescents are not all the same. Identification of more specific risk factors which are responsive to specific, targeted interventions is the best hope for success in prevention of substance abuse and related problems.

3. *What are the patterns of substance abuse and coexisting psychiatric problems?* We need to broaden our view as to what we are identifying and treating. Substance abuse may be a part—an important part—of larger behavioral and/or emotional syndromes. Both the component behaviors and symptoms become potential targets for intervention.

4. *What works—in treatment?* To improve treatment outcome in those adolescents who do not appear to benefit from past treatment approaches, several issues need to be addressed in future research.

- The development of age-appropriate diagnostic criteria for alcohol abuse or dependence should assist in the identification of youths with alcohol use disorders. Further research into the development of adolescent alcohol use is needed to recognize adolescents at risk for continued alcohol abuse and in need of treatment.

- Treatment studies need to use more rigorous experimental design and methodology. This includes comprehensive standardized assessments (before, during, and after treatment), thorough inventories of treatment content (i.e., what kind of modalities are used and in what intensity), manual-guided interventions with specific content and procedures for implementing a specific intervention, and the use of appropriate controls.

- Treatment outcomes must be evaluated more thoroughly, with careful follow-up for several years. Outcome studies not only should consider abstinence or relapse status, but also should include all changes in drinking patterns as well as changes in psychosocial functioning such as mental health and behavior, school functioning, family functioning, and use of prosocial forms of recreation such as sports, music, and other hobbies.

- More nontraditional treatments such as behavioral interventions (e.g., social and problem-solving training, cognitive therapy, parent-management training which assist parents in setting behavioral limits for their adolescents), and medication treatment should be evaluated further, especially in patients in whom more traditional approaches are not effective. As with adults, it is likely that certain types and levels of treatment may be more suitable for certain types of adolescents. Treatment-matching; that is, matching each patient to an individual treatment modality, will therefore be a critical element of treatment research.

- Different treatment approaches may not be effective for all adolescents alike. Treatment studies therefore need to evaluate efficacy in specific populations of adolescents with regard to age, sex, race, ethnicity, socioeconomic status, and comorbid psychiatric status.

5. *What works—prevention?* Considerations that are similar to those for treatment apply to the future of prevention efforts. The aim should be the development of comprehensive, but specific, interventions for specific populations of high-risk youth. Interventions should provide skills as well as knowledge. Most important, larger socioeconomic conditions must be addressed in order to provide an environment conducive to prevention.

CONCLUSION

Adolescents are training to be adults. They copy adults and reflect the choices that adults must also make. It is hardly surprising that both culturally sanctioned substance use in the forms of alcohol and tobacco and illicit use of other substances is prevalent in adults, as well as youth. Our society is struggling to deal with the negative consequences of our involvement with psychoactive substances. As we have had limited success in handling the problem of adult substance abuse, the similar but quite distinct problem of adolescent substance abuse offers difficulty as well. We must recognize these facts. As we ask our clients and patients to break through their denial, we, too, must identify what the problem of adolescent substance abuse is and how we can best deal with it.

REFERENCES

Abraham, J. (1926). Psychological relations between sexuality and alcoholism. *International Journal of Psychoanalysis, 7*(2).

Abrams, D. B., & Niaura, R. S. (1987). Social learning theory. In H. T. Blane & K. E. Leonard (Eds.), *Psychological theories of drinking and alcoholism* (pp. 131–180). New York: Guilford.

Achenbach, T. M., & Edelbrock, C. S. (1983). *Manual for the Child Behavior Checklist and Revised Child Behavior Profile.* Burlington, VT: T. M. Achenbach.

Adler, I., & Kandel, D. B. (1981). Cross-cultural perspectives on developmental stages in adolescent drug use. *Journal of the Study of Alcohol, 42,* 701–715.

Alcohol Drug Abuse and Mental Health Administration (ADAMHA). (1991). *National household survey on drug abuse: Population estimates 1990.* Washington, DC: U.S. Government Printing Office.

Alexander, J. F., & Parsons, B. V. (1973). Short-term behavioral intervention with delinquent families: Impact on family process and recidivism. *Journal of Abnormal Psychology, 18,* 219–225.

Alexander, J. F., Waldon, H. B., Newberry, A. M., & Liddle, N. (1990). The functional family therapy model. In A. S. Friedman & S. Granick (Ed.), *Family therapy for adolescent drug abuse* (pp. 183–200). Lexington, MA: Lexington Books.

Alford, G. S., Koehler, R. A., & Leonard, J. (1991). Alcoholic anonymous-narcotics anonymous model inpatient treatment of chemically dependent adolescents: A 2-year outcome study. *Journal of Studies on Alcohol, 52,* 118–126.

Alterman, A. I., & Tarter, R. E. (1986). An examination of selected topologies: Hyperactivity, familial and antisocial alcoholism. In M. Galanter (Ed.), *Recent developments in alcoholism* (Vol. 4, pp. 169–189). New York: Plenum.

Alterman, A. I., Tarter, R. E., Baughman, T. G., Bober, B. A., & Fabian, S. A. (1985). Differentiation of alcoholics high and low in childhood hyperactivity. *Drug and Alcohol Dependence, 15,* 111–121.

American College of Sports Medicine. (1987). Position statement on the use of anabolic steroids in sports. *Medical Science Sports Exercises, 19,* 534–539.

American Psychiatric Association. (1980, 1987, 1994). *Diagnostic and statistical manual of mental disorders,* (3rd ed., 3rd ed. rev., 4th ed.). Washington, DC: Author.

American Psychiatric Association, Work Group on Substance Related Disorders. (in press). *Practice guidelines for the treatment of patients with substance related disorders: Alcohol, cocaine, opiods.* Washington, DC: Author.

American Society for Addiction Medicine (ASAM). (1990). Definition of alcoholism. *ASAM News, 4.*

Andersson, T., & Magnusson, D. (1988). Drinking habits and alcohol abuse among young men: A prospective longitudinal study. *Journal of Studies on Alcohol, 49*, 245–252.

Anslinger, H., & Cooper, G. (1937). Marijuana: Assassin of youth. *American Magazine, 18*.

Apter, A., Bleich, A., Plutchik, R., Mendelsohn, S., & Tyano, S. (1988). Suicidal behavior, depression, and conduct disorder in hospitalized adolescents. *Journal of the American Academy of Child and Adolescent Psychiatry, 27*, 696–699.

Aries, P. (1962). *Centuries of childhood*. New York: Vintage Books.

Armstrong, T. L. (1991). *Intensive interventions with high-risk youth: Promising approaches in juvenile probation and parole*. Money, NY: Criminal Justice Press.

Arndt, I. O., Dorozynsky, L., Woody, G. E., McLellan, A. T., & O'Brien, C. P. (1992). Desipramine treatment of cocaine dependence in methadone-maintained patients. *Archives of General Psychiatry, 49*, 888–893.

Asberg, M., Traskman, L., & Thoren, P. (1976). 5-HIAA in the cerebrospinal fluid: A biochemical suicide predictor? *Archives of General Psychiatry, 33*, 1193–1197.

Atkin, C., Hocking, J., & Block, M. (1984). Teenage drinking: Does advertising make a difference? *Journal of Communication, 34*, 157–167.

August, G. J., Stewart, M. A., & Holmes, C. S. (1983). A four-year follow-up of hyperactive boys with and without conduct disorder. *British Journal of Psychiatry, 143*, 192–198.

Bacchetti, P., & Moss, A. R. (1989). Incubation period of AIDS in San Francisco. *Nature, 338*, 251–253.

Bachman, J. G., Wallace, J. M., O'Malley, P. M., Johnston, L. D., Kurth, C. L., & Neighbors, H. W. (1991). Racial/ethnic differences in smoking, drinking and illicit drug use among American high school seniors, 1976–89. *American Journal of Public Health, 81*, 372–377.

Balfour, D. J. K. (1990). *Psychotropic drugs of abuse*. New York: Pergamon.

Ballanger, J. C., Goodwin, F. K., Major, F. L., & Brown, G. L. (1979). Alcohol and central serotonin metabolism in man. *Archives of General Psychiatry, 36*, 224–227.

Bandura, A. (1969). *Principles of behavior modification*. New York: Holt, Rinehart, & Winston.

Barkley, R. A., Fischer, M., Edelbrock, C. S., & Smallish, L. (1990). The adolescent outcome of hyperactive children diagnosed by research criteria: I. An 8-year prospective follow-up study. *Journal of the American Academy of Child and Adolescent Psychiatry, 29*, 546–557.

Barnea, Z., Rahav, G., & Teichman, M. (1987). The reliability and consistency of self-reports on substance use in a longitudinal study. *British Journal of Addiction, 82*, 891–898.

Barnes, G. M., & Welte, J. W. (1986). Patterns of alcohol use among 7–11th grade students in New York state. *Journal of Studies on Alcohol, 47*, 3–62.

Battjes, R. J., & Bell, C. S. (1985). Future directions in drug abuse research. In C. S. Bell & R. J. Battjes (Eds.), *Prevention research: Deterring drug abuse among children and adolescents* (pp. 221–228). Rockville, MD: Department of Health and Human Services, National Institute on Drug Abuse.

Battjes, R. J., & Jones, C. L. (1985). Implications of etiological research for preventative interventions and future research. In C. L. Jones & R. J. Battjes (Eds.), *Etiology of drug abuse: Implications for prevention* (pp. 269–276). Rockville, MD: Department of Health and Human Services, National Institute on Drug Abuse.

Baumrind, D. (1983). Familial antecedents of adolescent drug use: A developmental perspective. In C. L. Jones & R. J. Battjes (Eds.), *Etiology of drug abuse: Implications for prevention* (NIDA Research Monograph 56, pp. 13–44). Rockville, MD: Department of Health and Human Services.

Baumrind, D., & Moselle, K. A. (1985). A developmental perspective on adolescent drug abuse. *Advances in Alcohol and Substance Abuse, 5,* 41–67.

Beck, A. T., Ward, C. H., Mendelsohn, M., Mock, J., & Erbaugh, J. (1961). An inventory for measuring depression. *Archives of General Psychiatry, 42,* 667–675.

Beck, A. T., Weissman, A., & Kovacs, M. (1976). Alcoholism, hopelessness and suicidal behavior. *Journal of Studies on Alcohol, 37,* 66–77.

Beck, A. T., Wright, F. D., Newman, C. F., & Liese, B. S. (1993). *The cognitive therapy of substance abuse.* New York: Guilford.

Begleiter, H., & Porjesz, B. (1988). Potential biological markers in individuals at high risk for developing alcoholism. *Alcoholism: Clinical and Experimental Research, 12,* 488–493.

Behar, D., Winokur, G., & Berg, C. J. (1984). Depression in abstinent alcoholic. *American Journal of Psychiatry, 141,* 1105–1107.

Benowitz, N. L. (1988). Pharmacologic aspects of cigarette smoking and nicotine addiction. *New England Journal of Medicine, 319,* 1318–1330.

Benson, G., & Holmberg, M. D. (1984). Drug-related criminality among young people. *Acta Psychiatrica Scandanavia, 70,* 487–502.

Berkson, J. (1946). Limitations of the application of four-fold table analysis to hospital data. *Biometry Bulletin,* 47–53.

Beschner, G. M., & Friedman, A. S. (1985). Treatment of adolescent drug abusers. *International Journal of the Addictions, 20,* 971–993.

Birmacher, B., Stanley, M., Greenhill, L., Twomey, J., Gavrilescu, A., & Rabinovich, H. (1990). Platelet imipramine binding in children and adolescents with impulsive behavior. *Journal of the American Academy of Child and Adolescent Psychiatry, 29,* 914–918.

Black, G. S. (1988). *The attitudinal basis of drug use—1987* and *Changing attitudes toward drug use—1988.* Reports from the Media-advertising Partnership for a Drug-free America, Inc. Rochester, NY: Gordon S. Black Corp.

Blane, H. (1970). The personality of the alcoholic. In M. E. Chafetz (Ed.), *Frontiers of alcoholism.* New York: Aronson.

Blane, H. (1976). Middle-aged alcoholics and young drinkers. In H. Blane & M. Chafetz (Eds.), *Youth, alcohol and social policy* (pp. 5–38). New York: Plenum.

Blouin, A. G., Bornstein, R., & Trites, R. (1978). Teenage alcohol use among hyperactive children: A five-year follow-up study. *Journal of Pediatric Psychology, 3,* 188–194.

Blum, K., Noble, E. P., Sheridan, P. J., Montgomery, A., Ritchie, J., Jagadeeswaren, P., Nogami, H., Briggs, A. H., & Cohen, J. B. (1990). Allelic association of human dopamine D_2 receptor gene in alcoholism. *Journal of the American Medical Association, 263,* 2055–2060.

Bohman, M., Cloninger, R., Sigvardisson, S., & Von Knorring, A. L. (1982). Predisposition to petty criminality in Swedish adoptees. *Archives of General Psychiatry, 39,* 1233–1241.

Bolos, A. M., Dean, M., Lucas-Derse, S., Ramsbury, M., Brown, G. L., & Goldman, D. (1990). Population and pedigree studies reveal a lack of association between the dopamine D_2 receptor gene and alcoholism. *Journal of the American Medical Association, 264,* 3156–3160.

Bonnie, R. J., & Whitebread, C. H., II. (1974). *The marijuana conviction: A history of marijuana prohibition in the United States* (pp. 26–27). Charlottesville: University Press of Virginia.

Botvin, G. J., Baker, E., Dusenbury, L., Tortu, S., & Botvin, E. M. (1990). Preventing adolescent drug abuse through a multimodal cognitive-behavioral approach: Results of a three-year study. *Journal of Consulting and Clinical Psychology, 58,* 437–446.

Botvin, G. J., Baker, E., Filazzola, A. D., & Botvin, E. M. (1990). A cognitive-behavioral approach to substance abuse prevention: One-year follow-up. *Addictive Behaviors, 15,* 47–63.

Botvin, G. J., Baker, E., Renick, N. L., Filazzola, A. D., & Botvin, E. M. (1984). A cognitive-behavioral approach to substance abuse prevention. *Addictive Behaviors, 9,* 137–147.

Botvin, G. J., & Botvin, E. M. (1992). Adolescent tobacco, alcohol and drug abuse: Prevention strategies, empirical findings and assessment issues. *Developmental and Behavioral Pediatrics, 13,* 290–301.

Bower, K. J. (1992a). Addictive potential of anabolic steroids. *Psychiatric Annals, 22,* 30–34.

Bower, K. J. (1992b). Clinical assessment and treatment of anabolic steroid users. *Psychiatric Annals, 22,* 35–40.

Bower, K. J., Blow, F. C., Young, J. P., & Hill, E. M. (1991). Symptoms and correlates of anabolic-androgenic steroid dependence. *British Journal of Addiction, 86,* 759–768.

Bradley, B. P., Phillips, G., Green, L., & Gossop, M. (1989). Circumstances surrounding the initial relapse to opiate use following detoxification. *British Journal of Psychiatry, 154,* 354–359.

Branchey, L., Branchey, M., Shaw, S., & Lieber, C. S. (1984). Depression, suicide and aggression in alcoholics and their relationship to plasma amino acids. *Psychiatric Research, 12,* 219–226.

Brent, D. A., Kalas, R., Edelbrock, C., Costello, A. J., Dulcan, M. K., & Conover, N. (1986). Psychopathology and its relationship to suicidal ideation in childhood and adolescence. *Journal of the American Academy of Child Psychiatry, 25*, 666–673.

Brent, D. A., & Kolko, D. J. (1990). The assessment and treatment of children and adolescents at risk for suicide. In S. J. Blumenthal & D. J. Kupfer (Eds.), *Suicide over the life cycle* (pp. 253–302). Washington DC: American Psychiatric Press.

Brent, D. A., Perper, J. A., & Allman, C. (1987). Alcohol, firearms and suicide among youth: Temporal trends in Allegheny County, Pennsylvania, 1960 to 1983. *Journal of the American Medical Association, 257*, 3369–3372.

Brent, D. A., Perper, J. A., Goldstein, C. E., Kolko, D. J., Allan, M. J., Allman, C. J., & Zelenak, J. P. (1988). Risk factors for adolescent suicide: A comparison of adolescent suicide victims with suicidal inpatients. *Archives of General Psychiatry, 45*, 581–588.

Brook, J. S., Hamburg, B. A., Balka, E. B., & Wynn, P. S. (1992). Sequences of drug involvement in African-American and Puerto Rican adolescents. *Psychological Reports, 71*, 179–182.

Brook, J. S., Linkoff, I. F., & Whiteman, M. (1977). Peer, family and personality domains as related to adolescent's drug behavior. *Psychological Reports, 41*, 1095–1102.

Brook, J. S., Linkoff, I. F., & Whiteman, M. (1980). Initiation into adolescent marijuana use. *Journal of General Psychology, 137*, 133–142.

Brook, J. S., Whiteman, M., & Gordon, A. S. (1982). Qualitative and quantitative aspects of adolescent drug use: Interplay of personality, family and peer correlates. *Psychological Reports, 51*, 1151–1163.

Brook, J. S., Whiteman, M., Gordon, A. S., & Brook, D. W. (1990). The psychosocial etiology of adolescent drug use: A family interactional approach. *General Social Psychology Monographs, 116*.

Brook, J. S., Whiteman, M., Gordon, A. S., & Cohen, P. (1986). Dynamics of childhood and adolescent personality traits and adolescent drug use. *Developmental Psychology, 22*, 403–414.

Brooks-Gunn, J., & Furstenberg, F. F. (1989). Adolescent sexual behavior. *American Psychologist, 44*, 249–257.

Brown, S. A., Vik, P. N., & Creamer, V. A. (1989). Characteristics of relapse following adolescent substance abuse treatment. *Addictive Behaviors, 14*, 291–300.

Brunswick, A. F., & Boyle, J. M. (1979). Patterns of drug involvement: Developmental and secular influences on age at initiation. *Youth in Society, 2*, 139–162.

Bry, B. H. (1983). Predictive drug abuse: Review and reformulation. *Journal of the Addictions, 18*, 223–233.

Bry, B. H. (1985). Empirical foundations of family-based approaches to adolescent substance abuse. In T. J. Glynn, C. G. Leukefeld, & J. P. Ludford (Eds.), *Preventing adolescent drug abuse* (pp. 115–140). Rockville, MD: National Institute on Drug Abuse.

Bry, B. H. (1988). Family-based approaches to reducing adolescent substance use: Theories, techniques and findings. In E. R. Radhert & J. Grabowski (Eds.), *Adolescent drug abuse: Analyses of treatment research.* Washington, DC: U.S. Government Printing Office.

Bry, B. H., Conboy, C., & Bisgay, K. (1986). Decreasing adolescent drug use and school failure: Long-term effects of targeted family problem-solving training. *Child and Family Behavior Therapy, 8,* 43–59.

Bry, B. H., McKeon, P., & Pandina, R. S. (1982). Extent of drug use as a function of number of risk factors. *Journal of Abnormal Psychology, 91,* 273–279.

Buckley, W. E., Yesalis, C. E., Friedl, K. E., Anderson, W. A., Streit, A. L., & Wright, J. E. (1988). Estimated prevalence of anabolic steroid use among male high school seniors. *Journal of the American Medical Association, 260,* 3441–3445.

Bukstein, O. G., Brent, D. A., & Kaminer, Y. (1989). Comorbidity of substance abuse and other psychiatric disorders in adolescents. *American Journal of Psychiatry, 146,* 1131–1141.

Bukstein, O. G., Brent, D. A., Perper, J. A., Mortiz, G., Schweers, J., Roth, C., & Balach, L. (1993). Risk factors for completed suicide among adolescents with a lifetime history of substance abuse: A case control study. *Acta Psychiatrica Scandinavia, 88,* 403–408.

Bukstein, O. G., Glancy, L. J., & Kaminer, Y. (1992). Patterns of affective comorbidity in a clinical population of dually diagnosed adolescent substance abusers. *Journal of the American Academy of Child and Adolescent Psychiatry, 31,* 1041–1045.

Bukstein, O. G., & Kaminer, Y. (1993). The nosology of adolescent substance abuse. *American Journal on Addictions, 3,* 1–13.

Bukstein, O. G., & Van Hasselt, V. B. (1993). Alcohol and drug abuse. In A. S. Bellack & M. Hersen (Eds.), *Handbook of behavior therapy in the psychiatric setting* (pp. 453–475). New York: Plenum.

Bulik, C. M. (1987). Drug and alcohol use by bulimic women and their families. *American Journal of Psychiatry, 144,* 1604–1606.

Bulik, C. M., Sullivan, P. F., Epstein, L. H., Weltzin, T., & Kaye, W. (1992). Drug use in women with anorexia and bulimia. *International Journal of Eating Disorders, 11,* 213–225.

Bulik, C. M., Sullivan, P. F., McKee, M., Weltzin, T. E., & Kaye, W. H. (1994). Characteristics of bulimic women with and without alcohol abuse. *American Journal of Drug and Alcohol Abuse, 20,* 273–283.

Burke, K. C., Burke, J. D., Regier, D. A., & Rae, D. S. (1990). Age of onset of selected mental disorders in five community populations. *Archives of General Psychiatry, 47,* 511–518.

Buydens-Branchey, L., Branchey, M., Noumair, D., & Lieber, C. S. (1989). Age of alcoholism onset. II: relationship to susceptibility to serotonin precursor availability. *Archives of General Psychiatry, 46,* 231–236.

Cabaj, R. P. (1992). Substance abuse in the gay and lesbian community. In J. H. Lowinson, P. Ruiz, & R. B. Millman (Eds.), *Substance abuse: A comprehensive textbook* (pp. 852–860). Baltimore: Williams & Wilkins.

Cadoret, R. J., Cain, G. A., & Grove, W. M. (1980). Development of alcoholism in adoptees raised apart from alcoholic biologic parents. *Archives of General Psychiatry, 37,* 561–563.

Cadoret, R. J., Troughton, E., O'Gorman, T. W., & Heywood, E. (1986). An adoption study of genetic and environmental factors in drug abuse. *Archives of General Psychiatry, 43,* 1131–1136.

Caetano, R. (1987). Concepts of alcohol dependence. *Alcohol and Alcoholism, 23,* 225–230.

Cahalan, D., & Cisin, I. H. (1976). Drinking behavior and drinking problems in the United States. In B. Kissin & H. Begleiter (Eds.), *The biology of alcoholism* (Vol. 4, pp. 77–115). New York: Plenum.

Cantwell, D. (1972). Psychiatric illness in the families of hyperactive children. *Archives of General Psychiatry, 27,* 414–417.

Cappell, C., & Heiner, R. B. (1990). The intergenerational transmission of family aggression. *Journal of Family Violence, 5,* 135–152.

Cappell, H., & Herman, C. P. (1972). Alcoholism and tension reduction: A review. *Quarterly Journal of Studies on Alcohol, 33,* 33–64.

Cappell, H., & Greeley, J. (1987). In H. T. Blane & K. E. Leonard (Eds.), *Psychological theories of drinking and alcoholism* (pp. 15–54). New York: Guilford.

Castellani, S., Petrie, W. M., & Ellinwood, E. (1985). Drug-induced psychosis. In A. I. Aterman (Eds.), *Substance abuse and psychopathology* (pp. 173–210). New York: Plenum.

Catalano, R. F., Hawkins, J. D., Wells, E. A., Miller, J., & Brewer, D. (1990–1991). Evaluation of the effectiveness of adolescent drug abuse treatment, assessment of risks for relapse, and promising approaches for relapse prevention. *International Journal of the Addictions, 25,* 1085–1140.

Cates, W. (1990). The epidemiology and control of sexually transmitted diseases in adolescents. In M. Schydlower & M. Shafer (Eds.), *Adolescent medicine: State of the art reviews* (pp. 409–428). Philadelphia: Hunley and Beltus.

Centers for Disease Control. (1985). *Suicide surveillance 1970–1980.* Atlanta: U.S. Department of Health and Human Services, Public Health Service; Violent Epidemiology Branch, Center for Health Promotion and Education.

Centers for Disease Control. (1992). Selected behaviors that increase risk for HIV infection among high school students vs. 1990. *Morbidity and Mortality Weekly Report (MMWR), 41,* 231–240.

Chaiken, M. R., & Chaiken, J. M. (1984). Offender types and public policy. *Crime and Delinquency, 30,* 195–226.

Chambless, D. L., Cherney, J., Caputo, G. C., & Rheinstein, B. J. G. (1987). Anxiety disorders and alcoholism. *Journal of Anxiety Disorders, 1,* 29–40.

Chaney, E. F. (1989). Social skills training. In R. K. Heste & W. R. Miller (Eds.), *Handbook of alcoholism treatment approaches.* New York: Pergamon.

Chassin, L., Rogosch, F., & Barrera, M. (1991). Substance use and symptomatology among adolescent children of alcoholics. *Journal of Abnormal Psychology, 4,* 449–463.

Chemical Dependency Adolescent Assessment Project (CDAAP). (1988). *Project update*. St. Paul, MN.

Chicago Tribune. (June 3, 1929).

Childress, A. R., McLellan, A. T., & O'Brien, C. P. (1988). Classically conditioned responses in cocaine and opiod dependence: A role in relapse? In B. A. Ray (Ed.), *Learning factors in drug dependence* (pp. 25–43). Rockville, MD: National Institute on Drug Abuse.

Cho, A. K. (1990). Ice: A new form of an old drug. *Science, 249,* 631–249.

Christiansen, B. A., Goldman, M. S., & Brown, S. A. (1985). The differential development of adolescent alcohol expectancies may predict adult alcoholism. *Journal of Addictive Behavior, 10,* 299–306.

Christiansen, B. A., Goldman, M. S., & Inn, A. (1982). Development of alcohol-related expectancies in adolescents: Separating pharmacological from social learning influences. *Journal of Consulting and Clinical Psychology, 50,* 336–344.

Christiansen, B. A., Smith, G. T., Roehling, P. V., & Goldman, M. S. (1989). Using alcohol expectancies to predict adolescent drinking behavior after one year. *Journal of Consulting and Clinical Psychology, 57,* 93–99.

Christie, K. A., Burke, J. D., Regier, D. A., Rae, D. S., Boyd, J. H., & Locke, B. Z. (1988). Epidemiologic evidence for early onset of mental disorders and higher risk of drug abuse in young adults. *American Journal of Psychiatry, 145,* 971–975.

Ciraulo, D. A., & Shader, R. I. (1991). *Clinical manual of chemical dependence*. Washington, DC: American Psychiatric Press.

Clark, D. B., & Jacob, R. G. (1992). Anxiety disorders and alcoholism in adolescents: A preliminary report (Abstract). *Alcoholism, Clinical and Experimental Research, 16,* 371.

Clark, D. B., Jacob, R. G., & Mezzich, A. (1994). Anxiety and conduct disorders in early onset alcoholism. In T. S. Babor, V. Hesselbrock, R. E. Meyer, & W. Shoemaker (Eds.), Types of alcoholics: Evidence from clinical, experimental and genetic research. *Annals of the New York Academy of Science, 708,* 181–186.

Clark, D. B., & Sayette, M. A. (1993). Anxiety and the development of alcoholism: Clinical and scientific issues. *American Journal on Addictions, 2,* 59–76.

Clark, W., & Widanik, L. (1982). Alcohol use and alcohol problems among U.S. adults: Results of the 1979 survey. In *Alcohol consumption and related problems* (Alcohol and Health Monograph I, Alcohol Consumption and Related Problems, pp. 3–52). Rockville, MD: National Institute on Alcohol Abuse and Alcoholism.

Cloninger, C. R. (1987). Neurogenetic adaptive mechanisms in alcoholism. *Science, 236,* 410–416.

Cloninger, C. R. (1991). D_2 dopamine receptor gene is associated but not linked with alcoholism. *Journal of the American Medical Association, 266,* 1833–1834.

Cloninger, C. R., Bohman, M., & Sigvardisson, S. (1981). Inheritance of alcohol abuse: Cross-fostering analysis of adopted men. *Archives of General Psychiatry, 38,* 861–868.

Cloninger, C. R., Bohman, M. C., Sigvardisson, S., & Von Knorring, A. (1985). Psychopathology in adopted-out children of alcoholics: The Stockholm adoption study. In M. Galanter (Ed.), *Recent Developments in Alcoholism* (Vol. 3, pp. 37–50). New York: Plenum.

Cloninger, C. R., Reich, T., & Wetzel, R. (1979). Alcoholism and affective disorders: Familial associations and genetic models. In D. W. Goodwin & C. K. Erickson (Eds.), *Alcoholism and affective disorders: Clinical, genetic and biochemical studies* (pp. 57–86). New York: SP Medical and Scientific Books.

Cohen, P., Cohen, J., & Brook, J. (1993). An epidemiological study of disorders in late childhood and adolescence—II. Persistence of disorders. *Journal of Child Psychology and Psychiatry, 34,* 869–877.

Cohen, P., Cohen, J., Kasen, S., Velez, C. M., Hartmark, C., Johnson, J., Rojas, M., Brook, J., & Streuning, E. L. (1993). An epidemiological study of disorders in late childhood and adolescence—I. Age and gender-specific prevalence. *Journal of Child Psychology and Psychiatry, 34,* 851–867.

Comings, D. E., Muhleman, D., Ahn, C., Gysin, R., & Flanagan, S. D. (1994). The dopamine D_2 receptor gene: A genetic risk factor in substance abuse. *Drug and Alcohol Dependence, 34,* 175–180.

Conger, J. J. (1956). Alcoholism: Theory, problems and challenge, II. Reinforcement theory and the dynamics of alcoholism. *Quarterly Journal of Studies on Alcohol, 17,* 296–305.

Conneally, P. M. (1991). Association between the D_2 dopamine receptor gene and alcoholism: A continuing controversy. *Archives of General Psychiatry, 48,* 664–666.

Cook, C. H. (1988a). The Minnesota model in the management of drug and alcohol dependency: Miracle, method or myth? Part I. The philosophy and the programme. *British Journal of Addiction, 83,* 625–634.

Cook, C. H. (1988b). The Minnesota model in the management of drug and alcohol dependency: Miracle, method or myth? Part II. Evidence and conclusion. *British Journal of Addiction, 83,* 735–743.

Cook, P. J., & Tauchen, G. (1984). The effect of minimum drinking age legislation on youthful auto fatalities, 1970–1977. *Journal of Legal Studies, 13,* 169–190.

Cornelius, J. R., Salloum, I. M., Cornelius, M. D., Ehler, J. G., & Perel, J. M. (1994, June). *Fluoxetine vs. placebo in depressed alcoholics.* Presented at the New Clinical Drug Evaluation Unit, (NCDEU) meeting, Marco Island, FL.

Cornelius, J. R., Salloum, I. M., Cornelius, M. D., Perel, J. M., Thase, M. E., Ehler, J. G., & Mann, J. (1993). Fluoxetine trial in suicidal depressed alcoholics. *Psychopharmacology Bulletin, 29,* 195–199.

Corneilius, M. D., Day, N. L., Corneilius, J. R., Geva, D., Taylor, P. M., & Richardson, G. A. (1993). Drinking patterns and correlates of drinking among pregnant teenagers. *Alcoholism: Clinical and Experimental Research, 17,* 290–294.

Cornell, D. G., Benedek, E. P., & Benedek, D. M. (1987). Characteristics of adolescents charged with homicide: Review of 72 cases. *Behavioral Sciences and the Law, 5,* 11–23.

Costello, A. J., Edelbrock, C., Dulcan, M., Kalas, R., & Klaric, S. H. (1984). *Development and testing of the NIMH Diagnostic Interview Schedule for children in clinic populations. Final report* Rockville, MD: National Institute for Mental Health.

Cotton, N. S. (1979). The familial incidence of alcoholism: A review. *Journal of Studies on Alcohol, 40,* 89–116.

Council on Scientific Affairs, American Medical Association. (1988). Drug abuse in athletes. *Journal of the American Medical Association, 259,* 1703–1705.

Courtwright, D., Joseph, H., & De Jarlais, D. (1989). *Addicts who survived: An oral history of narcotic use in America, 1923–1965* Knoxville: University of Tennessee Press.

Crumley, F. E. (1979). Adolescent suicide attempts. *Journal of the American Medical Association, 241,* 2404–2407.

Crumley, F. E. (1990). Substance abuse and adolescent suicidal behavior. *Journal of the American Medical Association, 263,* 3051–3056.

Cryer P. E., Haymond, M. W., Santiago, J. V., & Shah, S. P. (1976). Norepinephrine and epinephrine release and adrenergic medication of smoking-associated hemodynamic and metabolic events. *New England Journal of Medicine, 295,* 573–577.

Dackis, C. A., & Gold, M. S. (1985). More on self-medication and abuse. *American Journal of Psychiatry, 142,* 1259–1264.

Daley, D. C., & Marlatt, G. A. (1992). Relapse Prevention: Cognitive and behavioral interventions. In J. H. Lowinson, P. Ruiz, & R. B. Millman (Eds.), *Substance abuse: A comprehensive textbook* (pp. 533–542). Baltimore, MD: Williams & Wilkins.

D'Angelo, L. J., Gretson, P. R., Luban, L. L., & Gayle, H. D. (1991). Human immunodeficiency virus infection in urban adolescents: Can we predict who is at risk? *Pediatrics, 88,* 982–986.

Dawkins, M. P. (1976). Alcohol use among black and white adolescents. In F. D. Harper (Ed.), *Alcohol abuse and black America.* Alexandria, VA: Douglass.

Dawkins, M. P. (1988). Alcoholism prevention and black youth. *Journal of Drug Issues, 18,* 15–20.

DeLeon, G. (1988). The therapeutic community and behavioral science. In B. A. Ray (Ed.), *Learning factors in substance abuse* (pp. 74–99). Rockville, MD: National Institute on Drug Abuse.

DeMarsh, J., & Kumpfer, K. L. (1985). Family-oriented interventions for the prevention of chemical dependency in children and adolescents. *Journal of Children in Contemporary Society, 17,* 274–293.

DeMarsh, J., & Kumpfer, K. L. (1986). Family-oriented interventions for the prevention of chemical dependency in children and adolescents. In S. Griswold-Ezekoye, K. L. Kumpfer, & W. J. Bukowski (Eds.), *Children and chemical abuse: Prevention and intervention* (pp. 117–151). New York: Haworth.

Dembo, R., Williams, L., & Schmeidler, J. (1993). Addressing the problems of substance abuse in juvenile corrections. In J. A. Inciardi (Ed.), *Drug treatment and criminal justice* (pp. 97–126). Newbury Park, CA: Sage. DeMilio, L. (1989). Psychiatric syndromes in adolescent substance abusers. *American Journal of Psychiatry, 146,* 1212–1214.

Deutsch, L. (1952). *What can be done about the drug menace.* Public Affairs Pamphlet 15.

Deykin, E. Y., Buka, S. L., & Zeena, T. H. (1992). Depressive illness among chemically dependent adolescents. *American Journal of Psychiatry, 149,* 1341–1347.

Deykin, E. Y., Levy, J. C., & Wells, V. (1987). Adolescent depression, alcohol and
drug abuse. *American Journal of Public Health, 77,* 178–182.

DiClemente, R. J., Boyer, C. B., & Morales, E. S. (1988). Minorities and AIDS: Knowledge, attitudes and misconceptions among black and Latino adolescents. *American Journal of Public Health, 78,* 55–57.

DiClemente, R. J., & Ponton, L. E. (1993). HIV-Related risk behaviors among psychiatrically hospitalized adolescents and school-based adolescents. *American Journal of Psychiatry, 150,* 324–325.

DiClemente, R. J., Zorn, J., & Temshok, L. (1986). Adolescents and AIDS: A survey
of knowledge, attitudes and beliefs about AIDS in San Francisco. *American Journal of Public Health, 76,* 1443–1445.

Dilsaver, S. C. (1987). The psychopathologies of substance abuse and affective disorders: An integrative model. *Journal of Clinical Psychopharmacology, 7,* 1–10.

Dinkmeyer, D., & McKay, G. D. (1976). *Systematic training for effective parenting.*
Circle Pines, MN: American Guidance Service.

Dinwiddie, S. H., & Cloninger, C. R. (1991). Family and adoption studies in alcoholism and drug addiction. *Psychiatric Annals, 21,* 206–214.

Dinwiddie, S. H., & Reich, T. (1992). Epidemiological perspectives on children of
alcoholics. In M. Galanter (Ed.), *Recent developments in alcoholism* (Vol. 9,
pp. 287–299). New York, Plenum.

Dishion, T. J., & Loeber, R. (1985). Adolescent marijuana and alcohol use: The role
of parents and peers revisited. *American Journal of Drug and Alcohol Abuse, 11,*
11–25.

Dodes, L. M. (1988). The psychology of combining dynamic psychotherapy and alcoholics anonymous. *Bulletin of the Menninger Clinic, 52,* 283–293.

Donovan, J. E., & Jessor, R. (1978). Adolescent problem drinking: Psychosocial correlates in a national sample study. *Journal Studies on Alcohol, 39,* 1506–1524.

Donovan, J. E., & Jessor, R. (1983). Problem drinking and the dimension of involvement with drugs: A Guttman scalogram analysis of adolescent drug use. *American
Journal of Public Health, 73,* 543–552.

Donovan, J. E., & Jessor, R. (1985). Structure of problem behavior in adolescence and
young adulthood. *Journal of Consulting and Clinical Psychology, 53,* 890–904.

Donovan, J. E., Jessor, R., & Jessor, L. (1983). Problem drinking in adolescence and
young adulthood. *Journal of Studies on Alcohol, 44,* 109–137.

Drummond, D. C. (1990). The relationship between alcohol dependence and alcohol-
related problems in a clinical population. *British Journal of Addiction, 85,* 357–366.

Dunner, D. L., Hensel, B. M., & Fieve, R. R. (1979). Bipolar illness factors in drinking behavior. *American Journal of Psychiatry, 136,* 583–585.

Ecton, R. B., & Feindler, E. L. (1990). Anger control training for temper control disorders. In E. L. Feindler & G. R. Kalfus (Eds.), *Adolescent behavior therapy handbook* New York: Springer.

Edwards, G., Arif, A., & Hodgson, R. (1981). Nomenclature and classification of drug and alcohol related problems. *Bulletin of the World Health Organization, 59,* 225–242.

Edwards, G., & Gross, M. M. (1976). Alcohol dependence: Provisional description of a clinical syndrome. *British Medical Journal, 1,* 1058–1061.

Ellickson, P. L., & Bell, R. M. (1990). Drug prevention in junior high: A multi-site longitudinal test. *Science, 247,* 1299–1305.

Ellickson, P. L., & Hays, R. D. (1991). Antecedents of drinking among young adolescents with different alcohol use histories. *Journal of Studies on Alcohol, 52,* 398–408.

Ellickson, P. L., Hays, R. D., & Bell, R. M. (1992). Stepping through drug sequence: Longitudinal scalogram analysis of initiation and regular use. *Journal of Abnormal Psychology, 101,* 444–451.

Elliot, D. S., Huizinga, D., & Ageton, S. S. (1982). *Explaining delinquency and drug use. Report No. 21* Boulder, CO: Behavioral Research Institute.

Elliot, D. S., Huizinga, D., & Ageton, S. S. (1985). *Explaining delinquency and drug use* Beverly Hills, CA: Sage.

Elliot, D. S., Huizinga, D., & Menard, S. (1989). *Multiple problem youth* New York: Springer-Verlag.

Ensminger, M. E., Brown, C. H., & Kellam, S. G. (1982). Sex differences in antecedents of substance use among adolescents. *Journal of Social Issues, 38,* 25–42.

Esbensen, F. A., & Elliot, D. S. (1994). Continuity and discontinuity in illicit drug use: Patterns and antecedents. *Journal of Drug Issues, 24,* 75–97.

Evans, R. I. (1976). Smoking in children: Developing a social psychological strategy to deterrence. *Preventive Medicine, 5,* 122–127.

Fagerstrom, K. O. (1978). Measuring degree of physical dependence to tobacco smoking with reference to individualization of treatment. *Addictive Behaviors, 3,* 235–241.

Farrington, D. P., & West, D. J. (1975). The familial transmission of crime. *Medical Science and the Law, 15,* 177–186.

Fawcett, J., Clark, D. C., & Aagesen, C. A. (1987). A double-blind placebo controlled trial of lithium carbonate therapy for alcoholism. *Archives of General Psychiatry, 44,* 248–256.

Filmore, K. M. (1974). Drinking and problem drinking in early adulthood and middle age. *Quarterly Journal of Studies on Alcohol, 35,* 819–840.

Filstead, W. J. (1982). Adolescence and alcohol. In E. M. Pattison & E. Kaufman (Eds.), *Encyclopedic handbook of alcoholism.* New York: Gardner Press.

Fischer, P. M., Schwartz, M. P., Richards, J. W., Goldstein, A. O., & Rojas, T. H. (1991). Brand logo recognition by children aged 3 to 6 years. *Journal of the American Medical Association, 266,* 3145–3148.

Fischesser, M. (1991). The evolution of the ropes course. *Adolescent Counselor, 23,* 43.

Flavin, D. K., Franklin, J. E., & Francis, R. J. (1990). Substance abuse and suicidal behavior. In S. J. Blumenthal & D. J. Kupfer (Eds.), *Suicide over the life cycle* (pp. 177–204). Washington, DC: American Psychological Association Press.

Flay, B. R., & Sobel, J. L. (1983). The role of mass media in preventing adolescent substance abuse. In T. J. Glynn, C. G. Luekefeld, & J. P. Ludford (Eds.), *Preventing adolescent drug abuse: Intervention strategies* (NIDA Research Monograph No. 47., pp. 5–35). Washington, DC: U.S. Government Printing Office.

Fleisch, B. (1991). *Approaches in the treatment of adolescents with emotional and substance abuse problems* (DHSS Pub. No. ADM 91–1744). Washington, DC: U.S. Government Printing Office.

Fleming, J. P., Kellam, S. G., & Brown, C. H. (1982). Early predictors of age at first use of alcohol, marijuana and cigarettes. *Drug and Alcohol Dependence, 9,* 285–303.

Freeman, E. M. (1993). Treating runaway, drug-addicted adolescents. In E. M. Feeman (Ed.), *Substance abuse treatment: A family systems perspective* (pp. 48–70). Newbury Park, CA: Sage.

Friedman, A. S., & Beschner, G. M., (Eds.). (1985). *Treatment services for adolescent substance abusers* (DHSS Pub. No. ADM 85–1342). Washington, DC: U.S. Government Printing Office.

Friedman, A. S., & Glickman, N. W. (1987). Effects of psychiatric symptomatology on treatment outcome for adolescent male drug abusers. *Journal of Nervous and Mental Disease, 175,* 425–430.

Friedman, A. S., Granick, S., Kreisher, C., & Terras, A. (1993). Matching adolescents who abuse drugs to treatment. *American Journal on Addictions, 2,* 232–237.

Friedman, A. S., Schwartz, R., & Utada, A. (1989). Outcome of a unique youth drug abuse program: A follow-up study of clients of Straight, Inc. *Journal of Substance Abuse Treatment, 6,* 259–268.

Friedman, A. S., & Utada, A. (1989). A method for diagnosing and planning the treatment of adolescent drug abusers (The Adolescent Drug Abuse Diagnosis [ADAD] Instrument). *Journal of Drug Education, 19,* 285–312.

Friedman, I. M. (1985). Alcohol and unnatural deaths in San Francisco youths. *Pediatrics, 76,* 191–193.

Fullilove, M. T., Golden E., Fullilove, R. E., Lennon, R., Porterfield, D., & Schwarcz, Bolan, G. (1992). Crack cocaine use and high risk behaviors among sexually active black adolescents. *Journal of Adolescent Health, 14,* 295–300.

Fulton, A. I., & Yates, W. R. (1988). Family abuse of methylphenidate. *American Family Physician, 38,* 143–145.

Furnham, A. (1986). Social skills training with adolescents and young adults. In C. R. Hollin & P. Trower (Eds.), *Handbook of social skills training* (pp. 33–57). New York: Pergamon.

Furstenberg, F., Brooks-Gunn, J., & Chase-Lansdale, L. (1989). Teenage pregnancy and childbearing. *American Psychologist, 44,* 313–320.

Garfinkel, B., Froese, A., & Hood, J. (1982). Suicide attempts in children and adolescents. *American Journal of Psychiatry, 139,* 1257–1261.

Gawin, F. H., & Kleber, H. D. (1984). Cocaine abuse treatment: Open clinical trial with desipramine and lithium carbonate. *Archives of General Psychiatry, 41,* 903–909.

Giannini, A. J., Baumgartel, P., & DiMarzio, L. R. (1987). Bromocriptine therapy in cocaine withdrawal. *Journal of Clinical Pharmacology, 27,* 267–270.

Giannini, A. J., Malone, D. A., Giannini, M. C., Price, W. A., & Loiselle, R. H. (1986). Treatment of depression in chronic cocaine and phencyclidine abuse with desipramine. *Journal of Clinical Pharmacology, 26,* 211–214.

Gilcrist, L. D., & Schinke, S. P. (1985). Preventing substance abuse with children and adolescents. *Journal of Consulting and Clinical Psychology, 53,* 121–135.

Gilman, A. G., Rall, T. W., Nies, A. S., & Taylor, P. (1990). *Goodman and Gilman's the pharmacological basis of therapeutics.* New York: Pergamon.

Gittleman, R., Mannuzza, S., Shenker, R., & Bongura, N. (1985). Hyperactive boys almost grown up: I. Psychiatric status. *Archives of General Psychiatry, 42,* 937–947.

Globetti, G. A. (1970). Drinking patterns of Negro and white high school students in two Mississippi communities. *Journal of Negro Education, 39,* 60–69.

Glover, E. (1956). On the etiology of drug addiction. In E. Glover (Ed.), *On the early development of the mind.* New York: International Universities Press.

Gold, M. S., & Dackis, C. A. (1986). Role of the laboratory in the evaluation of suspected drug abuse. *Journal of Clinical Psychiatry, 47*(Suppl. 1), 17–23.

Goldstein, N. L. (1952). *Report by the attorney-general of New York to the New York legislature* (Legislative Document No. 27). Albany, NY.

Goodwin, D. W. (1982). *Alcoholism and affective disorders.* New York: Plenum.

Goodwin, D. W., Schlusinger, F., Hermansen, L., Guze, S. B., & Winokur, G. (1975). Alcoholism and the hyperactive child syndrome. *Journal of Nervous and Mental Disease, 160,* 349–353.

Goodwin, D. W., Schulsinger, F., Hermansen, L., Guze, S. B., & Winokur, G. (1993). Alcohol problems in adoptees raised apart from alcoholic parents. *Archives of General Psychiatry, 28,* 238–243.

Goodwin, D. W., Schulsinger, F., Moller, W., Hermansen, L., Winokur, G., & Guze, S. B. (1974). Drinking problems in adopted and non-adopted sons of alcoholics. *Archives of General Psychiatry, 31,* 164–169.

Goyer, P. F., Davis, G. C., & Rapoport, J. L. (1979). Abuse of prescribed stimulant medication by a 13-year old hyperactive boy. *Journal of the American Academy of Child Psychiatry, 18,* 170–175.

Grant, D. W. (1988). Genetic polymorphism of the alcohol metabolizing enzyme as a basis for alcoholic liver disease. *British Journal of Addiction, 83,* 1255–1259.

Green, W. H. (1991). *Child and adolescent clinical psychopharmacology.* Baltimore: Williams & Wilkins.

Greenbaum, P. E., Prange, M. E., Friedman, R. M., & Silver, S. E. (1991). Substance abuse prevalence and comorbidity with other psychiatric disorders among adolescents with severe emotional disturbances. *Journal of the American Academy of Child and Adolescent Psychiatry, 30,* 575–583.

Greenstein, R. A., Fudala, P. J., & O'Brien, C. P. (1992). Alternative pharmacotherapies for opiate addiction. In J. H. Lowinson, P. Ruiz, & R. B. Millman (Eds.), *Substance abuse: A Comprehensive Textbook* (pp. 562–573). Baltimore: Williams & Wilkins.

Grove, W. M., Andreasen, N. C., Winokur. G., Clayton, P. J., Endicott, J., & Coryell, W. H. (1987). Primary and secondary affective disorders: Unipolar patients compared on familial aggregation. *Comprehensive Psychiatry, 28,* 113–126.

Guze, S., Woodruff, R., & Clayton, P. (1971). Secondary affective disorder: A study of 95 cases. *Psychology in Medicine, 11,* 426–428.

Haggerty, K. P., Wells, E. A., Jenson, J. M., Catalano, R. F., & Hawkins, J. D. (1989). Delinquents and drug use: A model program for community reintegration. *Adolescence, 24,* 439–456.

Haley, J. (1976). *Problem-solving therapy.* San Francisco: Jossey-Bass.

Halikas, J. A. (1990). Substance abuse in children and adolescents. In B. D. Garfinkel, G. A. Carlson, & E. B. Weller (Eds.), *Psychiatric disorders in children and adolescents* (pp. 210–234). Philadelphia: Saunders.

Halikas, J. A., Melle, J., Morese, C., & Lyttle, M. D. (1990). Predicting substance abuse in juvenile offenders: Attention deficit disorder versus aggressivity. *Child Psychiatry and Human Development, 21,* 49–55.

Hallagan, J. B., Hallagan, L. F., & Snyder, M. B. (1989). Anabolic steroid use by athletes. *New England Journal of Medicine, 321,* 1042–1045.

Hansell, S., & White, H. R. (1991). Adolescent drug use, psychological distress and physical symptoms. *Journal of Health and Social Behavior, 32,* 288–301.

Hansen, W. B., Johnson, C. A., Flay, B. R., Graham, J. W., & Sobel, J. (1988). Affective and social influences approaches to the prevention of multiple substance abuse among seventh grade students: Results from Project SMART. *Preventive Medicine, 17,* 135–154.

Hardy, J. B., & Zabin, L. S. (1991). *Adolescent pregnancy in an urban environment.* Washington, DC: Urban Institute Press.

Harford, T. C. (1985). Drinking patterns among black and non-black adolescents: Results of a national survey. In R. Wright & T. D. Watts (Eds.), *Prevention of black alcoholism: Issues and strategies.* Springfield, IL: Thomas Publishing.

Harper, F. D. (1976). *Alcohol and blacks: An overview.* Alexandria, VA: Douglass.

Harper, F. D. (1979). *Alcoholism treatment and black Americans.* Rockville, MD: National Institute on Alcohol Abuse and Alcoholism.

Harper, F. D., & Hawkins, M. P. (1976). Alcohol and blacks: Survey of the periodical literature. *British Journal of Addiction, 71,* 29–36.

Harrison, P. A., & Hoffmann, N. (1989). *CATOR Report: Adolescent treatment completers one year later.* St. Paul, MN: Chemical Abuse/Addiction Treatment Outcome Registry.

Hasin, D. S., Grant, B., & Endicott, J. (1990). The national history of alcohol abuse: Implications for definitions of alcohol use disorders. *American Journal of Psychiatry, 147,* 1537–1541.

Hatsukami, D., Eckert, E., Mitchell, J., & Pyle, R. (1984). Affective disorder and substance abuse in women with bulimia. *Psychology in Medicine, 14,* 701–704.

Hawkins, J. D., Catalano, R. F., & Miller, J. Y. (1992). Risk and protective factors for alcohol and other drug problems in adolescence and early adulthood: Implications for substance abuse prevention. *Psychological Bulletin, 112,* 64–105.

Hawkins, J. D., Catalano, R. F., & Wells, E. A. (1986). Measuring the effects of a skills training intervention for drug abusers. *Journal of Consulting and Clinical Psychology, 54,* 661–664.

Hawkins, J. D., Lishner, D., & Catalano, R. F. (1985). Childhood predictors and the prevention of adolescent substance abuse. In C. L. Jones & R. J. Battjes (Eds.), *Etiology of drug abuse: Implications for prevention* (pp. 75–126). Rockville, MD: Department of Health and Human Services, National Institute on Drug Abuse.

Hawkins, J. D., Lishner, D. M., & Catalano, R. F. (1986). Childhood predictors of adolescent substance abuse. *Journal of Children in Contemporary Society, 18,* 1–65.

Hawks, R. D., Bahr, S. J., & Wang, G. (1994). Adolescent substance use and codependence. *Journal of Studies on Alcohol, 55,* 261–268.

Hechtman, L. (1989). Teenage mothers and their children: Risks and problems: A review. *Canadian Journal of Psychiatry, 34,* 569–575.

Hechtman, L., Weiss, G., & Perlman, T. (1984). Hyperactive as young adults: Past and current antisocial behavior and moral development. *American Journal of OrthoPsychiatry, 54,* 415–425.

Helzer, J. E, Burnam, A., & McEvoy, L. T. (1991). Alcohol abuse and dependence. In L. N. Robins & D. A. Regier (Eds.), *Psychiatric disorders in America* (pp. 81–115). New York: Free Press.

Helzer, J. E., & Winokur, G. (1974). A family interview study of male manic-depressive. *Archives of General Psychiatry, 31,* 73–77.

Henggeler, S. W. (1991). *Treating conduct problems in children and adolescents: An overview of the multi-systemic approach with guidelines for intervention design and implementation.* Columbia: South Carolina Department of Mental Health.

Henggeler, S. W. (1993, October). *Bringing psychotherapy treatment research from the laboratory into the community.* Symposium presented at the annual meeting American Academy of Child and Adolescent Psychiatry. San Antonio, TX.

Henggeler, S. W., Melton, G. B., & Smith, L. A. (1992). Family preservation using multisystemic therapy: An effective alternative to incarcerating serious juvenile offenders. *Journal of Consulting and Clinical Psychology, 60,* 953–961.

Henly, C., & Winters, K. (1988). Development of problem severity scales for the assessment of adolescent alcohol and drug abuse. *International Journal of the Addictions, 23,* 65–85.

Hesselbrock, M. N., Hesselbrock, V. M., Babor, T. F., Stabneau, J. R., Meyer, R. E., & Weidenman. (1987). Antisocial behavior, psychopathology and problem drinking in the natural history of alcoholism. In D. W. Goodwin, K. Drusen, & S. Mednick (Eds.), *Longitudinal research in alcoholism* (pp. 425–430). Boston: Kluwer-Nijhoff.

Hesselbrock, V. M., Hesselbrock, M. N., & Workman-Daniels, K. L. (1986). Effect of major depression and antisocial personality on alcoholism: Course and motivational patterns. *Journal of Studies of Alcohol, 47,* 207–212.

Hesselbrock, M. N., Meyer, R. E., & Keener, J. (1985). Psychopathology in hospitalized alcoholics. *Archives of General Psychiatry, 42,* 1050–1055.

Higgins, P. C., Albrecht, G. L., & Albrecht, M. H. (1977). Black-white adolescent drinking: The myth and reality. *Social Problems, 25,* 215–224.

Higgins, S. T., Budney, A. J., Bickel, W. K., Hughes, J. R., Foerg, F., & Badger, G. (1993). Achieving cocaine abstinence with a behavioral approach. *American Journal of Psychiatry, 150,* 763–769.

Hill, S. Y., Steinhauser, S. R., & Zubin, J. (1987). Biological markers for alcoholism: A vulnerability model conceptualization. In P. C. Rivers (Ed.), *Alcohol and addictive behavior* (pp. 207–256). Lincoln: University of Nebraska Press.

Hirschman, R. S., Leventhal, H., & Glynn, K. (1984). The development of smoking behavior: Conceptualization and supportive cross-sectional survey data. *Journal of Applied Social Psychology, 14,* 184–206.

Hoberman, H. M., & Garfinkel, B. D. (1988). Completed suicide in children and adolescents. *Journal of the American Academy of Child and Adolescent Psychiatry, 27,* 689–695.

Hoffmann, N. G., Halikas, J., & Mee-Lee, D. (1987). *The Cleveland admission, discharge, and transfer criteria: Model for chemical dependency treatment programs.* Cleveland, OH: Greater Cleveland Hospital Association.

Hovens, J. G., Cantwell, D. P., & Kiriakos, R. (1994). Psychiatric comorbidity in hospitalized adolescent substance abusers. *Journal of the American Academy of Child and Adolescent Psychiatry, 33,* 476–483.

Howland, J., & Hingson, R. (1988). Alcohol as a risk factor for drownings: a review of the literature 1950–1985. *Accidents and Annals of Prevention, 20,* 19–20.

Huba, G. J., & Bentler, P. M. (1980). The role of peer and adult modes for drug taking at different stages in adolescence. *Journal of Youth and Adolescence, 9,* 449–465.

Huba, G. J., & Bentler, P. M. (1982). A developmental theory of drug use: Deviation and assessment of a causal modeling approach. In P. B. Baltes & O. G. Brim (Eds.), *Life-span development and behavior* (Vol. 4, pp. 147–203). New York: Academic Press.

Huba, G. J., Wingard, J. A., & Bentler, P. M. (1981). A comparison of two latent variable causal models for adolescent drug use. *Journal of Personality and Social Psychology, 40,* 180–193.

Hubbard, R. L., Cavanaugh, E. R., Craddock, S. G., & Rachel, J. V. (1985). Characteristics, behaviors and outcomes for youth in TOPS. In A. S. Friedman & G. M. Beschner (Eds.), *Treatment services for adolescent substance abusers* (DHSS Pub. No. ADM 85-1342, pp. 49–65). Washington, DC: U.S. Government Printing Office.

Hubbard, S. D. (1920). New York City narcotic clinic and differing points of view on narcotic addiction. In *Monthly Bulletin of the Department of Health* (pp. 45–47). New York: Department of Health.

Hudson, J. I., Pope, H. G., Jonas, J. M., Yurgelun-Todd, D., & Frankenburg, F. R. (1987). A controlled family history study of bulimia. *Psychology in Medicine, 17,* 883–890.

Hughes, J. R., & Hatsukami, D. (1986). Signs and symptoms of tobacco withdrawal. *Archives of General Psychiatry, 43,* 289–294.

Hughes, S. O., Power, T. C., & Francis, D. J. (1992). Defining patterns of drinking in adolescence: A cluster analytic approach. *Journal of Studies on Alcohol, 53,* 40–47.

Huizinga, D., & Elliot, D. S. (1981). *A longitudinal study of drug use and delinquency in a national sample of youth: An assessment of causal order* (Project Report No. 16, A National Youth Study). Boulder CO: Behavioral Research Institute.

Hull, J. G. (1987). Self-awareness model. In H. T. Blane & K. E. Leonard (Eds.), *Psychological theories of drinking and alcoholism* (pp. 272–304). New York: Guilford.

Institute of Medicine. (1988). *Helplessness, health and human needs.* Washington, DC: National Academy Press.

Institute of Medicine. (1991). *Research on children and adolescents with mental, behavioral and developmental disorders: Mobilizing a national initiative.* Washington, DC: National Academy Press.

Jacobs, M. R., & Fehr, K. O. B. (1987). *Drugs and drug abuse: A reference text* Toronto: Addiction Research Foundation.

Jaffe, J. H., Babor, T. F., & Fishbein, D. H. (1988). Alcoholics, aggression and antisocial personality. *Journal of Studies on Alcohol, 49,* 211–218.

Jaffe, S. (1990). *The step workbook for adolescent chemical dependency recovery.* Washington, DC: American Academy of Child and Adolescent Psychiatry.

Jellinek, E. M. (1969). *The disease concept of alcoholism.* New Haven, CT: College and University Press.

Jemmott, J. B., Jemmott, L. S., & Fong, G. T. (1992). Reductions in HIV risk-association of sexual behaviors among black male adolescents: Effects of an AIDS prevention intervention. *American Journal of Public Health, 82,* 372–377.

Jessor, R. (1984). Adolescent problem drinking: Psychosocial aspects and developmental outcomes. In L. H. Towle (Ed.), *Proceedings: NIAAA-WHO collaborating center designation meeting and alcohol research seminar* (pp. 104–143). Washington, DC: Public Health Service.

Jessor, R., & Jessor, S. (1977). *Problem behavior and psychosocial development: A longitudinal study of youth.* New York: Academic Press.

Joanning, H., Quinn, W., Thomas, F., & Mullen, R. (1992). Treating adolescent drug abuse: A comparison of family system therapy, group therapy and family drug education. *Journal of Marital and Family Therapy, 18,* 345–356.

Johnson, C. A. (1986). Prevention and control of drug abuse. In J. M. Last (Ed.), *Maxcy-Rosenau public health and preventive medicine* (pp. 1075–1087). Norwalk, CT: Appleton-Century-Crofts.

Johnson, C. A., Pentz, M. A., Dwyer, J. H., Baer, N., MacKinnon, D. P., & Hansoen, W. B. (1990). Relative effectiveness of comprehensive community programming for drug abuse prevention with high risk and low risk adolescents. *Journal of Consulting and Clinical Psychology, 58,* 447–456.

Johnson, C. A., & Solis, J. (1983). Comprehensive community programs for drug abuse prevention. In *Preventing adolescent drug abuse: Intervention strategies* (pp. 76–114). Washington, DC: U.S. Department of Health and Human Services.

Johnson, E. M., Amatetti, S., Funkhouser, J. E., & Johnson, S. (1988). Theories and models supporting prevention approaches to alcohol problems among youth. *Public Health Reports, 103,* 578–586.

Johnston, L. D. (1973). *Drugs and American youth.* Ann Arbor: University of Michigan, Institute for Social Research.

Johnston, L. D. (1985). The etiology and prevention of substance use: What can we learn from recent historical changes. In C. L. Jones & R. J. Battjes (Eds.), *Etiology of drug abuse: Implications for prevention* (pp. 155–177). Rockville, MD: Department of Health and Human Services, National Institute on Drug Abuse.

Johnston, L. D., Bachman, J. G., & O'Malley, P. M. (1985). *Monitoring the Future: Questionnaire responses from the nations' high school seniors.* Ann Arbor, MI. Institute for Social Research.

Johnston, L. D., & O'Malley, P. M. (1986). Why do the nation's students use drugs and alcohol? Self-reported reasons from nine national surveys. *Journal of Drug Issues, 16,* 29–66.

Johnston, L. D., O'Malley, P. M., & Bachman, J. G. (1991). *Smoking, drinking and illicit drug use among American secondary school students, college students and young adults, 1975–1990.* U.S Department of Health and Human Services, National Institute on Drug Abuse. Washington, DC: U.S. Government Printing Office.

Johnston, L. D., O'Malley, P. M., & Bachman, J. G. (1993). *National survey results on drug use from the Monitoring the Future Study, 1975–1992.* U.S Department of Health and Human Services, National Institute on Drug Abuse. Washington, DC: U.S. Government Printing Office.

Johnston, L. D., O'Malley, P., & Eveland, L. (1978). Drugs and delinquency: A search for causal connections. In D. B. Kandel (Ed.), *Longitudinal research on drug use: Empirical findings and methodological issues* (pp. 137–156). Washington, DC: Hemisphere-Wiley.

Joint Committee of the American Bar Association and the American Medical Association on Narcotic Drugs. (1961). *Drug addiction: Crime or disease? Interim and final reports.* Bloomington: Indiana University Press.

Joksch, H. C. (1988). *The impact of severe penalties on drinking and driving.* Washington, DC: U.S. Government Printing Office.

Jones, E. E., & Berglas, S. (1978). Control of attributions about the self through self-handicapping strategies: The appeal of alcohol and the role of underachievement. *Personality and Social Psychology Bulletin, 4,* 200–206.

Kaminer, Y. (1992). Desipramine facilitation of cocaine abstinence in an adolescent. *Journal of the American Academy of Child and Adolescent Psychiatry, 31,* 312–317.

Kaminer, Y., Wagner, E., Plummer, B., & Seifer, R. (1993). Validation of the teen addiction severity index (T-ASI). *American Journal on Addictions, 2,* 250–254.

Kandel, D. B. (1974). Inter-and intragenerational influences in adolescent marijuana use. *Journal of Social Issues, 30,* 107–135.

Kandel, D. B. (1975a). Reaching the hard to reach: Illicit drug use among high school absentees. *Addictive Diseases, 1,* 465–480.

Kandel, D. B. (1975b). Stages in adolescent involvement in drug use. *Science, 190,* 912–914.

Kandel, D. B. (1978). Adolescent marijuana use: Role of parents and peers. *Science, 181,* 1067–1070.

Kandel, D. B. (1982). Epidemiological and psychosocial perspectives on adolescent drug use. *Journal of the American Academy of Child Psychiatry, 21,* 328–347.

Kandel, D. B., Kessler, R. C., & Margulies, R. Z. (1978). Antecedents of adolescent initiation into stages of drug use: A developmental analysis. In D. B. Kandel (Ed.),

Longitudinal research on drug use: Empirical findings and methodological issues (pp. 73–99). Washington, DC: Hemisphere (Halstead-Wiley).

Kandel, D. B., & Logan J. A. (1984). Patterns of drug use from adolescence to young adulthood: I. Periods of risk for initiation, continued use, and discontinuation. *American Journal of Public Health, 74,* 660–666.

Kandel, D. B., Simcha-Fagan, O., & Davies, M. (1986). Risk factors for delinquency and illicit drug use from adolescence to young adulthood. *Journal of Drug Issues, 16,* 67–90.

Kandel, D. B., Single, E., & Kessler, R. C. (1976). The epidemiology of drug use among New York State high school students: Distribution, trends and change in rates of use. *American Journal of Public Health, 66,* 43–53.

Kandel, D. B., & Yamaguchi, K. (1985). Developmental patterns of the use of legal, illegal and medically prescribed psychotropic drugs from adolescence to young adulthood. In C. L. Jones & R. J. Battjes (Ed.), *Etiology of drug abuse: Implications for prevention* (pp. 193–235). Rockville, MD: Department of Health and Human Services, National Institute on Drug Abuse.

Kandel, D. B., Yamaguchi, K., & Chien, K. (1992). Stages of progression in drug involvement from adolescence to adulthood: Further evidence for the gateway theory. *Journal of Studies on Alcohol, 53,* 447–457.

Kaplan, S., Pelcovitz, D., Salzinger, S., et al. (1983). Psychopathology of parents of abused and neglected children. *Journal of the American Academy of Child Psychiatry, 22,* 238–244.

Kashani, J. H., Beck, N. C., Hoeper, E. W., Fallahi, C., Corcoran, C. M., McAllister, J. A., Rosenberg, T. K., & Reid, J. C. (1987). Psychiatric disorders in a community sample of adolescents. *American Journal of Psychiatry, 144,* 584–589.

Kashani, J. H., Carlson, G. A., Beck, N. C., Hoeper, E. W., Corcoran, C. M., McAllister, J. A., Fallahi, C., Rosenberg, T. K., & Reid, J. C. (1987). Depression, depressive symptoms, and depressed mood among a community sample of adolescents. *American Journal of Psychiatry, 144,* 931–933.

Kashani, J. H., Keller, M. B., Solomon, N., Reid, J. C., & Mazzola, D. (1985). Double depression in adolescent substance abusers. *Journal Affective Disorders, 8,* 153–157.

Kashani, J. H., & Orvaschel, H. (1990). A community study of anxiety in children and adolescents. *American Journal of Psychiatry, 147,* 313–318.

Kashani, J. H., Orvaschel, H., Rosenberg, T. K., & Reid, R. C. (1989). Psychopathology in a community sample of children and adolescents: A developmental perspective. *Journal of the American Academy of Child and Adolescent Psychiatry, 28,* 701–706.

Kassett, J. A., Gershon, E. S., & Maxwell, M. E. (1989). Psychiatric disorders in first degree relatives of probands with bulimia nervosa. *American Journal of Psychiatry, 146,* 1468–1471.

Kaufman, E., & Kaufman, P. (1992). From a psychodynamic to a structural understanding of drug dependency. In E. Kaufman & P. Kaufman (Eds.), *Family therapy of drug and alcohol abuse.* New York: Gardner Press.

Kaufman, P. (1992). Family therapy with adolescent substance abusers. In E. Kaufman & P. Kaufman (Eds.), *Family Therapy of Drug and Alcohol Abuse* (pp. 63–71). New York: Gardner Press.

Kaye, W. H., Gwirtsman, H. E., Weiss, G. S, R., & Jimerson, D. C. (1986). Relationship of mood alterations to binging behavior in bulimia. *British Journal of Psychiatry, 149,* 479–485.

Kazdin, A. E. (1987). Treatment of antisocial behavior in children: Current status and future directions. *Psychological Bulletin, 102,* 187–203.

Kellam, S. G., Brown, C. H., Rubin, B. R., & Ensminger, M. E. (1983). Paths leading to teenage psychiatric symptoms and substance use: Development epidemiological studies in Woodlawn. In S. B. Guze, F. J. Earls, & J. E. Barrett (Eds.), *Childhood psychopathology and Development* (pp. 17–52). New York: Norton.

Kellam, S. G., Simon, M., & Ensminger, M. D. (1980). Antecedents in first grade of teenage drug use and psychological well-being: A ten-year community-wide prospective study. In D. Ricks & B. Dohrenwend (Eds.), *Origins of psychopathology: Research and public policy.* Cambridge: Cambridge University Press.

Kellam, S. G., Stevenson, D. L., & Rubin, B. R. (1983). How specific are the early predictors of teenage drug use? In L. Harris (Ed.), *Problems of Drug Dependence* (NIDA Research Monograph Series No. 43, pp. 329–334). Washington, DC: U.S. Government Printing Office.

Kett, J. (1977). *Rites of passage: Adolescence in America 1790 to the present.* New York: Basic Books.

Khantzian, E. J. (1985). The self-medication hypothesis of addictive disorders: Focus on heroin and cocaine dependence. *American Journal of Psychiatry, 142,* 1259–1246.

Kibble, M. W., & Ross, M. B. (1987). Adverse effects of anabolic steroids in athletes. *Clinical Pharmacology, 6,* 686–692.

Kipke, M. D., Futterman, D., & Hein, K. (1990). HIV Infection and AIDS during adolescence. *Medical Clinics of North America, 74,* 1149.

Kipke, M. D., Montgomery, S., & MacKenzie, R. G. (1993). Substance use among youth seen at a community-based health clinic. *Journal Adolescent Health, 14,* 289–294.

Klein, D. (1980). Anxiety reconceptualized. *Comprehensive Psychiatry, 21,* 411–427.

Klein, N. C., Alexander, J. F., & Parsons, B. V. (1976). The impact of family systems intervention on recidivism and sibling delinquency: A model primary prevention and program evaluation. *Journal of Consulting and Clinical Psychology, 45,* 469–474.

Kleinman, A. (1978). Onset of additional: A first attempt at prediction. *International Journal of the Addictions, 13,* 1217–1235.

Klitzner, M., Fisher, D., Stewart, K., & Gilbert, S. (1991). *Report to the Robert Wood Johnson Foundation on strategies for early intervention with children and youth to avoid abuse of addictive substances.* Bethesda, MD: Pacific Institute for Research and Evaluation.

Kogan, H. (1950). *Dope and Chicago's children* Chicago: Juvenile Protective Association.

Kosky, R., Siburn, S., & Zubrik, S. R. (1990). Are children and adolescents who have suicidal thoughts different from those who attempted suicide. *Journal of Nervous and Mental Disease, 178,* 38–43.

Kosten, T. R., Morgan, C. M., Falcone, F., & Schottenfeld, R. S. (1992). Pharmacotherapy for cocaine-abusing methadone-maintained patients using amantadine or desipramine. *Archives of General Psychiatry, 49,* 894–898.

Kotila, L., & Lonnggvist, J. (1988). Adolescent suicide attempts: Sex differences predicting suicide. *Acta Psychiatrica Scandanavia, 77,* 264–270.

Kraus, J. F., Fife, D., & Conroy, C. (1987). Incidence, severity and outcomes of brain injury involving bicycles. *American Journal of Public Health, 77,* 76–78.

Kreig, C. (1951). Teen age addicts. *National Education Journal, 40,* 341.

Kumpfer, K. L. (1989). Prevention of alcohol and drug abuse: A critical review of risk factors and prevention strategies. In D. Shaffer, I. Phillips, & N. B. Enzer (Eds.), *Prevention of mental disorders, alcohol and other drug use in children and adolescents* (pp. 309–272). Rockville, MD: U.S. Department of Health and Human Services.

Kushner, M. G., Sher, K. J., & Beitman, B. D. (1990). The relation between alcohol problems and anxiety disorders. *American Journal of Psychiatry, 147,* 685–695.

LaFromboise, T. D. (1988). American Indian mental health policy. *American Psychologist, 43,* 388–397.

Lahey, B. B., Piacentini, J. C., McBurnett, K., Stone, P., Hartdagen, S., & Hynd, G. (1988). Psychopathology in the parents of children with conduct disorder and hyperactivity. *Journal of the American Academy of Child and Adolescent Psychiatry, 27,* 163–170.

Lawrin, M. O., Naranjo, C. A., & Sellars, E. M. (1986). Identification and testing of new drugs for modulating alcohol consumption. *Psychopharmacology Bulletin, 22,* 1020–1025.

Leckman, J. F., Weissman, M. M., Merikangas, K. R., et al. (1983). Panic disorder and major depression. *Archives of General Psychiatry, 40,* 1055–1060.

Lender, M. E., & Martin, J. K. (1987). *Drinking in America.* New York: Free Press.

Levine, H. (1978). The discovery of addiction. *Journal of Studies on Alcohol, 39,* 143–174.

Levy, J. C., & Deykin, E. Y. (1989) Suicidality, depression and substance abuse in adolescents. *American Journal of Psychiatry, 146,* 1462–1467.

Lewinson, P. M., Clarke, G. N., Hops, H., & Andrews, J. (1990). Cognitive-behavioral treatment for depressed adolescent. *Behavior Therapy, 21,* 385–401.

Lewis, C. E., Rice, J., & Helzer, J. E. (1987). Diagnostic interactions: Alcoholism and antisocial personality. *Journal of Nervous and Mental Disease, 171,* 105–113.

Lewis, D. O., Shanok, S. S., Pincus, J. H., & Glaser, G. H. (1979). Violent juvenile delinquents: Psychiatric, neurological psychological and abuse factors. *Journal of Child Psychiatry, 18,* 307–319.

Lewis, R. A., Piercy, F. P., Sprenkle, D. H., & Trepper, T. S. (1990). Family-based interventions for helping drug-abusing adolescents. *Journal of Adolescent Research, 5,* 82–95.

Linnoila, M., DeJong, J., & Virkkunen, M. (1989). Family history of alcoholism in violent offenders and impulsive fire setters. *Archives of General Psychiatry, 46,* 613–616.

Liskow, B. I., & Goodwin, D. W. (1987). Pharmacological treatment of alcohol intoxicateion, withdrawal and dependence: A critical review. *Journal of the Study of Alcohol, 48,* 356–370.

Loeber, R. (1988). Natural histories of conduct problems, delinquency and associated substance use. In B. B. Lahey & A. E. Kazdin (Eds.), *Advances in clinical child psychology* (Vol. 11, pp. 73–124). New York: Plenum.

Loeber, R. (1990). Development and risk factors of juvenile antisocial behavior and delinquency. *Clinical Psychology Review, 10,* 1–41.

Loeber, R. (1991). Antisocial behavior: More enduring than changeable? *Journal of the American Academy of Child and Adolescent Psychiatry, 30,* 393–397.

Loeber, R., & Dishion, T. J. (1983). Early predictors of male delinquency: A review. *Psychological Bulletin, 94,* 68–99.

Lorion, R. P. (1990). Creating drug free environments: Beyond and back to the individual. In H. Resnik (Ed.), *Youth and drugs: Society's mixed messages* (pp. 169–174). Rockville, MD: Office for Substance Abuse Prevention.

Lorion, R. P., Price, R. H., & Eaton, W. W. (1989). The prevention of child and adolescent disorders: From theory to research. In D. Shaffer, I. Phillips, & N. B. Enzer (Eds.), *Prevention of mental disorders, alcohol and other drug use in children and adolescents* (pp. 55–96). Rockville, MD: U.S. Department of Health and Human Services.

Lourie, R. S. (1943). Alcoholism in children. *American Journal of OrthoPsychiatry, 13,* 322–338.

Ludwig, A. (1989). The mystery of craving. *Alcohol, Health and Research World, 11,* 12–17.

MacDonald, D. I. (1984). Drugs, drinking and adolescence. *American Journal of Diseases of Children, 138,* 117–125.

Maddahian, E., Newcomb, M. D., & Bentler, P. M. (1986). Single and multiple patterns of adolescent substance use: Longitudinal comparisons of four ethnic groups. *Journal of Drug Education, 15,* 311–326.

Maddahian, E., Newcomb, M. D., & Bentler, P. M. (1988). Risk factors for adolescent substance abuse: Ethnic differences among adolescents. *Journal of Substance Abuse, 1,* 11–23.

Maisto, S. A., & Carey, K. B. (1985). Origins of alcohol abuse in children and adolescents. In B. B. Lahey & A. E. Kazdin (Eds.), *Advances in clinical child psychology* (pp. 149–199). New York: Plenum.

Manson, S. M., & Trimble, J. E. (1982). American Indian and Alaska Native communities: Past efforts, future inquiries. In L. R. Snowden (Ed.), *Reaching the Undeserved: Mental health needs of neglected populations* (pp. 143–163). Beverly Hills, CA: Sage.

Margulies, R. Z., Kessler, R. C., & Kandel, D. B. (1977). A longitudinal study of onset of drinking among high school students. *Journal of Studies on Alcohol, 38,* 307–912.

Marlatt, G. A., & Gordon, J. R. (1985). *Relapse Prevention.* New York: Guilford.

Martin, C. S., Kaczynski, N. A., Maisto, S. A., Bukstein, O. G., & Moss, H. B. (submitted for publication). Patterns of alcohol abuse and dependence symptoms in adolescent drinkers.

Mascola, L., Lieb, L., Iwakoski, K. G., McCallister, A., Siminously, T., Giles, M., Run, G., Fannin, S. L., & Strants, I. H. (1989). HIV seroprevalence in intravenous drug users: Los Angeles, California, 1986. *American Journal of Public Health, 79,* 81–82.

Mayer, J. E., & Filstead, W. J. (1979). The Adolescent Alcohol Involvement Scale. *Journal of Studies on Alcohol, 40,* 291–300.

Mayfield, D. G. (1968). Psychopharmacology of alcohol: Affective change with intoxicateion, drinking behavior and affective state. *Journal of Nervous and Mental Diseases, 146,* 314–321.

McAlister, A., Perry, C. L., & Killen, J. (1980). Pilot study of smoking, alcohol and drug abuse prevention. *American Journal of Public Health, 70,* 719–721.

McCarthy, R. G., & Douglass, E. M. (1949). *Alcohol and Social Responsibility.* New York: Thomas Y. Crowell Co. and Yale Plan Clinic.

McCord, W., & McCord, J. (1960). *Origins of alcoholism.* Stanford, CA: Stanford University Press.

McKay, J. R. Murphy, R. T., Maisto, S. A., & Rivinus, T. R. (1992). Characteristics of adolescent psychiatric patients who engage in problematic behavior while intoxicated. *Journal of the American Academy of Child and Adolescent Psychiatry, 31,* 1031–1035.

McLellan, A. T., & Alterman, A. I. (1991). Patient treatment matching: A conceptual and methodological view with suggestions for future research. In *National Institute on Drug Abuse, improving drug abuse treatment* (pp. 114–35). Washington, DC: U.S. Department of Health and Human Services.

McLellan, A. T., Childress, A. R., & Woody, G. E. (1985). Drug abuse and psychiatric disorders: Role of drug choice. In A. I. Alterman (Ed.), *Substance abuse and psychopathology* (pp. 137–172). New York: Plenum.

McLellan, A. T., Luborsky, L., Woody, G. A., & O'Brien, C. P. (1980). An improved diagnostic evaluation instrument for substance abuse patients. The Addiction Severity Index. *Journal of Nervous and Mental Disease, 168,* 26–33.

McLellan, A. T., Woody, G. E., Luborsky, L., O'Brien, C. P., & Druley, K. A. (1983). Increased effectiveness of substance abuse treatment: A prospective study of patient-treatment "matching." *Journal of Nervous and Mental Disease, 171,* 597–605.

McManus, M., Lerner, H., Robbins, D., & Barbour, C. (1984). Assessment of borderline symptomatology in hospitalized adolescents. *Journal of the American Academy of Child Psychiatry, 23,* 685–694.

Meeks, J. D. (1987). Adolescent substance abuse: Etiology and dynamics. In J. D. Nosphitz (Ed.), *Basic handbook of child psychiatry* (Vol. V, pp. 388–393). New York: Basic Books.

Mee-Lee, D., & Hoffmann, N. G. (1992). *American Society of Addiction Medicine adolescent admission and continued stay criteria.* St. Paul, MN: CATOR/New Standards.

Meichenbaum, D. (1977). *Cognitive-behavioral modification: An integrative approach.* New York: Plenum.

Menninger, K. A. (1938). *Man against himself.* New York: Harcourt.

Menuck, M. (1983). Clinical aspects of dangerous behavior. *Journal of Psychiatry and Law, 11,* 277–304.

Merikangas, K. R., Leckman, J. F., Prusoff, B. A., Pauls, D. L., & Weissman, M. M. (1985). Familial transmission of depression and alcoholism. *Archives of General Psychiatry, 42,* 367–372.

Merikangas, K. R., Prusoff, B. A., & Weissman, M. M. (1988). Parental concordance for affective disorders: Psychopathology in offspring. *Journal of Affective Disorders,* 279–290.

Merikangas, K. R., Weissman, M. M., Prusoff, B. A., Pauls, D. L., & Leckman, J. F. (1985). Depressives with secondary alcoholism: Psychiatric disorders in offspring. *Journal of Studies on Alcohol, 46,* 199–204.

Messer, S. C., Kush, F., & Van Hasselt, V. B. (in press). Behavioral contracting in the treatment of dually diagnosed adolescent inpatients. *Journal of Adolescent Chemical Dependency.*

Metzger, D. S., Kushner, H., & McLellan, A. T. (1991). *Adolescent Problem Severity Index. Administration manual.* Philadelphia: Biomedical Computer Research Institute.

Meyer, R. E. (1986). How to understand the relationship between psychopathology and addictive disorders: Another example of the chicken and the egg. In R. E. Meyer (Ed.), *Psychopathology and addictive disorders* (pp. 284–291). New York: Guilford.

Meyer, R. E. (1992). New pharmacotherapies for cocaine dependence . . . revisited. *Archives of General Psychiatry, 49,* 900–904.

Meyer, R. E., Babor, T. F., & Mirkin, P. M. (1983). Topologies in alcoholism: An overview. *International Journal of Addictions* 18, 235–249.

Mezzich, A., Tarter, R. E., Kirisci, L., Clark, D., Bukstein, O. G., & Martin, C. (1993). Subtypes of early age onset alcoholism. *Alcoholism: Clinical and Experimental Research, 17,* 767–770.

Milan, R., Halikas, J. A., Meller, J. E., & Morse, C. (1991). Psychopathology among substance abusing juvenile offenders. *Journal of the American Academy of Child and Adolescent Psychiatry, 30,* 569–574.

Millon, T. (1987). On the nature of taxonomy in psychopathology: Issues in diagnostic research. In C. G. Last & M. Hersen (Eds.), *Psychiatric diagnosis* (pp. 3–35). New York: Plenum.

Mills, G. J., & Noyes, H. L. (1984). Patterns and correlates of initial and subsequent drug use among adolescents. *Journal of Consulting and Clinical Psychology, 52,* 231–243.

Milstein, S. G., & Irwin, C. E. (1987). Accident-related behaviors in adolescents: A biopsychosocial view. *Alcohol, Drugs and Driving, 4,* 21–29.

Minuchin, S. (1974). *Families and family therapy.* Cambridge, MA: Harvard University Press.

Mitic, W. R., McGuire, D. P., & Neumann, B. (1985). Perceived stress and adolescents' cigarette use. *Psychological Reports, 57,* 1043–1048.

Molina, B. S. G., Chassin, L., & Curran, P. J. (1994). A comparison of mechanisms underlying substance use for early adolescent chidden of alcoholics and controls. *Journal of Studies on Alcohol, 55,* 269–275.

Moncher, M. S., Holden, G. W., & Trimble, J. E. (1990). Substance abuse among Native American youth. *Journal of Consulting and Clinical Psychology, 58,* 408–415.

Moore, W. V. (1988). Anabolic steroid use in adolescence. *Journal of the American Medical Association, 260,* 3484–3486.

Morrison, J. R. (1974). Bipolar affective disorder and alcoholism. *American Journal of Psychiatry, 131,* 1130–1133.

Morrison, J. R., & Stewart, M. A. (1971). A family study of the hyperactive child syndrome. *Biologic Psychiatry, 3,* 189–195.

Moskowitz, J. M. (1989). The primary prevention of alcohol problems: A critical review of the research literature. *Journal of Studies on Alcohol, 50,* 54–88.

Moskowitz, J. M., & Jones, R. (1985). Evaluating the effects of parent groups on the correlates of adolescent substance abuse. *Journal of Psychoactive Drugs, 17,* 173–178.

Mullaney, J. A., & Trippett, C. J. (1979). Alcohol dependence and phobias: Clinical description and relevance. *British Journal Psychiatry, 135,* 565–573.

Murphy, G. E., Armstrong, J. W., Hermele, S. L., Fischer, U. R., & Clendenin, W. W. (1979). Suicide and alcoholism: Interpersonal loss confirmed as predictor. *Archives of General Psychiatry, 36,* 65–69.

Murray, D. M., & Perry, C. L. (1985). The prevention of adolescent drug abuse: Implications of etiology, developmental, behavioral and environmental models. In C. L. Jones & R. J. Battjes (Eds.), *Etiology of drug abuse: Implications for prevention* (pp. 236–256). Rockville, MD: Department of Health and Human Services, National Institute on Drug Abuse.

Naranjo, C. A., Kadlec, K. E., Sanheuza, P., Woodley-Remus, D., & Sellars, E. M. (1990). Fluoxetine differentially alters alcohol intake and other consummatory behavior in problem drinkers. *Clinical and Pharmacological Therapy, 47,* 490–498.

Nathan, P. E. (1988). Alcohol dependency prevention and early intervention. *Public Health Reports, 103,* 683–689.

National Center for Health Statistics. (1982). *Vital statistics of the U.S.: Mortality.* Washington, DC: U.S. Government Printing Office.

National Center for Health Statistics. (1992). *Advance reports of Final mortality statistics, 1990 monthly vital statistics* (Report 41, Suppl. 7, pp. 1–52). Washington, DC: U.S. Government Printing Office.

National Institute on Alcohol Abuse and Alcoholism (NIAAA). (1990). *Seventh special report to the U.S. Congress on alcohol and health* (DHSS Pub. No. ADM 90-1656). Washington, DC: Supt. of Docs., U.S. Government Printing Office.

National Institute on Drug Abuse (NIDA). (1991). *Annual data 1990, data from the Drug Abuse Warning Network (DAWN).* (Statistical Series I). Washington, DC: U.S. Government Printing Office.

National Institute on Drug Abuse (NIDA). (1992). *Drug abuse treatment research: A five year plan.* Rockville, MD: National Institute on Drug Abuse.

National Institute on Drug Abuse and National Institute on Alcohol Abuse and Alcoholism. (1989). *National drug and alcoholism treatment unit survey (NDATUS), 1987 final report* (DHSS Pub. No. ADM 89-1626). Washington, DC: Supt. of Docs., U.S. Government Printing Office.

National Institute on Drug and Abuse and National Institute on Alcohol Abuse and Alcoholism. (1992). *State resources and services related to alcohol and other drug abuse problems, fiscal year 1990.* Rockville, MD: U.S. Department of Health and Human Services.

National Institute on Drug and Alcohol Abuse and National Institute on Alcohol Abuse and Alcoholism. (1986). *State resources and services related to alcohol and other drug abuse problems, fiscal year 1985.* Rockville, MD: U.S. Department of Health and Human Services.

Newcomb, M. D., & Bentler, P. M. (1986a). Frequency and sequence of drug use: A longitudinal study from early adolescence to young adulthood. *Journal of Drug Education, 16,* 101–120.

Newcomb, M. D., & Bentler, P. M. (1986b). Substance use and ethnicity: Differential impact of peer and adult model. *Journal of Psychology, 120,* 83–95.

Newcomb, M. D., & Bentler, P. M. (1988). *Consequences of adolescent drug abuse.* Newbury Park, CA: Sage.

Newcomb, M. D., Maddahian, E., & Bentler, P. M. (1986). Risk factors for drug use among adolescents: Concurrent and longitudinal analyses. *American Journal of Public Health, 76,* 525–531.

Newman, R. (1987). *Analysis of all terrain vehicles related injuries and deaths.* Washington, DC: U.S. Consumer Product Safety Commission.

Nichols, M. (1984). Family therapy: Concepts and method. New York: Gardner Press.

Nobeles, W. W. (1984). Alienation, human transformation and adolescent drug use: Toward a reconceptualization of the problem. *Journal of Drug Issues, 14,* 243–252.

Nystrom, K. F., Bal, A. L., & Labreque, V. (1979). Substance Abuse. In J. D. Noshipitz (Ed.), *Basic Handbook of Child Psychiatry* (Vol. II, pp. 660–636). New York: Basic Books.

O'Malley, P. M., Bachman, J. G., & Johnston, L. D. (1988). Period, age and cohort effects on substance use among young Americans: A decade of change, 1976–1986. *American Journal of Public Health, 78,* 1315–1321.

O'Malley, P. M., & Wagenaar, A. C. (1991). Effects of minimum drinking age laws on alcohol use, related behaviors and traffic crash involvement among American youth: 1976–1987. *Journal of Studies on Alcohol, 52,* 478–491.

O'Malley, S. S., Jaffe, A. J., Chang, G., Schottenfeld, R. S., Meyer, R. E., & Rounsaville, B. (1992). Naltexone and coping skills therapy for alcohol dependence. *Archives of General Psychiatry, 49,* 881–887.

Oetting, E. R., & Beauvais, F. (1987). Common elements in youth drug abuse: peer clusters and other psychosocial factors. *Journal of Drug Issues,* 133–151.

Oetting, E. R., & Beauvais, R. (1990). Adolescent drug use: Findings of national and local surveys. *Journal of Consulting and Clinical Psychology, 58,* 385–394.

Oetting, E. R., Edwards, R., Goldstein, G. S., & Garcia, M. V. (1980). Drug use among adolescents of five Southwestern Native American tribes. *International Journal of the Addictions, 15,* 439–445.

Office of Juvenile Justice and Delinquency Prevention. (1993). *Comprehensive strategy for serious and chronic juvenile offenders.* Washington, DC: Office of Juvenile Justice and Delinquency Prevention.

Offord, D. R. (1989). Conduct disorder: Risk factors and prevention. In D. Shaffer, I. Phillips, & N. B. Enzer (Eds.), *Prevention of mental disorders, alcohol and other drug use in children and adolescents.* (pp. 273–308). Rockville, MD: U.S. Department of Health and Human Services.

Ogloff, J. R. (1987). The juvenile death penalty: A frustrated society's attempt for control. *Behavioral Science and the Law, 5,* 447–455.

Orlandi, M. A. (1986). Community-based substance abuse prevention: A multicultural perspective. *Journal of School Health, 56,* 394–40.

Padilla, A. M., & Salgado de Snyder, V. N. (1929). Hispanics: What the culturally informer evaluator needs to know. In M. A. Orlandi (Ed.), *Cultural competence for evaluators* (pp. 117–146). Rockville, MD: U.S. Department of Health and Human Services, Public Health Service Alcohol, Drug Abuse and Mental Health Administration.

Pandina, R. J. (1986). Methods, problems, and trends in studies of adolescent drinking practices. *Annals of Behavioral Medicine, 8,* 20–26.

Pandina, R. J., & Schuele, J. (1983). Psychosocial correlates of adolescent alcohol and drug use. *Journal of Studies on Alcohol, 44,* 950–973.

Paton, S., Kessler, R. C., & Kandel, D. B. (1977). Depressed mood and illegal drug use: A longitudinal analysis. *Journal of Genetic Psychology, 131,* 267–289.

Patterson, C. R. (1982). *Coercive family process.* Eugene, OR: Castalia Publishing.

Patterson, G. R., Chamberlain, P., & Reid, J. B. (1982). A comparative evaluation of a parent training program. *Behavior Therapy, 13,* 638–650.

Pentz, M. A. (1985). Social competence skills and self-efficacy as determinants of substance use in adolescence. In S. Shiffman & T. A. Wills (Ed.), *Coping and substance use* (pp. 1–2). Academic Press.

Pentz, M. A., Brannon, B. R., Charlin, V. L., Barret, E. J., MacKinnon, D. P., & Flay, B. R. (1989). The power of policy: The relationship of smoking policy to adolescent smoking. *American Journal of Public Health, 79,* 857–862.

Pentz, M. A., Dwyer, J. H., MacKinnon, D. P., Flay, B. R., Hansen, W. B., Wang, E. Y. I., & Johnson, C. A. (1989). A multi-community trial for the primary prevention of adolescent drug abuse: Effects on drug use prevalence. *Journal of the American Medical Association, 261,* 3259–3266.

Perkower, L., Dew, M. A., & Kinsley, L. A. (1991). Behavioral, health and psychosocial factors and risk for HIV infection among sexually active homosexual men: The multicenter AODS Cohort study. *American Journal of Public Health, 81,* 194–196.

Perry, C. L. (1986). Community-wide health promotion and drug abuse prevention. *Journal of School Health, 56,* 359–363.

Pfeffer, C. R., Newcorn, J., Kaplan, G., Mizruchi, M. S., & Plutchik, R. (1988). Suicidal behavior in adolescent psychiatric inpatients *Journal of the American Academy of Child and Adolescent Psychiatry, 27,* 357–361.

Pfeffer, C. R., Plutchik, R., & Mizruchi, M. S. (1983). Suicidal and assaultive behavior in children, classification, measurement and interrelation. *American Journal of Psychiatry, 140,* 154–157.

Pfeffer, C. R., Plutchik, R., Mizruchi, M. S., & Lipkens, R. (1986). Suicidal behavior in child psychiatric inpatients and outpatients and in nonpatients. *American Journal of Psychiatry, 143,* 733–738.

Piaget, J. (1969). The intellectual development of the adolescent. In G. Caplan & S. Lebovici (Eds.), *Adolescence: Psychosocial perspectives* (pp. 22–26). New York: Basic Books.

Pickens, R. W., Leukefeld, C. G., & Schuster, C. R. (1991). *Improving drug abuse treatment.* Rockville, MD: National Institute on Drug Abuse.

Plaut, J., & Kelley, T. (1989). *Childwatch: Children and drugs.* New York: Interface.

Polich, J. M., Ellickson, P. L., Reuter, P., & Kahan, J. P. (1984). *Strategies for controlling adolescent drug use.* Santa Monica, CA: Rand.

Porjesz, B., & Begleiter, H. (1990). Event-related potentials in individuals at high risk for alcoholism. *Alcohol, 7,* 465–469.

Poteet, D. J. (1987). Adolescent suicide: A review of 87 cases of completed suicide in Shelby County, Tennessee. *American Journal Forensic Medicine and Pathology, 8,* 12–17.

Powell, B., Penick, E., Othner, E., Bingham, S. F., & Rice, A. S. (1982). A prevalence of additional psychiatric syndromes among male alcoholics. *Journal of Clinical Psychiatry, 43,* 404–407.

Price, R. H., Cowen, E. L., Lorion, R. P., & Ramos-McKay, J. (1989). The search for effective prevention programs. *American Journal of OrthoPsychiatry, 59,* 49–58.

Prosser, W. L. (1954). The narcotic problem. *UCLA Law Review, 1,* 405–546.

Puig-Antich, J., & Chambers, W. (1978). *The Schedule for Affective Disorders and Schizophrenia for School-aged Children, Unpublished interview schedule.* New York: New York State Psychiatric Institute.

Pyle, R. L., Mitchell, J. E., & Eckert, E. D. (1981). Bulimia: A report of 34 cases. *Journal of Clinical Psychiatry, 42,* 60–64.

Rachel, J. V., Hubbard, R. L., William, J. R., & Tuchfield, B. S. (1976). Drinking levels and problem drinking among junior and senior high school students. *Journal of Studies on Alcohol, 37,* 1751–1761.

Rausch, M. H., Monteiro, M. G., & Schuckit, M. A. (1991). Platelet serotonin uptake in men with family history of alcoholism. *Neuropsychopharmacology, 4,* 83–86.

Reese, F., Chassin, L., & Molina, B. S. G. (1994). Alcohol expectancies in early adolescents: Predicting drinking behavior from alcohol expectancies and parental alcoholism. *Journal of Studies on Alcohol, 55,* 276–284.

Regier, D. A., Farmer, M. E., Rae, D. S., Locke, B. Z., Keith, S. J., Judd, L. L., & Goodwin, F. R. (1990). Comorbidity of mental disorders with alcohol and other drug abuse. *Journal of the American Medical Association, 264,* 2511–2518.

Reich, L. H., Davies, R. K., & Himmelhoch, J. N. (1974). Excessive alcohol use in manic-depressive illness. *American Journal of Psychiatry, 131,* 83–86.

Reich, T., Cloninger, C. R., Van Eerdewegh, P., Rice, J. P., & Mullaney, J. (1988). Secular trends in the familial transmission of alcoholism. *Alcoholism: Clinical and Experimental Research, 12,* 458–464.

Reichler, B. D., Clement, M. S., & Dunner, D. L. (1983). Chart review of alcohol problems in adolescent psychiatric patients in an emergency room. *Journal of Clinical Psychiatry, 4,* 338–339.

Reilly, D. M. (1979). Family factors in the etiology and treatment of youthful drug abuse. *Family Therapy, 11,* 149–171.

Reinherz, H. Z., Giaconia, R. M., Lefkowitz, E. S., Pakiz, B., & Frost, A. K. (1993). Prevalence of psychiatric disorders in a community population of older adolescents. *Journal of the American Academy of Child and Adolescent Psychiatry, 32,* 369–377.

Remafedi, G., Resnick, M., Blum, R., & Harris, L. (1992). Demography of sexual orientation in adolescents. *Pediatrics, 89,* 714–721.

Rich, C. L., Young, D., & Fowler, R. C. (1986a). San Diego suicide study: I. Young vs. old subjects. *Archives of General Psychiatry, 43,* 577–582.

Rich, C. L., Young, D., & Fowler, R. C. (1986b). San Diego suicide study: II. Substance abuse in young cases. *Archives of General Psychiatry, 43,* 962–965.

Rimmele, C. T., Miller, W. R., & Dougher, M. J. (1989). Aversion therapies. In R. K. Hester & W. R. Miller (Eds.), *Handbook of alcoholism treatment approaches.* New York: Pergamon.

Rinaldi, R. C., Steindler, E. M., Wilford, B. B., & Goodwin, D. (1988). Clarification and standardization of substance abuse terminology. *Journal of the American Medical Association, 259,* 555–557.

Robbins, D. R., & Alessi, N. E. (1985). Depressive symptoms and suicidal behavior in adolescents. *American Journal of Psychiatry, 142,* 588–592.

Robertson, M. J. (1989). *Homeless youth in Hollywood: Patterns of alcohol use.* Berkeley, CA: Alcohol Research Group.

Robin, A. L. (1981). A controlled evaluation of problem-solving communication training with parent-adolescent conflict. *Behavior Therapy, 12,* 593–609.

Robin, A. L., & Foster, S. L. (1988). *Negotiating parent adolescent conflict: A behavioral-family systems approach.* New York: Guilford.

Robins, L. (1966). *Deviant children grown up.* Baltimore: Williams & Wilkins.

Robins, L. N. (1978). Sturdy childhood predictors of adult antisocial behavior: Replications from longitudinal studies. *Psychological Medicine, 8,* 611–622.

Robins, L. N. (1980). The natural history of drug abuse. In D. J. Lehier, M. Sayers, & H. W. Pearson (Eds.), Evaluation of treatment of drug abusers. *Acta Psychiatrica Scandanavia, 284,* 7–20.

Robins L. N., & McEvoy, L. (1990). Conduct problems as predictors of substance abuse. In L. N. Robins & M. Rutter (Eds.), *Straight and devious pathways from childhood to adulthood* (pp. 182–204). Cambridge, England: Cambridge University Press.

Robins, L. N., & Przybeck, T. R. (1985). Age of onset of drug use as a risk factor in drug and other disorders. In C. L. Jones & R. J. Battjes (Eds.), *Etiology of drug abuse: Implications for prevention* (pp. 178–192). Rockville, MD: Department of Health and Human Services, National Institute on Drug Abuse.

Rosenberg, D., Holttrum, J., & Gerhon, S. (1994). *Child and adolescent psychopharmacology.* Philadelphia: Saunders.

Rotheram, M. J., Roasiro, M., & Koopman, C. (1991). Minority youths at high risk: Gay males and runaways. In S. Gore & M. E. Colton (Eds.), *Adolescence, stress and coping* (pp. 181–200). New York: Aldine.

Rotheram-Borus, M. J., & Koopman, C. (1991). Sexual risk behaviors, AIDS knowledge and beliefs about AIDS among runaways. *American Journal of Public Health, 81,* 208–210.

Rotheram-Borus, M. J., Koopman, C., & Ehrhardt, A. A. (1991). Homeless youths and HIV infection. *American Psychologist, 46,* 1188–1197.

Rothman, D. (1971). *The discovery of the asylum: Social order and disorder in the new republic.* Boston: Little Brown.

Rounsaville, B. J. (1987). An evaluation of the DSM-III substance use disorders. In G. L. Tischler (Ed.), *Diagnosis and classification in psychiatry* (pp. 175–194). Cambridge: Cambridge University Press.

Rounsaville, B. J., Bryant, K., Babor, T., Kranzler, H., & Kadden, R. (1993). Cross system agreement for substance use disorders: DSM-III-R, DSM-IV and ICD-10. *Addiction, 88,* 337–348.

Rounsaville, B. J., Dolinsky, Z. S., Babor, T. F., & Meyer, R. E. (1987). Psychopathology as a predictor of treatment outcome in alcoholics. *Archives of General Psychiatry, 44,* 505–513.

Rounsaville, B. J., Kosten, T. R., Weissman, M. M., & Kleber, H. D. (1986). Prognostic significance of psychiatric disorders in treated opiate addicts. *Archives of General Psychiatry, 43,* 739–745.

Rounsaville, B. J., Rosenberger, P., Wilber, C., Weissman, M. M., & Kleber, H. D. (1980). A comparison of SADS/RDC and the DSM-III. *Journal of Nervous and Mental Disease, 168,* 90–97.

Rounsaville, B. J., Spitzer, R. L., & Williams, J. B. W. (1986). Proposed changes in DSM-III substance use disorders: Description and rationale. *American Journal of Psychiatry, 143,* 463–468.

Rowe, D., & Grills, C. (1993). African-American drug treatment: An alternative conceptual paradigm for drug counseling with African-American clients. *Journal of Psychoactive Drugs 5,* 21–33.

Roy, A., DeJong, J., Lamparski, D., Adinoff, B., George, T., Moore, V., Garnett, D., Kerich, M., & Linnoila, M. (1991). Mental disorders among alcoholics. *Archives of General Psychiatry, 48,* 423–427.

Roy, A., & Linnoila, M. (1986). Alcoholism and suicide. *Suicide and Life Threatening Behavior, 16,* 244–273.

Rudorfer, M. V. (1993). Challenges in medication clinical trials. *Psychopharmacology Bulletin, 29,* 35–44.

Runeson, B. (1990). Psychoactive substance use disorder in youth suicide. *Alcohol and Alcoholism, 25,* 561–568.

Runyan, C. W., & Gerken, E. A. (1989). Epidemiolgy and prevention of adolescent injury: A review and research agenda. *Journal of the American Medical Association, 262,* 2273–2279.

Rush, T. V. (1985). Predicting treatment outcomes for juvenile and young-adult clients in the Pennsylvania substance abuse system. In G. M. Beschner & A. S. Friedman (Eds.), *Youth, drug abuse: Problems, issues and treatment* (pp. 629–656). Lexington, MA: Heath.

Rutter, M. (1979). *Changing youth in a changing society: Patterns of adolescent development and disorder.* London: Nuffield Provincial Hospitals Trust.

Rutter, M. (1985). Resilience in the face of adversity: Protective factors and resistance to psychiatric disorder. *British Journal of Psychiatry, 147,* 598–611.

Rutter, M. (1989). Psychiatric disorder in parents as a risk factor for children. In D. Shaffer, I. Phillips, & N. B. Enzer (Eds.), *Prevention of mental disorders, alcohol and other drug use in children and adolescents* (pp. 157–190). Rockville, MD: U.S. Department of Health and Human Services.

Ryan, N., Puig-Antich, J., Ambrosini, P., Rabinovich, H., Robinson, D., Nelson, B., Iyengao, N., & Twomay, J. (1987). The clinical picture of major depression in children and adolescents. *Archives of General Psychiatry, 44,* 854–861.

Rydeluis, P. (1983a). Alcohol abusing teenage boys: Testing a hypothesis on alcohol abuse and personality factors, using a personality inventory. *Acta Psychiatrica Scandinavia, 68,* 381–385.

Rydeluis, P. (1983b). Alcohol abusing teenage boys: Testing a hypothesis on alcohol abuse and social background factors, criminality and personality in teenage boys. *Acta Psychiatrica Scandinavia, 68,* 386–389.

Saffer, H., & Grossman, M. (1987). Beer, taxes, the legal driving age and motor vehicle fatalities. *Journal of Legal Studies, 16,* 351–374.

Sameroff, A. J., & Fiese, B. H. (1989). Conceptual issues in prevention. In D. Shaffer, I. Phillips, & N. B. Enzer (Eds.), *Prevention of mental disorders, alcohol and other drug use in children and adolescents* (pp. 23–54). Rockville, MD: U.S. Department of Health and Human Services.

Savada, S. W. (1987). Interfactional theory. In H. T. Blane & K. E. Leonard (Eds.), *Psychological theories of drinking and alcoholism* (pp. 90–130). New York: Guilford.

Schilling, R. F., & McAlister, A. L. (1990). Preventing drug use in adolescents through media interventions. *Journal of Consulting and Clinical Psychology, 58,* 416–424.

Schinke, S. P., & Gilcrist, L. D. (1984). *Life skills counseling with adolescents.* Baltimore: University Park Press.

Schinke, S. P., & Gilcrist, L. D. (1985). Preventing cigarette smoking with youth. *Journal of Primary Prevention, 5,* 48–56.

Schinke, S. P., Gordon, A. N., & Weston, R. E. (1990). Self-instruction to prevent HIV infection among African-American and Hispanic-American adolescents. *Journal of Consulting and Clinical Psychology, 58,* 432–436.

Schinke, S. P., Moncher, M. S., Palleja, J., Zayas, L. II., & Schilling, R. F. (1988). Hispanic youth, substance abuse and stress: Implications for prevention research. *International Journal of the Addictions, 23,* 809–826.

Schuckit, M. A. (1983). Alcoholic patients with secondary depression. *American Journal of Psychiatry, 140,* 711–714.

Schuckit, M. A. (1984). Subjective responses to alcohol in sons of alcoholics and control subjects. *Archives of General Psychiatry, 41,* 879–884.

Schuckit, M. A. (1985a). Clinical implications of primary diagnostic groups among alcoholics. *Archives of General Psychiatry, 42,* 1043–1049.

Schuckit, M. A. (1985b). Studies of populations at high risk for alcoholism. *Psychiatric Developments, 3,* 31–63.

Schuckit, M. A. (1986). Genetic and clinical implications of alcoholism and affective disorder. *American Journal of Psychiatry, 143,* 140–147.

Schuckit, M. A. (1987). Biological vulnerability to alcoholism. *Journal of Consulting and Clinical Psychology, 55,* 301–309.

Schuckit, M. A. (1988). A simultaneous evaluation of multiple markers of ethanol/placebo challenges in sons of alcoholics and controls. *Archives of General Psychiatry, 45,* 211–216.

Schuckit, M. A. (1994). A clinical model of genetic influences in alcohol dependence. *Journal of Studies on Alcohol, 55,* 5–17.

Schuckit, M., Helzer, J., Crowley, T., Nathan, P., Woody, G., & Davis, W. (1991). Substance use disorders. *Hospital and Community Psychiatry, 42,* 471–473.

Schwartz, R. H. (1988). Urine testing in the detection of drugs of abuse. *Internal Medicine, 148,* 2407–2412.

Schwartz, R. H., & Berman, A. (1990). Suicide attempts among adolescent drug users. *American Journal of Diseases of Children, 144,* 310–314.

Searles, J. S. (1988). The role of genetics in the pathogenesis of alcoholism. *Journal of Abnormal Psychology, 97,* 153–167.

Seig, A. (1975). Why adolescence occurs. In H. D. Thornberg (Ed.), *Contemporary adolescence: Readings* (2nd ed.). Monterey, CA: Brooks/Cole Publishing Co.

Selik, R. M., Castro, K., & Pappaiosuou, M. (1988). Racial/ethnic differences in the risk of AIDS in the United States. *American Journal of Public Health, 78,* 1539–1545.

Selik, R. M., Chu, S. Y., & Buehler, J. W. (1993). HIV infection as a leading cause of death among young adults in U.S. cities and states. *Journal of the American Medical Association, 269,* 2991–2994.

Sells, S. B., & Simpson, D. D. (1979). Evaluation of treatment outcome for youths in the drug abuse reporting program (DARP) 1979. A follow-up study. In G. M. Beschner & A. S. Friedman (Eds.), *Youth drug abuse: Problems, issues and treatment* (pp. 571–628). Lexington, MA: Heath.

Selzer, M. L. (1971). The Michigan Alcoholism Screening Test: The quest for a new diagnostic instrument. *American Journal of Psychiatry, 12,* 89–94.

Shaffer, D. (1974). Suicide in childhood and early adolescence. *Journal of Child Psychology and Psychiatry, 15,* 275–291.

Shaffer, D., Garland, A., Gould, M., Fisher, P., & Trautman, P. (1988). Preventing teenage suicide: A critical review. *Journal of the American Academy of Child and Adolescent Psychiatry, 27,* 675–687.

Shaffi, D., Carrigan, S., Whittinghill, J. R., & Derrick, A. (1985). Psychological autopsy of completed suicide in children and adolescents. *American Journal of Psychiatry, 42,* 1061–1064.

Shane, P. G. (1989). Changing patterns among homeless and runaway youth. *American Journal of OrthoPsychiatry, 59,* 208–214.

Sher, K. J. (1987). Stress response dampening. In H. T. Blane & K. E. Leonard (Eds.), *Psychological theories of drinking and alcoholism* (pp. 227–271). New York: Guilford.

Sher, K. J., Walitzer, K. S., Wood, P. K., & Brent, E. E. (1991). Characteristics of children of alcoholics: Putative risk factors, substance use and abuse and psychopathology. *Journal of Abnormal Psychology, 4,* 427–448.

Shiffman, S. M. (1979). The tobacco withdrawal syndrome. In N. A. Krasnegor (Ed.), *Cigarette smoking as a dependence process* (NIDA Research Monograph 23, pp. 158–185). Bethesda, MD: National Institute on Drug Abuse. Silverman, M. M. (1989). The integration of problem and prevention perspectives: Mental health disorders associated with alcohol and drug use. In D. Shaffer, I. Phillips, & N. B. Enzer (Ed.), *Prevention of mental disorders, alcohol and other drug use in children and adolescents* (pp. 7–22). Rockville, MD: U.S. Department of Health and Human Services.

Silverstein, D., Kelly, E., Swan, J., & Kozlowski, L. T. (1982). Physiological predisposition toward becoming a cigarette smoker: Evidence for a sex difference. *Addictive Behaviors, 7,* 83–86.

Smart, R. G., Adlaf, E. M., & Walsh, G. W. (1994). The relationship between declines in drinking and alcohol problems among Ontario students: 1979–1991. *Journal of Studies on Alcohol, 55,* 338–341.

Smith, G. N., & Fogg, C. P. (1978). Psychological predictors of early use, late use and nonuse of marijuana among teenage students. In D. B. Kandel (Ed.), *Longitudinal research on drug use: Empirical findings and methodological issues* (pp. 101–113). Washington, DC: Hemisphere/Wiley.

Sobell, L. C., & Sobell, M. B. (1990). Self-report across addictive behaviors: Issues and future directions in clinical and research settings. *Behavioral Assessment, 12,* 1–4.

Sorenson, R. C. (1973). *Adolescent sexuality in contemporary America.* New York: World Publishing.

Spicer, J. (1994). *The Minnesota Model.* Center City, MN: Hazelden Educational Materials.

Stevenson, E. K., Hudgens, R. W., Held, C. P., Meredith, C. H., Hendrix, M. E., & Carr, D. L. (1972). Suicidal communication by adolescents: Study of two matched groups of 60 teenagers. *Diseases Nervous System, 33,* 112–122.

Stewart, M. A., DeBlois, S., & Cummings, C. (1980). Psychiatric disorder in the parents of hyperactive boys and those with conduct disorder. *Journal Child Psychology and Psychiatry, 21*, 283–292.

Stinchfield, R. D., Niforopulos, L., & Feder, S. H. (1994). Follow-up contact bias in adolescent substance abuse treatment outcome research. *Journal of Studies on Alcohol, 55*, 285–289.

St. Louis, M. E., Conway, G. A., Haymancr, S., Miller, C., Peterson L. R., & Dondero, T. J. (1991). Human immunodeficiency virus infection in disadvantaged adolescents. *Journal of the American Medical Association, 266*, 2387–2391.

Stowell, R. J. (1991). Dual diagnosis issues. *Psychiatric Annals, 21*, 98–104.

Strunin, L., & Hingson, R. (1992). Alcohol, drugs and adolescent sexual behavior. *International Journal of the Addictions, 27*, 129–146.

Sue, D. W., & Sue, D. (1989). *Counseling the culturally different.* New York: Wiley.

Swanson, J. W., Holzer, C. E., Ganju, V. K., & Tsutomu Jono, R. (1990). Violence and psychiatric disorder in the community: Evidence from the epidemiologic catchment area surveys. *Hospital and Community Psychiatry, 41*, 761–770.

Swisher, J. D., & Hsu, T. W. (1983). Alternatives to drug abuse: Some are and some are not. In T. J. Glynn, C. G. Luekefeld, & J. P. Ludford (Eds.), *Preventing adolescent drug abuse: Intervention strategies* (NIDA Research Monograph No. 47, pp. 141–153). Washington, DC: U.S. Government Printing Office.

Szapocznik, J., Kurtines, W. M., Foote, F. H., Perez-Vidal, A., & Hervis, O. (1983). Conjoint versus one-person family therapy: Some evidence for the effectiveness of conducing family therapy through one person. *Journal of Consulting and Clinical Psychology, 51*, 889–899.

Szapocznik, J., Kurtines, W. M., Foote, F. H., Perez-Vidal, A., & Hervis, O. (1986). Conjoint versus one-person family therapy: Some evidence for the effectiveness of conducing family therapy through one person with drug-abusing adolescents. *Journal of Consulting and Clinical Psychology, 54*, 395–397.

Tabakoff, B., Hoffman, P. L., Lee, J. M., Saito, T., Willard, B., & DeLeon-Jones, F. (1988). Differences in platelet enzyme activity between alcoholics and nonalcoholics. *New England Journal of Medicine, 318*, 134–139.

Tanner, J. M. (1962). *Growth at Adolescence* (2nd ed.). Oxford: Blackwell.

Tardiff, K., Gross, E., & Messner, S. (1981). A study of homicide in Manhattan. *American Journal of Public Health, 76*, 139–143.

Tarter, R. E. (1990). Evaluation and treatment of adolescent substance abuse: A decision tree method. *American Journal of Drug and Alcohol Abuse, 16*, 1–46.

Tarter, R. E. (1992). Prevention of drug abuse: Theory and application. *American Journal on Addictions 1*, 2–20.

Tarter, R. E., Alterman, A. I., & Edwards, K. L. (1985). Vulnerability to alcoholism in men: A behavior-genetic perspective. *Journal of Studies on Alcohol, 46*, 329–356.

Tarter, R. E., Hegedus, American, and Gavaler, J. S. (1985). Hyperactivity in the sons of alcoholics. *Journal of Studies of Alcohol, 46*, 259–261.

Tarter, R. E., Kirisci, L., Hegedus, A., Mezzich, A., & Vanyukov, M. (1994). Heterogeneity of adolescent alcoholism. In T. S. Babor, V. Hesselbrock, R. E. Meyer,

& W. Shoemaker (Eds.), Types of alcoholics: Evidence from clinical, experimental and genetic research. *Annals of the New York Academy of Science, 708,* 172–180.

Tarter, R. E., Laird, S. B., Mostefa, K., Bukstein, O. G., & Kaminer, Y. (1990). Drug abuse severity in adolescents is associated with magnitude of deviation in temperamental traits. *British Journal of Addiction, 85,* 1501–1504.

Tarter, R. E., McBride, H., Buonpane, N., & Schneider, D. U. (1977). Differentiation of alcoholics: Childhood history of minimal brain dysfunction, family history and drinking pattern. *Archives of General Psychiatry, 34,* 761–768.

Teicher, J. D., Sinay, R. D., & Stumphauzer, J. S. (1976). Training community-based paraprofessionals as behavior therapists with families of drug-abusing adolescents. *American Journal of Psychiatry, 133,* 847–850.

Temple, M. T., & Filmore, K. M. (1986). The variability of drinking patterns and problems among young men, age 16–31: A longitudinal study. *International Journal of the Addictions, 20,* 595–1620.

Tennant, F. S., & Sagerian, A. A. (1987). Double-blind comparison of amantadine and bromocriptine for ambulatory withdrawal from cocaine dependence. *Archives of Internal Medicine, 147,* 109–112.

Tennant, F. S., & Tarver, A. L. (1984). Double-blind comparison of desipramine and placebo in withdrawal from cocaine dependence. In L. S. Harris (Ed.), *Problems in drug dependence* (NIDA Research Monograph, No. 55. pp. 159–163). Washington, DC: U.S. Government Printing Office.

Thompson, T., & Simmons-Cooper, C. (1988). Chemical dependency treatment and black adolescents. *Journal of Drug Issues, 18,* 21–31.

Tobler, N. S. (1986). Meta-analysis of 143 adolescent drug prevention programs: Quantative outcome results of program participants compared to a control or comparison group. *Journal of Drug Issues, 16,* 537–568.

Trimble, J. E., Padilla, A. M., & Bell, C. S. (1987). *Drug abuse among ethnic minorities.* Washington, DC: U.S. Government Printing Office.

Tuchfeld, B. S., Clayton, R. R., & Logan, J. A. (1982). Alcohol, drug use and delinquent and criminal behaviors among male adolescents and young adults. *Journal of Drug Issues, 2,* 185–198.

Tucker, J. A., Vuchinich, R. E., & Sobell, M. B. (1981). Alcohol consumption as a self-handicapping strategy. *Journal of Abnormal Psychology, 90,* 220–230.

U.S. Congress. Senate. Special Committee to Investigate Organized Crime in Interstate Commerce. (1951). *Final report* (82nd Congress, 1st Session). Washington, DC: U.S. Government Printing Office.

U.S. Bureau of the Census. (1984). *Projections of the population of the United States, by age, sex and race: 1983 to 2030* (Current Population Reports Series P-25, No. 985). Washington, DC: U.S Government Printing Office.

U.S. Bureau of the Census. (1986). *Persons below the poverty level, by family status, type of family, race and Spanish origin, 1959, 1960, 1965, 1968 to 1984. Characteristics of the population below the poverty level: 1984.* (Current Population Reports Series P-60, No. 152). Washington, DC: U.S. Government Printing Office.

U.S. Bureau of the Census. (1990). *The Hispanic population in the United States: March 1989* (Current Population Reports Series P-20, No. 444). Washington DC: U.S. Government Printing Office.

U.S. Department of Health and Human Services. (1988). *The health consequences of smoking: Nicotine addiction. A Report of the surgeon general.* Rockville, MD: U.S. Department of Health and Human Services, Public Health Service, Office of Smoking and Health.

U.S. Department of Health and Human Services, Centers for Disease Control. (1991). Alcohol and other drug use among high school students—United States, 1990. *Morbidity and Mortality Weekly Report, 777.* Washington, DC: U.S. Government Printing Office.

U.S. Department of Health and Human Services, National Institute on Drug Abuse. (1989). Data from the *Drug Abuse Warning Network.* Washington, DC: U.S. Government Printing Office.

U.S. Department of Health and Human Services, National Institute on Drug Abuse. (1991). *National household survey on drug abuse: Main findings, 1990.* Washington, DC: U.S. Government Printing Office.

U.S. General Accounting Office (GAO). (1987). *Drinking-age laws: An evaluation synthesis of their impact on highway safety.* Washington, DC: Author.

U.S. General Accounting Office (GAO). (1989). *Homelessness: Homeless and runaway youth receiving services at federally funded shelters.* Washington, DC: Author.

U.S. Public Health Service. (1938). *Clinical records of hospitalized drug addicts: A statistical analysis* (Suppl. No. 143). Washington, DC: U.S. Government Printing Office.

University of Michigan. (1994). *1993 Monitoring the Future Survey* Ann Arbor, MI: Institute for Social Research.

Valdiserri, R. O., Lyter, D. W., Leviron, L. C., Callahan, C. M., Kingsley, L. A., & Rinaldo C. R. (1988). Variables influencing condom use in a cohort of gay and bisexual men. *American Journal of Public Health, 78,* 801–805.

Van Hasselt, V. B., Ammerman, R. T., Glancy, L. J., & Bukstein, O. G. (1992). Maltreatment in psychiatrically hospitalized dually diagnosed adolescent substance abusers. *Journal of the American Academy of Child and Adolescent Psychiatry, 31,* 868–874.

Van Hasselt, V. B., Hersen, M., & Milliones, J. (1978). Social skills training for alcoholics and drug addicts: A review. *Addictive Behaviors, 3,* 221–233.

Van Hasselt, V. B., Hersen, M., Null, J., Ammerman, R. T., Bukstein, O. G., McGillivray, J., & Hunter, A. (1993). Drug abuse prevention for high-risk African-American children and their families: A review and model program. *Addictive Behaviors, 18,* 213–234.

Van Hasselt, V. B, Null, J. A., Kempton, T., & Bukstein, O. G. (1993). Social skills and depression in adolescent substance abusers. *Addictive Behaviors, 18,* 9–18.

Van Valkenburg, C., Winokur, G., Lowry, M., Behar, D., & Van Valkenburg, D. (1983). Depression in chronically anxious persons. *Comprehensive Psychiatry, 24,* 285–289.

Vermund, S. H., Hein, K., Gayle, H. D., Cary, J. M., Thomas, P. A., & Drucker, E. (1989). Acquired immunodeficiency syndrome among adolescents. *American Journal of Diseases of Children, 143,* 1220–1225.

Vingilis, E., & Smart, R. G. (1981). Physical dependence on alcohol in youth. In Y. Israel, F. B. Gleser, & H. Kalant (Eds.), *Research advances in alcohol and drug problems* (Vol. 6. pp. 197–215). New York: Plenum.

Wagenaar, A. C. (1983). *Alcohol, young drivers and traffic accidents.* Lexington, MA: Lexington Books.

Wallack, L., & Corbett, K. (1990). Illicit drug, tobacco and alcohol use among youth: Trends and promising approaches in prevention. In H. Resnik (Ed.), *Youth and drugs: Society's mixed messages* (pp. 5–30). Rockville, MD: Office for Substance Abuse Prevention.

Warburton, D. M. (1987). The functions of smoking. In W. R. Martin, C. R. VanLoon, E. T. Wamoto, & L. Davis (Eds.), *Advances in behavioral biology. Vol. 31: Tobacco smoking and nicotine: A neurobiological approach* (pp. 51–61). New York: Plenum.

Webb, J. A., Baer, P. E., McLaughlin, R. J., McKelvy, R. D., & Card, C. D. (1991). Risk factors and their relation to initiation of alcohol use among early adolescents. *Journal of the American Academy of Child and Adolescent Psychiatry, 30,* 563–568.

Wechsler, H. (1979). Patterns of alcohol consumption among the young: High school, college and general population studies. In H. Blane & M. Chafetz (Eds.), *Youth, alcohol and social policy* (pp. 39–58). New York: Plenum.

Wechsler, H., & Thum, D. (1973). Teenage drinking, drug use, and social correlates. *Quarterly Journal of Studies on Alcohol, 34,* 1220–1227.

Weiss, G., & Hechtman, L. T. (1986). *Hyperactive children grown up.* New York: Guilford.

Weiss, G., Hechtman, L., Milroy, T., & Perlman, J. (1985). Psychiatric status of hyperactives as adults: A controlled prospective 15-year follow-up of 63 hyperactive children. *Journal of the American Academy Child Psychiatry, 24,* 211–220.

Weiss, K. J., & Rosenberg, D. J. (1985). Prevalence of anxiety disorder among alcoholics. *Journal of Clinical Psychiatry, 46,* 3–5.

Weissman, M. M., Gammon, G. D., John, K., Merikangas, K. R., Warner, V., Prusoff, B. A., & Sholomskas, D. (1987). Children of depressed parents. *Archives of General Psychiatry, 44,* 847–853.

Weissman, M. M., Gershon, E. S., Kidd, K., Prusoff, B. A., Leckman, J. F., Dibble, E., Hamovitt, J., Thompson, W. D., Pauls, D. L., & Guroff, J. J. (1984). Psychiatric disorders in the relatives of probands with affective disorder: The Yale University, National Institute of Mental Health collaborative family study. *Archives of General Psychiatry, 41,* 13–21.

Weissman, M. M., Leckman, J. F., Merikangas, K. R., Gammon, G. D., & Prusoff, B. A. (1984). Depression and anxiety disorders in parents and children. *Archives of General Psychiatry, 41,* 845–852.

Weissman, M. M., & Myers, J. (1980). Clinical depression in alcoholism. *American Journal of Psychiatry, 137,* 372–373.

Welte, J. W., & Barnes, G. M. (1985). Alcohol: The gateway to other drug use among secondary school students. *Journal of Youth and Adolescence, 14,* 487–498.

Welte, J. W., & Barnes, G. M. (1987). Alcohol use among adolescent minority groups. *Journal of Studies on Alcohol, 48,* 329–336.

Werry, J. S., & Aman, M. G. (1993). *Practitioner's guide to psychoactive drugs for children and adolescents.* New York: Plenum.

Wesnes, K., & Warburton, D. M. (1983). Smoking, nicotine and human performance. *Pharmacological Therapy, 23,* 189–208.

Wheeler, K., & Malmquist, J. (1987). Treatment approaches in adolescent chemical dependency. *Pediatric Clinics of North America, 34,* 437–447.

White, H. R., Brick, J., & Hansell, S. (1993). A longitudinal investigation of alcohol use and aggression in adolescence. *Journal of Studies on Alcohol, 11,* 62–77.

Whitman, H. (1951). How can we stop narcotic sales to children. *Women's Home Companion, 78,* 32.

Wieder, H., & Kaplan, E. H. (1969). Drug use in adolescents: Psychodynamic meaning and pharmacologic effect. *Psychoanalytic Study of the Child, 24,* 399.

Williams, A. F. (1985). Fatal motor vehicle crashes involving teenagers. *Pediatrician, 12,* 37–40.

Wills, T. A. (1986). Stress and coping in early adolescence. Relationships to smoking and alcohol use in urban school samples. *Health Psychology, 5,* 503–529.

Wills, T. A., & Schiffman, S. (1985). Coping and substance use: A conceptual framework. In S. Schiffman & T. A. Wills (Eds.), *Coping and substance use* (pp. 1–12). New York: Academic Press.

Wilson, J. D. (1988). Androgen use by athletes. *Endocrine Review, 9,* 181–199.

Wilson, J. R., & Crowe, L. (1991). Genetics of alcoholism: Can and should youth at risk be identified. *Alcohol Health and Research World, 15,* 11–17.

Wilson, J. R., & Nagoshi, C. T. (1988). Adult children of alcoholics: Cognitive and psychomotor characteristics. *British Journal of Addiction, 83,* 809–820.

Windle, M. (1989). Substance use and abuse among adolescent runaways: A four-year follow-up study. *Journal of Youth and Adolescence, 18,* 331–335.

Windle, M. (1991). Alcohol use and abuse: Some findings from the National Adolescent Student Health Survey. *Alcohol Health and Research World, 15,* 5–10.

Windle, M., Barnes, G. M., & Welte, J. (1987). Causal models of adolescent substance use: An examination of gender differences using distribution-free estimators. *Journal of Personality and Social Psychology, 56,* 132–142.

Winokur, G. (1979). Alcoholism and depression in the same family. In D. W. Goodwin & C. K. Erickson (Eds.), *Alcoholism and affective disorder: Clinical, genetic and biochemical studies* (pp. 49–56). New York: SP Medical and Scientific Books.

Winokur, G., Clayton, P., & Reich, T. (1969). *Manic depressive illness.* St. Louis: Moseby.

Winokur, G., Reich, T., Rimmer, J., & Pitts, F. N. (1970). Alcoholism: III. Diagnosis and familial psychiatric illness in 259 alcoholic probands. *Archives of General Psychiatry, 23,* 104–111.

Winters, K. (1990). The need for improved assessment of adolescent substance involvement. *The Journal of Drug Issues, 20*, 487–502.

Winters, K., & Henly, G. (1988). *Personal Experience Inventory (PEI)*. Los Angeles: Western Psychological Services.

Woodruff, R., Guze, S., & Clayton, P. (1971). Alcoholics who see a psychiatrist compared with those who do not. *Quarterly Journal of Studies on Alcohol, 34*, 1162–1171.

Woody, G. E., McLellan, A. T., Luborsky, L., & O'Brien, C. P. (1985). Sociopathy and psychotherapy outcome. *Archives of General Psychiatry, 42*, 1081–1086.

World Health Organization (in press). *International Classification of Diseases or Related Health Problems* (10th rev.).

Wright, J. D., & Weber, E. (1987). *Homelessness and health*. New York: McGraw-Hill.

Yamaguchi, K., & Kandel, D. B. (1984). Patterns of drug use from adolescence to young adulthood. II. Sequences of progression. *American Journal of Public Health, 74*, 668–672.

Yates, A., Beutler, L. E., & Crago, M. (1984). Characteristics of young, violent offenders. *Journal of Psychiatry and the Law*, 40–47.

Yates, G., MacKenzie, R., Pennbridge, J., & Cohen, E. (1988). A risk profile comparison of runaway and non-runaway youth. *American Journal of Public Health, 78*, 820–821.

Yesalis, C. E. (1992). Epidemiology and patterns of anabolic androgenic steroid use. *Psychiatric Annals, 22*, 7–18.

Yesalis, C. E., Vicary, J. R., Buckle, W. E., Streit, A. L., Katz, D. L., & Wright, J. E. (1990). Indications of psychological dependence among anabolic-androgenic steroid abusers. *National Institute of Drug Abuse Monograph, 102*, 196–214.

Young, J. C., Robinson, J. C., & Wickert, P. (1981). How good are the numbers for cigarette tar at predicting deliveries of carbon monoxide, hydrogen cyanide, and acrolein? *Journal of Toxicology and Environmental Health, 7*, 801–808.

Zelnik, M., & Shah, F. K. (1983). First intercourse among young Americans. *Family Planning Perspectives, 15*, 64–70.

Zigler, E., Taussig, C., & Balck, K. (1992). Early childhood intervention: A promising preventative for juvenile delinquency. *American Psychologist, 47*, 997–1006.

Zucker, R. A. (1979). Developmental aspects of drinking through the young adult years. In H. Blane & M. Chafetz (Eds.), *Youth, alcohol and social policy* (pp. 91–146). New York: Plenum.

Zucker, R. A. (1994). Pathways to alcohol problems and alcoholism: A developmental account of the evidence for multiple alcoholisms and for contextual contributions to risk. In R. A. Zucker, J. Howard, & G. M. Boyd (Eds.), *The development of alcohol problems: Exploring the biopsychosocial matrix of risk* (pp. 255–290). Rockville, MD: National Institute on Alcohol Abuse and Alcoholism.

Author Index

Subject Index